# SEMANTICS
## and PHILOSOPHY

# SEMANTICS
# and PHILOSOPHY

*Edited by*
*Milton K. Munitz*
*and Peter K. Unger*

*New York:* NEW YORK UNIVERSITY PRESS

*1974*

Copyright © 1974 by New York University
Library of Congress Catalog Card Number: 74-15427
ISBN: 0-8147-5366-3
ISBN: 0-8147-5376-0 (paperback)

Manufactured in the United States of America

# Contents

The following essays represent the contributions to a seminar held under the auspices of New York University Institute of Philosophy during the academic year 1972-73. The general theme of the seminar was 'Semantics of Natural Language'. All contributions are previously unpublished.

# Meaning and Semantics *

## GILBERT HARMAN

*Princeton University*

In his *Introduction to Logical Theory* P. F. Strawson observes, concerning what he calls statement-making sentences, "To know the meaning of a sentence of this kind is to know under what conditions someone who used it would be making a true statement; to explain the meaning is to say what these conditions are" (p. 211). In this essay I want to consider whether such a connection between truth and meaning tells us anything about the nature of meaning or only tells us something about the nature of truth. More specifically, I shall be concerned with the question whether a theory of truth for a language can tell us something about meaning that is not revealed by a method for translating that language into ours. By a theory of truth for a language, I mean a formal theory that implies a statement of truth conditions for every sentence in the language. My question is whether such a theory sheds light on meaning.

The question arises because theories of truth for artificial languages, containing one or another device, often do seem to illuminate meaning. The truth functional analysis of sentential connectives

* I am indebted to discussions with Donald Davidson, to W. V. Quine's *Philosophy of Logic*, and to Barbara Humphries' comments on a version of this paper which was presented at a colloquium at Georgetown University. I discuss some of the issues that emerge below in *Thought* (Princeton, N.J.: Princeton University Press, 1973); "Is Modal Logic Logic?," *Philosophia*, II (1972), 75-84; "Logical Form," *Foundations of Language*, IX (1972), 38-65; "Against Universal Semantic Representation," forthcoming. NSF support is gratefully acknowledged.
[1] Alfred Tarski, "The Concept of Truth in Formalized Languages," *Logic, Semantics, Metamathematics* (Oxford; Oxford University Press, 1956).

1

seems to determine the meaning of those connectives. The Frege-Tarski analysis of quantification, which culminates in Tarski's theory of truth [1] for quantificational languages, appears to give an account of the meaning of the quantifiers. Kripke's semantics for modal logic [2] and Stalnaker's analysis of the conditional,[3] both concerned with defining truth conditions in terms of possible worlds, seem to tell us something about meaning (even if not everything we might want to know). Similarly for Davidson's analysis of the logical form of action sentences, which explains truth conditions in terms of events.[4] In these cases a formal theory of truth seems to tell us something about meaning that no mere translation scheme could reveal. That is no doubt why there is a use of the term "semantics" among logicians simply to mean a theory of truth in this sense for a language. So, there is empirical evidence that semantics (in this sense) sheds light on meaning.

On the other hand, it is not obvious why. As far as I can see, nothing in the extensive recent discussion of this subject explains why the theories of truth I have mentioned should shed any sort of light on meaning in the way that they do. At the end of this essay, I will suggest a way in which a formal theory of truth can be relevant to the meaning of certain expressions; but, if I am right, the relevance of such a theory to meaning is much more indirect and less central than certain philosophers have suggested.

I begin by considering the views of three philosophers who have suggested that a theory of meaning might take the form of a theory of truth—Donald Davidson, David Wiggins (who, however, has doubts about this, as I shall note below), and David Lewis. I will start with Davidson, who has argued in a number of places that a theory of meaning should take the form of a formal theory that satisfies a "convention *T*," borrowed from Tarski. Roughly speaking, the theory is to imply all relevant instances of the schema "*s* is true if and only if *p*," where what replaces "*s*" names a sentence and what replaces "*p*" is that very sentence or a translation of that sentence into the metalanguage in which the theory of truth is stated.[5] According to Davidson, such a theory of truth can be a theory of meaning since "to give

[2] Saul A. Kripke, "Semantical Considerations on Modal Logic," *Acta Philosophica Fennica*, XVI (1963).

[3] Robert Stalnaker, "A Theory of Conditionals," in *Studies in Logical Theory*, ed. by Nicholas Rescher (Oxford, Oxford University Press, 1958).

[4] Donald Davidson, "The Logical Form of Action Sentences," in *The Logic of Decision and Action*, ed. by Nicholas Rescher (Pittsburgh: University of Pittsburgh Press, 1967).

[5] This has to be modified somewhat to allow for complications concerning demonstrative pronouns, tense, and so forth. I here ignore these complications since the way in which the theories of truth I have mentioned seem to shed light on meaning has nothing to do with these complications. See also footnote 17.

truth conditions is a way of giving the meaning of a sentence. To know the semantic concept of truth for a language is to know what it is for a sentence—any sentence—to be true, and this amounts, in one good sense we can give to the phrase, to understanding the language."[6]

Wiggins advocates a similar thesis. He argues that everyone must accept the following "minimum contention": "Any satisfactory theory of meaning ... must entail the following proposition: *To know the sense of an indicative sentence* s *is to know some condition* p *which is true if and only if* s *is true and which is the designated condition for* s."[7]

Similarly, in the following passage Lewis complains about theories of meaning that do not mention truth conditions:

> My proposals concerning the nature of meanings will not conform to the expectations of those linguists who conceive of semantic interpretation as the assignment to sentences and their constituents of compounds of 'semantic markers' or the like.

Here Lewis is referring to Katz and Postal's 1964 book, *An Integrated Theory of Linguistic Description*. Lewis continues:

> Semantic markers are *symbols*: items in the vocabulary of an artificial language we may call *Semantic Markerese*. Semantic interpretation by means of them amounts merely to a translation algorithm from the object language to the auxiliary language Markerese. But we can know the Markerese translation of an English sentence without knowing the first thing about the meaning of the English sentence: namely, the conditions under which it would be true. Semantics with no treatment of truth conditions is not semantics. Translation into Markerese is at best a substitute for real semantics, relying either on our tacit competence (at some future date) as speakers of Markerese or on our ability to do real semantics at least for the one language, Markerese. Translation into Latin might serve as well, except insofar as the designers of Markerese may choose to build into it useful features—freedom from ambiguity, grammar based on symbolic logic—that might make it easier to do real semantics for Markerese than for Latin.[8]

[6] Donald Davidson, "Truth and Meaning," *Synthese*, XVII (1967).
[7] David Wiggins, "On Sentence-Sense, Word-Sense, and Differences of Word-Sense," in *Semantics*, ed. by Steinberg and Jakobovits (Cambridge: Cambridge University Press, 1972), p. 22.
[8] David Lewis, "General Semantics," in *Semantics of Natural Language*, ed. by Davidson and Harman (Dordrecht: Reidel, 1971), pp. 169-170.

On the other hand, many philosophers and linguists do not seem to believe that a theory of meaning must involve a theory of truth in any way that is important for the theory of meaning. Of course, everyone would agree that there is some connection between truth and meaning, since whether a sentence is true depends on its meaning. But not everyone would conclude that a theory of meaning should take the guise of a formal theory of truth. There is no suggestion that such a theory of truth might provide a theory of meaning in the book by Katz and Postal that Lewis refers to. Nor does any such suggestion appear in Katz and Fodor's paper, "The Structure of a Semantic Theory." [9] Furthermore, there is no reference to truth conditions in Grice's "Meaning." [10]

Even where philosophers explicitly concede the obvious connection between truth and meaning, they do not always suppose that the connection illuminates the theory of meaning. In his comments on David Wiggins's paper, William Alston concedes that linguistic rules which give meaning to certain sentences may cite their truth conditions; but he evidently takes this point to have limited significance. [11] Thus, when Alston develops his own theory in a popular introductory text, [12] which also surveys what he takes to be the important philosophical theories of meaning, he nowhere mentions the view that a theory of meaning might be presented as a formal theory of truth. Presumably he does not think that this is one of the important philosophical theories of meaning.

I began this paper with a quotation from P. F. Strawson, "To know the meaning of a sentence of [a statement-making] kind is to know under what conditions someone who used it would be making a true statement; to explain the meaning is to say what these conditions are." But Strawson's recent inaugural lecture is in fact an attack, with special reference to Davidson's views, on the idea that a formal theory of truth could be a theory of meaning. [13]

In this light of this sort of disagreement, it is appropriate to ask what reasons could be given for the supposition that a formal theory of truth—a formal "semantics"—for a language could be a theory of meaning for that language that reveals anything more about meaning than a translation procedure would. There is, of course, the empirical evidence that I have already mentioned. Partial theories of

---

[9] *Language*, XXXIX (1963).
[10] *Philosophical Review*, LXVI (1957).
[11] William Alston, "How Does One Tell if a Word Has One, Several, or Many Senses?," in Steinberg and Jakobovits, *op. cit.*, p. 36.
[12] William Alston, *Philosophy of Language* (Englewood Cliffs, N.J.: Prentice-Hall, 1964).
[13] P. F. Strawson, "Meaning and Truth," *Logico-Linguistic Papers*.

truth for certain portions of language do seem to shed light on meaning which mere translation does not. But this evidence does not conclusively establish that a theory of truth is directly relevant to a theory of meaning; perhaps its relevance is indirect. In any event, we want to know *why* a theory of truth should tell us something about meaning.

I have found three sorts of argument for the thesis that a formal theory of truth should tell us about meaning. There is, first, an argument that the thesis follows from the fact that knowing the meaning of certain sentences is knowing their truth conditions. Second, there is an argument that appeals to an analogy from what is expected of a theory of meaning and what is expected of a theory of truth. And, third, there is an argument that the normal use of language in communication rests on a background of conventions that correlate sentences with truth conditions. I will discuss each of these arguments in turn and will eventually be led to give my own positive account.

The first argument might be put like this: "For certain sentences, anyway, to know their meanings is to know their truth conditions and to know their truth conditions is to know their meanings. So, the meanings of these sentences are their truth conditions, and a theory of truth that gives the truth conditions of these sentences amounts to a theory of meaning."

In reply to this argument it can be said (a) that whatever is correct about the redundancy theory of truth is sufficient to account for why knowing meaning is knowing truth conditions and (b) that to specify meaning simply by specifying truth conditions would seem to involve not a full-fledged theory of meaning but only a translational theory that specifies the meaning of an expression by providing another expression with the same meaning.

Let me elaborate these replies. The first points to the fact that one can take it to be a remark about the nature of truth rather than meaning that knowledge of meaning is knowledge of truth conditions for certain sentences. "Snow is white" is true if and only if snow is white; and similarly for many other sentences. To understand the meaning of the word "true" is to understand at least that much. That is what is correct about the redundancy theory of truth. Now, if you understand the sentence "snow is white", that is, if you know what the sentence means, and you also understand what truth is, then you can figure out what the truth conditions of the sentence "snow is white" are; and similarly for other sentences. But the point has to do with what "true" means, not with what "means" means. That is the first reply to the argument that knowing meaning is knowing truth conditions.

The second reply indicates that there is a sense in which a theory that would explain meaning in terms of truth conditions would be open to Lewis's objection to Katz and Postal's theory of semantic markers. Lewis says, you will recall, "But we can know the Markerese translation of an English sentence without knowing the first thing about the meaning of an English sentence: namely the conditions under which it would be true." Similarly, there is a sense in which we can know the truth conditions of an English sentence without knowing the first thing about the meaning of the English sentence. To borrow David Wiggins's example, we might know that the sentence "All mimsy were the borogroves" is true if and only if all mimsy were the borogroves. However, in knowing this we would not know the first thing about the meaning of the sentence, "All mimsy were the borogroves."

The truth theorist will, no doubt, respond that he envisions stating truth conditions in a metalanguage that is already completely understood. If the sentence, "All mimsy were the borogroves" is not antecedently understood, it will not be part of this metalanguage, and, if its truth conditions are to be given, it must be translated into terms that are antecedently understood. But then it is not clear how the theory of truth can say anything more about meaning than a straightforwardly translational theory that gives the meanings of sentences in one language by giving translations of those sentences into a language that is antecedently understood. Lewis complains that Katz and Postal give a translational theory of this sort and that they must therefore rely on a tacit and unexplained competence in Markerese; someone who explains meaning in terms of truth conditions similarly relies on a tacit and unexplained competence in the metalanguage.

In this connection, we should also consider a second argument, from analogy, for the thesis that a theory of truth is a theory of meaning. The argument appears in Davidson's paper, "Truth and Meaning." From more recent writings of Davidson and from conversation with him, I gather that he would no longer make use of this argument; but it is useful to mention the argument just for the record. Like the previous argument, this takes a theory of meaning to be equivalent to what I am calling a translational theory. Briefly put, the argument is that a theory of meaning should imply results of the form "$s$ means $p$", where what replaces "$s$" names a sentence of the object language and what replaces "$p$" is that sentence itself or its translation into the metalanguage. Davidson observes that such a condition is similar to convention $T$, which, you will remember, requires of a theory of truth that it imply relevant instances of "$s$ is true if and only if $p$."

It is easy to see that a theory of meaning in this sense is equivalent to a formal theory of translation. Suppose that we have a formal procedure for translating a language $L$ into our language. Suppose in particular that we have a recursive procedure for recognizing the relevant instances of "$s$ (in $L$) translates into our language as $t$." Then we can easily formulate a recursive procedure for recognizing relevant instances of "$s$ (in $L$) means $p$" or "$s$ (in $L$) is true if and only if $p$" (where what replaces "$s$" is the same name of a sentence as that which replaced "$s$" in the previous schema and what replaces "$p$" is the sentence named by what replaces "$t$" in the previous schema).[14] Then we can treat each of the instances of one of the latter schemas as axioms in a formal theory of meaning or a formal theory of truth, since each of the infinitely many axioms in the theory will be formally specifiable and recognizable. Similarly, given a formal theory of truth or a formal theory of meaning in this sense, we can easily state a formal theory of translation.

Now, the light that is shed on meaning by the theories of truth I have mentioned, of Tarski, Kripke, Stalnaker, and Davidson, is not due merely to the fact that those theories tell us how to translate sentences of the object language into the metalanguage; so Davidson's analogy gives us no explanation of the fact that these formal theories of truth shed the sort of light they do on meaning.

Perhaps that is why, as I have indicated, Davidson no longer takes the interest for meaning of a theory of truth to lie only in the $T$ sentences, "$s$ is true if and only if $p$". He now also emphasizes the recursion clauses in a *finite theory* of truth that implies those T sentences.[15] This seems all to the good. The unilluminating theories of

---

[14] I ignore demonstratives, etc. (see footnote 18) and ambiguity. Ambiguity might be eliminated by supposing that sentences are identified not just as strings of words but as also having enough syntactic structure to eliminate ambiguity. For details see *Thought*, pp. 77–78. I also suppose that only statement making sentences are in question. The complications involved in allowing for demonstrative reference, imperative sentences, etc. play no role in the formal theories of truth I have mentioned that shed light on meaning (Tarski's, Kripke's, Stalnaker's, and Davidson's).

During a discussion of this essay at New York University it was suggested that a theory concerning how to tell whether a theory of truth for a foreign language is an adequate theory would constitute a general theory of meaning. That is irrelevant, since it does not by itself explain why the theories of truth mentioned shed the light they do on meaning. Similarly, a theory concerning how to tell whether translation is adequate could constitute a general theory of meaning without making any reference to theories of truth.

[15] Donald Davidson, "Semantics for Natural Languages," *Linguaggi nella società e nella tecnica* (Milan: Edizione di Comunita, 1970).

truth that are equivalent to theories of translation are infinite theories in which all the $T$ sentences are treated as axioms. The theories of truth that do shed light on meaning are finite theories. Our current difficulty is that we do not understand why this should be so. Why should we expect a finite theory of truth to shed light on meaning? Is it just an accident that the theories in question (Tarski's etc.) shed such light? Is it possible that these theories only seem to shed light on meaning? I will return to those questions later.

The third argument that I want to consider asserts that normal linguistic communication exploits conventions that correlate sentences and truth conditions. David Lewis gives a very clear statement of the argument in his book, *Convention*.[16] In brief, he argues that the theory of meaning for a language spoken in some community must be a theory of the linguistic conventions that speakers normally observe; and, he claims, these conventions include in effect the principle that speakers are to try to say what is true in the language in question.

Lewis argues that normal linguistic communication is made possible by the fact that there are certain regularities in the use of the language by speakers and by hearers. People adhere to these regularities because others do and because it is common knowledge that they do. Lewis considers a number of different uses of language, but for our purposes we can confine the discussion to the normal use of language in a situation of communication of information using ordinary statement-making sentences. According to Lewis, it is a relevant background regularity that normally speakers try to observe certain general principles which, if consistently observed in all cases, would have such implications as these: speakers would say "It is raining" only if it were raining; speakers would say "It is snowing" only if it were snowing; speakers would say "Snow is white" only on the condition that snow is white; they would say "Grass is green" only on the condition that grass is green; and so forth. Furthermore, in gaining information from what has been said, hearers (according to Lewis) normally rely on the fact that speakers normally try to adhere to these regularities. Speakers normally rely on hearers' doing this; and so forth.

Now it may seem that, if Lewis is right about the conventions of a language that are relied on in normal linguistic communication and is also right that a theory of meaning is a theory of these conventions, then a theory of meaning would have to involve something like a theory of truth. For it may seem that the conventional regularities that he is thinking of would have to connect sentences and their truth

16 David Lewis, *Convention* (Cambridge, Mass.: Harvard University Press, 1969).

conditions. And it may seem that the recursion clauses in a finite theory of the conventional regularities would exactly match the recursion clauses in a finite theory of truth in that language. So it may seem that, if Lewis is right, a good way to give an account of the conventions of a particular language *L* would be, first, to give a theory of truth in *L* and, second, to say that linguistic communication using *L* exploits the conventional regularity that speakers normally try to say only what is true in *L*.

However, it is not obvious that Lewis's theory (even if correct) has this consequence. According to Lewis, the basic convention is that speakers try to say what is true in *L*. But to try to say what is true is to say what you believe. So, for Lewis, normal linguistic communication in a language *L* exploits the expectation that a speaker normally says something only if he believes it. What is conventional about language has to do with what sentences express what beliefs. This seems to yield the theory that the meaning of a statement making sentence depends on the belief it could normally be used to express. Meaning is taken to be a matter of the belief expressed rather than a matter of truth conditions.

Notice that it seems more accurate to say that hearers rely on an expectation that speakers will normally say what they believe than an expectation that speakers will normally say what is true. The expectation that speakers normally say what is true is more optimistic than the expectation that they normally say what they believe. The optimistic expectation would seem to rest not just on an understanding of the conventions of the language but also on an estimate of the reliability of speakers' beliefs.

This point can be denied. It is sometimes said that, if speakers did not normally speak the truth, the language could not be learned. We are supposed to conclude that it follows from linguistic conventions that speakers normally say what is true; and such a conclusion would support the idea that meaning is a matter of truth conditions. But, this sort of paradigm case argument is not compelling. If as a result of false beliefs speakers did not normally speak the truth, the language could still be learned by someone who shared with speakers those false beliefs.

To be sure, there is a legitimate issue here. How wrong can we take someone's beliefs to be before we must decide that we have misinterpreted them? It can and has been argued that the thesis that people are normally right in their beliefs is not an empirical generalization but rather a presupposition of ascribing any beliefs to them at all. However, I do not see how this sort of argument could possibly show that linguistic conventions correlate sentences with their truth conditions. For one would have to argue that it follows from *linguistic* conventions that people are normally right in their beliefs. But the argument would, it seems, apply not only to beliefs that can be expressed in language but also to beliefs, or expectations, or whatever else are analogous to beliefs and expectations, in dumb animals and children who have not yet learned a spoken language. There would be the same sorts of limits to the interpretation of the beliefs, expectations, or what have you of these creatures. So these limits do not seem to be derived from linguistic conventions.

Taking the point one step further, observe that there is no general convention among English speakers to say only what one believes. Speakers violate no linguistic conventions when they make suppositions, give examples, joke, tell stories, and so forth. Furthermore, when speakers do such things, they utilize the same linguistic conventions they make use of when they try to say only what is true, and they use these conventions in the same way. Of course, it may be that speakers are supposed to assert only what they believe; but that is not a general linguistic convention; it is a particular point about assertion.[17]

The relevant linguistic conventions do not associate sentences only with beliefs but more generally with propositions or, as I shall say, thoughts, which are sometimes believed, sometimes supposed, sometimes just presented for consideration. The meaning of a sentence is determined by the thought with which the sentence is conventionally correlated, that is, the thought which, by convention, speakers would normally intend to communicate to a hearer by using that sentence.

Thoughts in this sense are not mysterious objects; they are just beliefs, hopes, suppositions, and so forth, more generally described. The term "thought", as I use it here, is simply a more general term than "belief", "hope", and "supposition". A belief that cigarettes are good for you, a hope that cigarettes are good for you, and a supposition that cigarettes are good for you are all thoughts that cigarettes are good for you, in this sense of "thought".

The relevant thoughts are to be identified, not in terms of truth conditions, but rather in terms of their potential role in a speaker's "conceptual scheme"—the system of concepts constituted by the speaker's beliefs, plans, hopes, fears, and so on, ways the speaker has of modifying his beliefs, plans, hopes, fears, and so on, and ways these modify what the speaker does. I have defended a "functionalist" theory of this sort in my book, *Thought*, and will say more about it

---

[17] Here I am indebted to Donald Davidson.

below. Supposing that such a theory is correct, there is a sense in which meaning depends on role in conceptual scheme. The meaning of a sentence is determined by the role in a conceptual scheme of the thoughts that the sentence would normally be used to express.

Now, to get to the main point, the implications that a thought has are very important to its role in a conceptual scheme; and logical implications are particularly important. Furthermore, logical implication is a matter of truth and logical form. $P$ logically implies $Q$ if and only if, whenever a proposition with the same logical form as $P$ is true, the corresponding proposition with the same logical form as $Q$ is also true. And this, according to me, is how truth is relevant to meaning. It is not relevant to the meaning of those syntactic elements of sentences that determine logical form. For the meaning of those elements depends on their role in logical implication; and logical implication is to be defined in terms of truth.

That is a summary of my view. Let me elaborate. I say that meaning depends on role in conceptual scheme rather than on truth conditions. That is, meaning has to do with evidence, inference, and reasoning, including the impact sensory experience has on what one believes, the way in which inference and reasoning modify one's beliefs and plans, and the way beliefs and plans are reflected in action. For me, the meaning of the relevant sort of sentence is determined by the thought it would normally express. The nature of that thought is not in the first instance determined by its truth conditions; it is, rather, a matter of psychology. For a thought, as I am using this term, is a psychological state, defined by its role in a system of states that are modified by sensory input, inference, and reasoning, and that have an influence on action. To specify a thought is to specify its role in such a conceptual system. To specify the meaning of a sentence of the relevant sort is to specify a thought, so to specify its meaning is to specify a role in a conceptual scheme.

The idea that meaning is a matter of role in conceptual scheme is not a philosophical novelty. It appears, in simplified form, in verification theories of meaning. Quine's theory in *Word and Object* is a better version because it corrects the mistaken assumption of verificationist theories that evidence can have a direct bearing on individual statements apart from considerations of theory. But Quine, like the earlier verificationists, considers only role in relation to sensory experience, evidence, and theoretical inference. He leaves the practical side out. Other writers, for example, Hampshire in *Thought and Action*, take that aspect of role to be important for meaning (and a similar idea is characteristic of pragmatism). Meaning is a matter of role because meaning is a matter of the thought expressed; and a thought is defined by its role in a psychological system that includes not only the effect of sensory stimulation and inference but also the impact on the environment of this system via action.

It would be a mistake to suppose that the relevant thoughts have an existence independent of the language in which one expresses them. Learning a language is not just learning a way to encode thoughts one already has. It is rather in part to acquire the possibility of new thoughts, thoughts that are *in* that language. That is why a language carries with it aspects of a world view. Learning a language is not to be distinguished from learning a theory. One acquires a new system of representation for thought. One learns a new way of thinking.

The conventions of language would be difficult to state and harder to learn if they correlated sentences with thoughts that had to be specified independently of each other. But, as a first approximation, the rule is simple: a sentence expresses the thought that one would have if one thought exactly those words. That is only a first approximation because thoughts in words are not just strings of words. They are sentences under an analysis that reveals logical form. They are words with more structure than a string. The thought which a speaker intends to communicate with his words is a complex structure of words. In the normal case, communication is successful if the hearer perceives what is said as having the intended structure. The difference between two possible interpretations of "Jack dislikes pleasing students" is like the difference between the two interpretations of an ambiguous drawing of a staircase. To hear one interpretation is to hear the sentence as having a particular structure. One does not need to decode the sentence into a completely nonlinguistic thought. The conventions of language that are relevant to communication are the conventions of grammar, the conventions that correlate sentences with their underlying logical forms.

But the conventions of language that are thus relevant to communication are not the only conventional regularities involving language that are relevant to meaning. Also relevant are regularities concerning the way in which language is used in thought. For example, a community will conventionally accept a number of basic principles that partially determine the roles and therefore the meanings of various terms. These principles, sometimes called "meaning postulates", might include such things as statements of transitivity for "more than" and so forth. Furthermore, there will be certain conventional regularities in the way in which beliefs are formed as the result of sensory experience. It is conventional regularities of this sort that are primarily relevant to the roles in belief and therefore the meanings, of color words. And then there will also be some conventional regularities relevant to the meanings of logical words, like "and", "or", "if", "every", "some", "not", and so forth.

It is not easy to say how the latter conventions, concerning logic, are to be expressed. It is not that *all* the truths of logic are conventionally accepted, for they are not. It would be more accurate to say that what is conventionally accepted are general principles like, "Every thought of the form 'If *P*, then *P*' is true." That does bring out the way in which the relevant conventions involve truth; but it makes such general principles of logic seem too similar to other general principles conventionally accepted, like the principle expressing the transitivity of "more than".

That there is a difference between principles of logic and other general principles is the moral of Lewis Carroll's fable concerning Achilles and the Tortoise. The point of that story is that principles of logic have a function in reaching new conclusions that nonlogical principles do not have.

The point is sometimes expressed by saying that there is a difference between a premise and a rule of inference. But that is not a good way to put things. Although rules of logic are sometimes called rules of inference, they are really best thought of as rules of implication. They are certainly not rules that tell one when to infer certain conclusions given certain antecedent beliefs, since one can always escape a deductive argument by denying a premise rather than accepting the conclusion.

I think that deduction is relevant to inference because it is relevant to explanation and inference is inference to the best explanation. But I cannot defend that answer on this occasion.

In any event, principles of logic differ from other general principles one accepts in two respects. First, logical principles have a special role in inference. Second, general logical principles cannot be stated directly in the object language but only indirectly by talking about language and truth. A general logical principle must say that all thoughts of a specified form are true.

The meaning of a logical term is a matter of its role in one's conceptual scheme; and that is a matter of the way such a term is involved in principles of logic which have the special role in inference. Logical principles say that all thoughts of certain specified logical forms are true, where forms are specified with reference to the logical constructions that they involve. A truth of logic can be said to hold by virtue of its form, since any other thought with the same logical form is also true. Logical terms have an important role in logical truths, since the truths hold by virtue of their logical terms. That is why consideration of truth conditions can sometimes tell us something about meaning. It can tell us something about the meanings of logical elements of structure since it can provide an account of the role of such elements in determining what the logical truths are.

I have already mentioned Davidson's idea that what a formal theory of truth tells us about meaning is not given by the $T$ sentences it implies but rather by the recursion clauses of the theory. We can now make sense of that idea, at least as it applies to logical terms. Consider a logical term like "and", representing logical conjunction. The infinite number of $T$ sentences by themselves tell us nothing about the meaning of "and" since these $T$ sentences by themselves tell us nothing in particular about the function of "and". What is relevant is the clause in a formal theory of truth that says a conjunction is true if and only if both conjuncts are. For that tells us something about conjunction that is relevant to its logical role. Since to specify the meaning of "and" is to specify this role, the relevant clause of the theory of truth tells us something about the meaning of "and".

We can easily envision formal theories of truth that would tell us nothing about the meaning of "and", for example the theory that simply took all $T$ sentences as axioms. A theory that sheds light on the meaning of "and" and other logical terms does not do so simply in virtue of being a theory of truth but rather because it contains specific clauses saying how conjunction and the other logical terms contribute to the truth or falsity of complex sentences.

Now it seems to me that consideration of those cases in which a theory of truth appears to tell us something about meaning supports my account over the thesis that meaning is generally a matter of truth conditions. For consider some of the examples I have already mentioned: the truth functional account of the *logical* connectives, the Frege-Tarski analysis of *logical* quantification, or Kripke's semantics for operators of *modal* logic.

Davidson's theory concerning the *logical form* of action sentences illustrates the point in a different way. Davidson does not give clauses in a truth definition for any new logical operator. His aim is rather to argue that the logical form of action sentences can be represented in ordinary quantificational logic on the assumption that these sentences involve disguised quantification over events. Davidson suggests that a sentence like "John walks" has the logical form, "$(\exists x)$ (John walks $x$)". The sentence "John walks in the rain" has the form, "$(\exists x)$ (John walks $x$ & $x$ is in the rain)". That the first of these sentences is implied by the second is taken by Davidson to be an instance of a simple implication of ordinary quantificational logic.

Davidson's theory tells us something about meaning because it tells us about logical form, and meaning is partly a matter of logical form. The linguistic conventions that are relevant to meaning include those grammatical conventions that correlate surface forms of sentences with their logical forms. So to say something about the logical form of a sentence is to say something about its meaning. But Davidson's theory does not tell us everything we might want to know about the meaning of action sentences, since the theory sees quantification over events in these sentences. Although a theory of truth can explain the meaning of the quantification, it cannot fully explicate the reference to events. For that, something more is needed, a theory of events along with some indication of how we are to confirm or disconfirm statements about events.

A similar point can be made about Kripke's semantics for modal logic. It does not fully specify the meaning of "possible" or "necessary" because it accounts for truth conditions in terms of quantification over possible worlds. No theory of truth can by itself explain that reference to possible worlds. What is needed is a theory of possible worlds and an indication of how we are to confirm or disconfirm statements about possible worlds.

Recall the sentence, "All mimsy were the borogroves." As Wiggins remarks, the thing that we lack here is not an understanding of what the relevant clauses in a truth theory would look like (for we know *that*), but rather an understanding of evidence and inference. I say that this will always be the case for nonlogical terms.[18]

---

[18] As noted earlier, I have ignored complications concerning demonstrative pronouns, tense, and so forth, since the interest of the relevant theories of truth that I have mentioned does not involve such complications. When these complications are taken into account, my conclusion will have to be modified. For example, the clause in a theory of truth for the first-person singular pronoun will say that it is used by a speaker to refer to himself; that says something important about the meaning of the pronoun, which is not a logical term. This second connection between truth and meaning has a different source than the connection with respect to logical terms. It reflects the point that the truth of a remark is typically not an absolute matter but is relative to speaker, audience, time of utterance, and so forth. "I am sick" is true for one speaker, false for another; true for a speaker at one time, false for the same speaker at another time. That is why convention *T* has to be modified as indicated in note 5 above. I cannot correctly say that your remark, "I am sick," is true if and only if I am sick. Truth is typically relative to an assignment of someone, the speaker, as the referent of the first-person pronoun; someone else, the audience, as the referent of the second person pronoun; a time, the time of utterance, as referent of "now" (which may be implicit); a demonstrated object as referent of an occurrence of a demonstrative pronoun; and so forth.

A theory of truth sheds light on the meaning of logical terms because of the particular connection in the case of such terms between truth and role in conceptual scheme. If a theory of truth sheds light on demonstrative pronouns and so forth it does so because truth is relative to an assignment of objects to demonstrative pronouns and so forth. Theories of truth do not shed light on the meaning of other sorts of terms in the way that they can shed light on logical terms and demonstratives.

If by "semantics" we mean a formal theory of truth, we must not identify semantics with the theory of meaning. Semantics in this sense can tell us something important about the meanings of logical terms and other aspects of logical structure, but it cannot in the same way illuminate the meaning of nonlogical terms.

# Semantic Rules

## WILLIAM P. ALSTON

*Douglass College*

*Rutgers University*

In recent decades there has been rather widespread acceptance of the view that linguistic meaning is a matter of rules; more explicitly:

(R) What it is for a linguistic expression to have a certain meaning is for the employment of that expression to be governed by certain rules.[1]

I shall henceforth refer to this as the "rule theory of linguistic meaning." The following list of quotations displays something of the breadth of support for this idea.

> The meaning of a word or a combination of words is, in this way, determined by a set of rules which regulate their use. . . . Stating the meaning of a sentence amounts to stating the rules according to which the sentence is to be used. . . .
> —Moritz Schlick, "Meaning and Verification,"
> *Philosophical Review*, XLV, 4 (July, 1936), 341.

> . . . to talk about the meaning of an expression or sentence is not to talk about its use on a particular occasion, but about the rules,

---

[1] Other formulations of the same position are: "the *fact* that a linguistic expression has a certain meaning is the *fact* that its employment is governed by certain rules"; "the *concept* of linguistic meaning is (should be) the *concept* of being governed by a certain kind(s) of rule".

17

habits, conventions governing its correct use, on all occasions, to refer or to assert. . . . The question whether the sentence is significant or not is the question whether there exists such language habits, conventions or rules that the sentence logically could be used to talk about something. . . .

> —P. E. Strawson, "On Referring," in A. Flew, ed., *Essays in Conceptual Analysis* (New York: St. Martin's Press, 1956), pp. 30, 31, 33.

. . . to know what an expression means is to know how it may and may not be employed.

> —Gilbert Ryle, "The Theory of Meaning," in C. A. Mace, ed., *British Philosophy in the Mid-Century* (New York: Macmillan, 1957), p. 255.

It is quite clear that, in some sense, one who knows a natural language tacitly knows a system of rules ... the semantic component [of a description of a language] is a statement of the rules by which he [the user of the language] interprets sentences as meaningful messages.

> —J. J. Katz, *Philosophy of Language* (New York: Harper & Row, 1966), pp. 100, 111.

I have said that the hypothesis of this book is that speaking a language is performing acts according to rules. The form this hypothesis will take is that the semantic structure of a language may be regarded as a conventional realization of a series of sets of underlying constitutive rules, and that speech acts are acts characteristically performed by uttering expressions in accordance with these sets of constitutive rules.

> —J. R. Searle, *Speech Acts* (Cambridge: Cambridge University Press, 1969), pp. 36–37.

*I*

It is not my main purpose in this paper to argue for this thesis but rather to point out some of the difficulties in implementing it and to propose a first step in circumventing those difficulties. However, at the outset I will just sketch what I take to be the rationale for this approach to semantics.

Whatever else may be true of linguistic meaning, it is clear that the fact that a given word, phrase, or sentence in a language has a

certain meaning is in some way dependent upon facts about the
society in which that language is spoken, rather than on any intrinsic
features of the expression (as an acoustic or orthographical type), and
rather than on any nomological connections in which such physical
types stand. This is shown by the mere fact that the same acoustic
type, for example, 'low' can have very different meanings in different
languages; for example, in French and English. Consider further the
fact that it is possible to change the meaning of a word in a language
by an explicit agreement or by (a successfully enforced) fiat; thus we
could, if enough of us so chose, change the meaning of the English
word 'snow' from what it is now to the meaning currently possessed
by 'fire'. It seems that any fact that is dependent on the constitution
of a society, and moreover dependent in such a way that it could be
changed by agreement, convention, or decree, must be a fact about
what rules (conventions, norms) are in force in the society; for this is
the kind of fact that behaves in just this way. Both of the above points
hold, for example, of the fact that in the United States the right side
of the road is the one on which to drive.

More direct indications of the "rulish" character of semantic
facts come from the pervasive application of rule-derived distinctions
to the semantic side of the use of language.[2] One may use the *right* or
the *wrong* word, the *correct* or *incorrect* phrase, to say what one set
out to say. If one is learning a language one is often corrected by one's
tutors, told that one is not to say _____ in those circumstances, or that
what one *can* say is _____. One may *misuse* expressions in the language to the point at which what one says does not make sense. Such
metatalk reflects the presence of rules governing the use of language.
It is where rules are in force—permitting some moves, forbidding
others, requiring others—that one can speak of a certain action in a
certain context as being right or wrong, correct or incorrect; that one
can speak of what a person can, must, or must not do; that one can be
said to *misuse* something; that one's behavior can be corrected. These
considerations lend powerful credence to the idea that when a person
learns a language (more specifically, when he learns the meanings of
elements of the language) what he learns is the practical mastery of a
system of rules; that what makes someone a fluent speaker of a
language (more specifically what constitutes one's knowledge of the
meanings of expressions in the language) is the practical mastery of a

---

[2] A proper defense of the rule theory of linguistic meaning would appear as just one
facet of a defense of the more general contention that a language is best conceived as
being a system of rules—syntactical and phonological as well as semantic. Actually all
the points we are making in this section apply equally well to the phonological and
syntactic aspects of language. However, we will not have time to go into the more
general problem in this paper.

set of rules, and that what a linguist is trying to uncover when he sets out to describe the language (and, more specifically, the semantics of the language) is just that system of rules. No doubt, much more could and should be said about these points, but this will have to suffice for a brief indication of the main sources of antecedent plausibility for the rule theory.

## II

So long as we confine ourselves just to asserting that linguistic meaning is *somehow or other* a matter of rules governing linguistic expressions, and supporting that assertion with equally unspecific considerations, there is not much to do with the theory except contemplate it. But if that very unspecific assertion is correct, there will be more specific things to be said concerning the ways in which the meanings of particular types of linguistic expressions consist in subjection to particular types of rules, and the acceptability of the general thesis depends on the possibility of its being developed along these lines. What should be expected from a more specific elaboration of the rule theory? Ideally such a theory would take the form of a systematically organized set of theoretical definitions of semantic terms. At the base might be a definition of '$x$ has a meaning'. This would be in the form of a specification of the types of rules that are such that it is necessary and sufficient for $x$ to have a meaning that utterances of $x$ are governed by a rule of one of these types.[3] It seems reasonable to think that we would have to correlate different types of rules with different types of linguistic expressions, for example, names, predicates, and sentences; and if the theory is to be adequate these rules will have to interrelate in ways that mirror the semantic relations between these different sorts of expressions.[4] From these definitions of '$x$ has a meaning' we would presumably go on to define whatever other semantic terms are deemed worth the trouble; for

[3] Such a formulation will be more or less ambitious, depending on whether or not the range of the variable is limited to entities already ratified as linguistic expressions. If not, then we are claiming to make explicit, in terms of rule-governance, what gives any entity whatever (or perhaps any type of perceptible occurrence) a meaning in the same generic sense in which linguistic expressions have meaning. (This could be something like a rule-account of Grice's notion of nonnatural meaning.) Then if it turns out that rules of the specified types can govern types other than linguistic types, it will be a further question whether the differentia for the subclass of meaningful linguistic expressions consists of some difference in the kinds of semantic rules involved (that is, in a different sort of meaning), or in something else, for example, involvement in a syntactical system.
This point is sketchily illustrated for the relation of words and sentences in the final section of the paper.

example, '$x$ is synonymous with $y$', '$x$ connotes property $p$', '$x$ denotes class C', and so on.[5]

It is clear that at present we are a long way from being able to spell out such a system of theoretical definitions along the lines of the rule theory. Indeed I think it not unfair to say that no approach to the understanding of semantic concepts has thus far succeeded in coming very close to any such system, at least any such system that is at all illuminating in ways to be made explicit shortly. If that is the case, then in order to evaluate the rule theory we must ask the following question: What can reasonably be demanded of the rule theorist at this stage, short of the actual delivery of a set of theoretical definitions, as a token of the promise his approach holds out? Granted that the final and definitive evaluation of any view as to the nature of linguistic meaning must be in terms of how it works out in the grand enterprise sketched above, what could the rule theorist be expected to do at present that would give us some grounds for supposing that the job *can* be done along his lines? I would suppose that the least we are entitled to expect is one or more plausible illustrations of his position. That is, he should present some particular semantic rules, and, even if he is not in a position to specify in a completely general fashion what are the necessary and sufficient conditions for something's being a semantic rule, still he should be able to say something helpful as to what it is about his examples that make *them* semantic rules.

I am afraid that one who approaches rule theorists with this very modest demand is in for a disappointment. Many philosophers of this persuasion, including some of those quoted initially, confine themselves to enunciating the completely unspecific principle, (R), and make no serious effort to indicate how it might be put in practice. And those who do make the effort have not been markedly successful in providing rules that do the desired job. Here is a representative list of recent attempts by philosophers to give examples of semantic rules.

I.   Rudolf Carnap—*Introduction to Semantics* (Cambridge, Mass.: Harvard Univ. Press, 1942), p. 24.[6]

---

[5] The account should also have a bearing on the explication of various quasi-semantic concepts like knowing the meaning of a word, learning the meaning of a word, understanding what someone is saying, and being true by virtue of meaning.

[6] Unlike the other authors from whom I have taken semantic rules, Carnap does not proffer his rules *as* exemplifications of the rule theory as I have construed it. (Or at least it is not clear that he is doing so.) However, I wanted to include Carnapian rules as representative of the "formal semantic" tradition, in which there is much talk of linguistic rules, semantic and otherwise. For whatever the intentions of formal semanticists, it is of interest to determine whether the sorts of rules they envisage *can* illustrate the way in which having a meaning consists in being governed by certain rules. Much of what I have to say about the Carnapian rules will also apply to later

A. Rules of truth:

    1. $pr_1$ ($in_1$) is true if and only if Chicago is large.

    2. $pr_2$ ($in_1$) is true if and only if Chicago has a harbor.

B. Rules of designation

    1. $in_1$ designates Chicago
    2. $pr_1$ designates the property of being large
    3. $pr_2$ designates the property of having a harbor.

II. Rudolf Carnap—*Meaning and Necessity* (Chicago: University of Chicago Press, 1947), pp. 4-56.

Rules of designation for individual constants

    1. 's' is a symbolic translation of 'Walter Scott.'
    2. 'w'—(the book) Waverley

B. Rules of designation for predicates

'Hx'—'x is human (a human being)'
'RAx'—'x is a rational animal'
'Fx'—'x is (naturally) featherless'
'Bx'—'x is a biped'
'Axy'—'x is an author of y.'

C. Rule of truth for the simplest atomic sentences. An atomic sentence in $S_1$ consisting of a predicate followed by an individual constant is true if and only if the individual to which the individual constant refers possesses the property to which the predicate refers.

D. Rule of truth for 'v'. A sentence 'pvq' is true in $S_1$ if and only if at least one of the two components is true.

III. Max Black, "Necessary Statements and Rules," in *Models and Metaphors* (Ithaca, N.Y.: Cornell University Press, 1962), p. 66.

---

developments in "formal semantics", insofar as they couch their proposals in terms of rules. For a good presentation of some recent developments see David Lewis, "General Semantics", in *Semantics of Natural Language*, ed. D. Davidson and G. Harman (Dordrecht: Reidel, 1972), and the literature referred to in Lewis's article.

"Monday" may be replaced by "the day before Tuesday" and vice versa.

IV.  P. F. Strawson—"On Referring," in A. Flew, ed., *op. cit.*, p. 42.

The requirement for the correct application of an expression in its ascriptive use to a certain thing is simply that the thing should be of a certain kind, have certain characteristics. The requirement for the correct application of an expression in its referring use to a certain thing is something over and above any requirement derived from such ascriptive meaning as the expression may have; it is, namely, the requirement that the thing should be in a certain relation to the speaker and to the context of utterance.

V.  J. J. Katz, *op. cit.*

A.  Dictionary entries (p. 155)
     bachelor→N, $N_1$, ..., $N_k$;
(1)  (Physical object),
     (Living), (Human),
     (Male), (Adult), (Never
     married); <SR>

(2)  (Physical object),
     (Living), (Human), (Young),
     (Knight), (Serving under
     the standard of
     another); <SR>

B.  Projection rules (p. 166)

*Given* two readings,
$R_1$: $(a_1)$, $(a_2)$, ..., $(a_n)$; <$SR_1$>
$R_2$: $(b_1)$, $(b_2)$, ..., $(b_m)$; <$SR_2$>

such that $R_1$ is assigned to a node $X_1$ and $R_2$ is assigned to a node $X_2$. $X_1$ dominates a string of words that is a head and $X_2$ dominates a string that is a modifier, and $X_1$ and $X_2$ branch from the same immediately dominating node X, *then* the derived reading

$R_3$: $(a_1)$, $(a_2)$, ... , $(a_n)$, $(b_1)$, $(b_2)$, ... , $(b_m)$; $<SR_1>$ is assigned to the node X just in case the selection restriction $<SR_2>$ is satisfied by $R_1$.

*VI.  J. R. Searle, op. cit.*

A. Rules for the use of a device, Pr, for promising (in part): (p. 63)

1. Pr is to be uttered only in the context of a sentence (or larger stretch of discourse) T, the utterance of which predicates some future act A of the speaker S.

2. Pr is to be uttered only if it is not obvious to both S and H that S will do A in the normal course of events.

3. Pr is to be uttered only if S intends to do A.

B. Rules for the use of R to make singular definite reference (p. 96)

1. R is to be uttered only in the context of a sentence (or some similar stretch of discourse) the utterance of which could be the performance of some illocutionary act.

2. R is to be uttered only if there exists an object X such that either R contains an identifying description of X or S is able to supplement R with an identifying description of X, and such that, in the utterance of R, S intends to pick out or identify X to H.

3. The utterance of R counts as the identification or picking out of X to (or for) H.

C. Rules for the use of any predicating device P (p. 127)

1. P is to be uttered only in the context of a sentence or other stretch of discourse T the utterance of which could be the performance of some illocutionary act.

2.  P is to be uttered in T only if the utterance of T
    involves a successful reference to X.

3.  P is to be uttered only if X is of a type or category
    such that it is logically possible for P to be true or
    false of X.

4.  The utterance of P counts as raising the question of
    the truth or falsity of P of X (in a certain illocution-
    ary mode determined by the illocutionary force in-
    dicating device of the sentence).

It is my contention that none of these formulations are wholly
satisfactory as illustrations of the way in which having a certain
meaning *is* being governed by a certain rule. To substantiate this
charge, and to provide a basis for my own constructive efforts, I shall
now lay down four requirements that a rule must satisfy in order to be
suitable for the task at hand.

(1) *Distinctiveness*. It must be a rule in some distinctive sense, as
contrasted, for example, with definitions, empirical generalizations,
and nomological principles. The word 'rule' is used rather freely,
especially in learned and quasi-learned discourse; and many items so
called do not count as belonging to the category of rules, *rather than*
to some of the other categories listed above.[7] If the rule theory is to be
supported by the rationale sketched in section i, the rules involved will
have to be such that, unlike empirical generalizations and natural
laws, they have implications as to the conditions under which a certain
kind of behavior is right or wrong, correct or incorrect; and they will
have to be such that they are modifiable at will. And an adequate
formulation of a rule will have to represent it in such a way that these
implications are made clear.

The Carnap examples do not satisfy this requirement. His formulations do present facts about a language (assuming that we know
how to interpret the connectives, "designates," and "---", the author
not being very helpful on these matters). But as they stand they do

---

[7] To illustrate this with something outside semantics, Arthur Koestler, in his recent
book, *The Ghost in the Machine*, develops an extremely general notion of a "holon."
One of his general principles is: "Functional holons are governed by fixed sets of rules
and display more or less flexible strategies" (p. 342). In applying this to atoms conceived as holons, he speaks of "the rule-governed interactions between nucleus and
outer electron shells" (p. 62). However, it is clear that these "rules" are more felici-
tously called "natural laws." They are not rules in a distinctive sense in which the fact
that a rule holds sets up implications as to what behavior is right or wrong, correct or
incorrect.

not formulate *rules* in any distinctive sense of the term. If it is a fact that in a certain language $pr_1$ designates the property of being large, then it follows from the rule theory that this is the case because there is some rule governing the employment of $pr_1$ in that language. But Carnap does not tell us what that rule is. He does not specify what may, must, or must not be done with $pr_1$, or the conditions under which it may, must, or must not be uttered. His formulation does nothing to make explicit the conditions under which behavior involving the expression is correct or incorrect, right or wrong. The same holds true of his rules of truth. They make explicit the necessary and sufficient conditions of a sentence having a certain property, but they do not make explicit what moves with the sentence are permitted, required, or forbidden. Thus they are not formulations of *rules* in any distinctive sense, any more than any other statements of necessary and sufficient conditions, for example, "lead melts if and only if it is heated to 327 degrees F".[8] And if the lexicon in the Fodor-Katz model for the semantic description of a language is to be taken as a set of rules, the same comments would apply to the dictionary entry quoted from Katz (V. A.).[9] In all these cases we are presented with semantic statements that the rule theory aims to explicate in terms of rules, rather than the rules themselves; we are given the explicandum, not the explicans.

(2) *Translinguistic connection.* It must effect a connection between a linguistic expression and what, in this connection, is quaintly called "the world", that is, between the expression and those states of affairs, largely though not exclusively nonlinguistic, which the expression is used to talk about. For the meaning of an expression is what enables it to be used in talking about one thing rather than another, in communicating some distinctive "content". This is the requirement that lies behind the Carnap-Morris idea that semantics, as contrasted with syntactics on the one side and pragmatics on the other, is concerned with the relation between symbols and their "designata"; it also lies behind the popular view that to have a meaning is to "refer" to something. These latter formulations reflect the idea in much too restrictive a way, for it is not the case that all meaningful linguistic expressions designate or refer to something, in any dis-

---

[8] The same stricture applies to the recently popular view that the meaning of a predicate is a "function" from possible worlds (perhaps together with other items) to extensions. (See D. Lewis, *op. cit.*) Such formulations do not make explicit what may or may not be done with any expression.

[9] Katz says, "Accordingly we may regard the dictionary as a finite list of rules, called 'dictionary entries,' each of which pairs a word with a representation of its meaning in some normal form." *Op. cit.*, p. 154.

tinctive sense of the terms 'designate' or 'refer'.[10] Indeed any formulation that, like those just mentioned, views all meaningful linguistic expressions as performing the same semantic function, is bound to fail; for it is of the essence of linguistic structure that members of structurally different linguistic categories perform different semantic functions. (That is what linguistic structure is all about.) My formulation in terms of "what an expression is used to talk about" is overgeneralized in a way that is opposite to those just criticized; that is, it characterizes all meaningful linguistic expressions in terms that are distinctively appropriate to sentences. It is a sentence that is usable to say something, to communicate a "content". A word, except where used elliptically for a sentence, cannot be the vehicle of a complete message. So far as I can see, the least complicated way of making the point in question (that is, the formulation that involves the least differentiation of linguistic types) is one based on a distinction between sentences and components of sentences, such as words. Making that distinction, we can say that (a) it is by virtue of having a certain meaning that a *sentence* is rendered usable for saying one thing rather than another, for communicating a "message" with a distinctive "content" and (b) it is by virtue of having a certain meaning that a *word* is rendered usable to make a certain distinctive contribution to the "content" communicated by a given sentence in which it occurs. In accordance with (a), it is because 'the strike is over' has the meaning it does that it is usable to make a particular assertion, rather than usable to make some other assertion, or usable to make some request or suggestion. And it is because they have the same meaning that the sentences 'What time is it?' and '*Quelle heure est-il?*' are usable to ask the same question. And, in accordance with (b), depending on whether we insert 'strike', 'play', or 'trial' in the sentence frame, 'The _____ is over', the resulting sentence will be usable to make one rather than another assertion. Thus sentence meaning ties a sentence to a "complete" communicable content, while word-meaning ties a word to something that is potentially a part of many complete communicable contents. And since these "contents" in general have to do with extralinguistic matters, semantic rules will in general have to relate the expression to the extralinguistic world.[11]

[10] Indeed, as far as 'refer' is concerned, I would agree with Strawson that no linguistic expression refers to anything, but rather that some expressions are such that one can use a given expression of this type to refer to various different things on various different occasions. But that is another story.

[11] The necessity for this requirement is also indicated by the oft-noted point that one could have practical mastery of an indefinite number of purely intralinguistic rules that govern a particular language, for example, Japanese, and still not know the meanings of any Japanese words or be able to understand Japanese sentences and use

To be sure, not *all* semantic rules have to be of this form. Once some expressions have been given meaning by translinguistic rules, the meanings of other expressions can be specified by rules of intersubstitutability, as in the classic form of definition. If we have already specified the meanings of 'female' and 'fox', then the meaning of 'vixen' can be given by formulating a rule that permits the substitution of 'vixen' for 'female fox'. That is relatively unproblematical. The real difficulty comes in giving appropriate formulations of the basic semantical rules, those the application and status of which do not presuppose other semantic rules. And for those the present requirement holds.

Among our examples, II A. and B., and III run afoul of this requirement. In these cases what is presented as a semantical rule is simply a definition of the standard replacement type. Whether it is explicitly formulated as a rule, as in the Black example, or not, as in the Carnap example, it equally fails to satisfy the present requirement.

(3) *Noncircularity.* If a rule-formulation is to function as an illustration of the way in which having a certain meaning can consist in being governed by a rule, then it cannot contain any semantic terms, like 'means', 'designates', or 'denotes'. Why do I say this? It is not a matter of avoiding circularity of definition, for we are not now considering *definitions* of semantic terms. It is rather like this. We begin by trying to understand what it is for a word to have a certain meaning. For example, what sort of fact is the fact that 'thermometer' means *instrument for measuring temperature*? We are told that the word's having this meaning is a matter of its being governed by a certain rule. "Like what?" we reply. "Well, for example, the rule: 'Thermometer' may be used to denote instruments for measuring temperature (connote the complex characteristic of being an instrument for measuring temperature)." (Or more blatantly, " 'Thermometer' may be used with the meaning, *instrument for measuring temperature*.") But this fails to provide the illumination we seek; we are not making the right sort of progress. For any semantic term we use in the rule formulation ('denote', 'connote', or whatever) expresses the

---

them properly in communication. By virtue of knowing such rules one could know how to construct grammatical phrases and sentences and how to avoid constructing ungrammatical ones; one could know which substitutions could be made without changing meaning, and what sentences are paraphrases of a given sentence. One could know all this on the basis of intralinguistic rules, but if such rules were all one had mastered, one would not know the meanings of any Japanese words or sentences. However, this familiar line of argument, unlike the one we presented, does not proceed on the basis of any positive notion of the nature and function of linguistic meaning.

kind of concept we are trying to elucidate via the rule approach. To use any such term in our paradigmatic rule formulations is to incorporate bodily into our account the very sort of thing the structure of which the account is supposed to lay bare.

To be sure, one may quite properly set out to exhibit the *interrelations* between various semantic concepts; for example, meaning, synonymy, connotation, and denotation. However, that is not what the rule theory is supposed to do. The rule theory is designed to give us a fundamental insight into the general nature of semantic facts *via* exhibiting them as a special case of a pervasive and comparatively unproblematic sort of fact, namely, rule governance. We begin by rejecting the seductive picture of a semantic fact as involving a mysterious, *sui generis* kind of relation, connecting a linguistic element with an equally mysterious entity, its meaning. And then we find it difficult to replace this model with a more acceptable one that still does justice to the facts. The rule theory holds out hope here; it makes the initially plausible suggestion that a semantic fact (such as the fact that 'thermometer' means *instrument for measuring temperature*) can be construed as the fact that a certain rule holds in a given society. Although there are difficult conceptual and methodological problems connected with the concept of a rule being in force in a society, it is an eminently viable concept, one that is successfully employed in many connections in the social sciences; and the problems it engenders are by no means confined to language, and certainly not to the semantic side of language. But now if in trying to give a characterization of semantic facts along these lines, the only basic rules we can mention contain semantic terms, then the promise is not being fulfilled. For now the question, "Just what is it that the rule permits us to use 'thermometer' to do?" is just the kind of question we set out to answer in the first place.[12]

It is obvious that Carnap's designation rules from *Introduction to Semantics* violate this requirement, and if the rules of designation from *Meaning and Necessity* are so construed that the '−' is something like 'means the same as', then they do also. The examples from Strawson and Searle violate the requirement in a somewhat more

---

[12] The exclusion of semantic terms from rule formulations is in order only when we are thinking of using those formulations in the context under consideration. No such restrictions can be placed on rules that are to be used in the actual semantic description of languages. There we are free to use any terms, including semantic ones, so long as they are sufficiently intelligible. Indeed, since some meaningful words and sentences have to do with linguistic meaning, for example, the word 'synonymous' and the sentence, " 'auspicious' means *favorable*," it would seem that the rules that give *these* expressions the meaning(s) they have, must be formulated in terms of semantic concepts, on pain of irrelevance.

subtle fashion. Searle's rule-formulations and the kinds of rule-for-mulations adumbrated by Strawson, employ such notions as 'ascribe', 'refer', 'identify', and 'predicate'. Now I take it that when I speak of *ascribing* the property of roundness to this table, of *referring* to this table, of *identifying* this object as the table I inherited from my grandfather, or of *predicating* roundness of this table, I am using notions that we would eventually want to explicate in terms of the rule approach for the same reasons we would want to explicate such terms as '*means*', '*denotes*', and '*synonymous*' along the lines of that approach. The notion that in saying something I am *predicating* roundness of the table and the notion that I am *referring* to that table present the same kind of initial obscurity and puzzlement that attach to semantic terms like 'means'; hence an explication of 'means' that is based on rules formulated in terms of any of these notions (where they have not been earlier explicated by more basic rules not em-ploying such notions) does not really give us what we were hoping to get out of the rule approach.[13]

As for the Katz items, it seems that the projection rules definitely violate (3). Katz equates the term 'reading' with 'representation of a sense of a linguistic expression', and surely 'sense', and any term defined by means of it, will be among the semantic terms we want to explicate via the rule approach. Presumably the dictionary entries do not violate (3). (Although each entry *is* a reading, the term 'reading' does not occur in the entry.) If the material on the right-hand side of the arrow designated a complex linguistic expression, then we would have to interpret the arrow as 'is synonymous with', and (3) would be violated. However, Katz denies that this is his intent (p. 156).

(4) *Scope*. The rules must govern first-level speech behavior, rather than (just) secondary metalinguistic activity on the part of grammarians, lexicographers, and other persons involved in describ-ing and theorizing about language.

This requirement, like (1), stems from the basic rationale for the rule theory. What emerged from those considerations was the thesis that a language consists of a system of rules, and that what one learns when one learns a language is the practical mastery of that set of rules. More specifically with respect to the semantic side of language, the upshot was that in learning the meanings of words and in learning how to interpret sentences in a language, one acquires practical mas-tery of rules and comes to act in the light of them. Now the rules that are such that learning a language consists in acquiring a practical

---

[13] See below where I make a similar point about the use of unanalyzed illocutionary act terms in our rule formulations.

mastery of those rules, must be rules governing activities engaged in by any fluent speakers of a language, activities such as making a variety of assertions, requests, promises, asking questions, and expressing feelings and attitudes. This is the sort of thing I am calling "first-level speech behavior."

With the possible exception of V, all of our examples that are rules in a distinctive sense govern first-level speech.[14] The status of the Katz rules is not so clear. In the article by Katz and J. A. Fodor, "The Structure of a Semantic Theory," [15] the authors maintain that the use of projection rules like V. B. is an essential part of the fluent speaker's exercise of his fluency.

> What the fluent speaker has at his disposal ... are rules for applying the information in the dictionary which take account of semantic relations between morphemes and the interaction between meaning and syntactic structure in determining the correct semantic interpretation for any of the infinitely many sentences the grammar generates. (p. 493)

Again Katz in *Philosophy of Language* speaks of the "semantic component" as "a statement of the rules by which he (a speaker of the language) interprets sentences as meaningful messages" (p. 111). But sometimes the relation between the rules formulated by the linguist in describing the language and the rules utilized by the native speaker of the language is specified as something short of identity.

> Hence, for the semantic component to reconstruct the principles underlying the speaker's semantic competence, the rules of the semantic component must simulate the operation of these principles by projecting representations of the meaning of higher level constituents from representations of the meaning of the lower level constituents that comprise them. (p. 152)

> Thus, these rules (projection rules) provide a reconstruction of the process by which a speaker utilizes his knowledge of the dictionary to obtain the meanings of any syntactically compound constituent, including sentences. (pp. 161-162)

[14] To turn again to the recently popular idea that a meaning is a function from possible worlds to extensions, it would seem that insofar as the statements of such a function can be construed as a rule in a distinctive sense, it will govern only a very sophisticated higher-level behavior, namely assigning extensions to expressions in various possible worlds.
[15] *Language*, XXXIX (1963), 170–210.

Whatever the exact intent of these authors, there are some problems here. First, although we can well imagine a *hearer* interpreting sentences by constructing readings for those sentences in the manner indicated by the projection rules, it is not at all clear how such rules would be used by the *speaker*. He is going in the opposite direction; he doesn't assign a "reading" to a given sentence, but (if he does anything of this general character) he finds a sentence to match a given "reading." Thus if he *uses* any rules of this ilk, they will have to be somewhat differently constituted. Second, even if a hearer does, in some sense, make use of the projection rules, it is not clear that these rules function in this context as rules in the distinctive sense outlined above. If hearers derive readings for sentences in anything like the way described by Fodor and Katz, they certainly don't do so consciously. But it is not clear that "rules" governing unconscious cognitive operations are rules in our distinctive sense, in which they determine certain moves as right or wrong, correct or incorrect. Perhaps they are better understood as describing the normal operation of a *mechanism*, in which case they would no more furnish a basis for accusing someone of a rule violation than would an account of the normal operations of a gasoline engine. Of course a linguist could consciously and deliberately construct a reading for a sentence in accordance with projection rules; and then the rule would be functioning as a rule in the distinctive sense of the term. But in that case the rule would not be governing first-level speech. These issues are exceedingly thorny, and I shall not pursue them further.

## III

In view of the failure of all the attempts surveyed, one may feel that there are but dim prospects for the rule-theory. However, I believe that one can formulate a quite different sort of rule, one which satisfies all the above requirements and which constitutes at least an opening wedge for construing linguistic meaning in terms of rules. I will work up to my suggestions by indicating the route by which I arrived at the kind of rule in question. The following exposition is based on earlier presentations of what I termed an "illocutionary-act-potential theory of meaning," [16] but in those previous publications the focus was not on *rules* to the extent it is here; and I might add that I believe myself able now to see various aspects of the subject more clearly.

[16] See my "Meaning and Use," *Philosophical Quarterly*, XIII (1963), 107–124, and *Philosophy of Language* (Englewood Cliffs, N.J.: Prentice-Hall, 1964, ch. 2.

In trying to get started on a rulish account of linguistic meaning, one is well advised to begin at the sentence level. I do not believe that this judgment can be adequately supported without making a comprehensive survey of possible semantic rules, something that we will not have time for in this paper. However, a short justification can be extracted from the remarks we made in support of the Trans-Linguistic Connection requirement. There it was pointed out that sentences and sentence-components are "tied" to distinctive contents in different ways, more specifically that the sentence is "tied" to its content in a more direct first-level way, while a word "has" its content in a more derivative, second-order fashion. That is, a sentence has a certain content in the sense that it is itself usable to issue a complete message with some distinctive content; whereas a word (when used at its "proper level" as a sentence-component, rather than as elliptically for a sentence) has a certain content only in the sense that it makes a certain distinctive contribution to the contents of sentences in which it occurs. This suggests that semantic rules governing words would be higher-level affairs, having to do with the way in which the occurrence of a given word in a given sentence affects the constitution of the semantic rule(s) governing that sentence. That is, sentence rules, or generalized references thereto, will enter into the formulation of word-rules, but not vice versa. Thus the first order of business is to get clear about the nature of semantic rules governing sentences. In this paper I shall almost entirely restrict myself to that stage of the enterprise.

From this standpoint it is fortunate that we have ready to hand in ordinary language an indefinitely large repertoire of terms for making explicit *what* someone said in uttering a certain sentence (in an appropriate sense of 'what *x* said' where that involves specifying the "content" of his utterance, rather than specifying what sentence he uttered). Such terms typically are made up of an act-type term, 'predict', 'suggest', 'advise', 'promise', or whatever, together with a phrase which, following Searle, we may call a proposition specifying phrase, a phrase that makes explicit what it is that is predicted, suggested, advised, promised, or whatever. Here is a sample of sentences predicating such terms of speakers:

*A* asked *B* for a match.
*A* suggested to *B* that they go to a movie.
*A* congratulated *B* on his performance.
*A* predicted that the strike would be over soon.
*A* remarked that the weather was warming up.
*A* told *B* that he had left his lights on.

*A* advised *B* to sell his utilities stock.
*A* expressed considerable enthusiasm for *B*'s proposal.
*A* expressed his intention to stay here all summer.
*A* told *B* that it was his duty to stay.
*A* reminded *B* that it was almost 9:00.
*A* assured *B* that everything would be all right.
*A* exhorted *B* to try hard to finish before the week was out.

The list can be extended indefinitely.

As I have in past publications, I shall call such sentences "illocutionary act reports", the terms "illocutionary act-terms", and the acts reported "illocutionary acts". I have taken this term, of course, from John Austin. In fact I have appropriated Austin's terminological triad, 'locutionary', 'illocutionary', 'perlocutionary'. Thus I would contrast act-concepts of the above sort with locutionary-act concepts, an attribution of such a concept simply making explicit what sentence a speaker uttered, and perlocutionary-act concepts, the attribution of each of which makes explicit a certain effect of the speaker's utterance. There will then be still other speech-act concepts that fall into none of these three groups. These additional categories may be exemplified as follows.

*Locutionary Acts*

*A* said, "Do you have a match?"
*A* said, "Let's go to a movie."

*Perlocutionary Acts*

*A* got *B* to give him a match.
*A* made *B* feel good.
*A* irritated *B*.
*A* brought *B* to realize that he had left his lights on.
*A* persuaded *B* to sign the petition.

*Other Speech Acts*

*A* scolded her for what she had done.
*A* described his trip for us.
*A* repeatedly alluded to the incident.
*A* finally explained his strange behavior.
*A* interrupted me in the middle of a sentence.

> *A* discussed the proposal at some length.
> *A* made an afterdinner speech.

At this hour of the day I regret my terminological appropriation, for the differences between my usage of 'locutionary' and 'illocutionary', and Austin's usage of those terms has undoubtedly led to misinterpretation. In my sense of the term a (complete) illocutionary act concept contains a specification of the "content" of the utterance, while Austin (though *How To Do Things with Words* is, in my opinion, not at all consistent on this point), unmistakably wanted to draw a distinction between the full locutionary act, which involved uttering a sentence with a certain sense and reference, and the "illocutionary force," which was supposed to be something that could vary with the sense and reference of the sentence fixed, and which is represented in my scheme, if at all, only by the *act-type* verb—'request', 'promise', or whatever. However, I am afraid it is too late in the day for restitution, though not for repentance, and so, while remaining penitent, I shall continue to enjoy the fruits of my crime, both for good and for ill.

Now we can reformulate the points made earlier about sentence-meaning by saying that on this approach a sentence's having a certain meaning consists in its being usable to perform illocutionary acts of a certain type, in having, as I have put it elsewhere, a certain "illocutionary-act potential". And an alternative way of saying what we are looking for in the way of a rule is this. We are seeking a kind of rule such that being governed by a rule of that kind gives a sentence a certain illocutionary-act potential. What sort of rule is it that makes the sentence 'Let's go to the movies' usable to suggest going to the movies?

At this point one may grab the bull by the horns and boldly respond: a rule that permits the use of the sentence 'Let's go to the movies' to perform the illocutionary act of suggesting going to the movies. More generally a sentence, S, has a certain illocutionary act potential by virtue of being governed by a rule of the form:

S can be used to perform illocutionary acts of Type I.

However, rules of this sort will not pass our noncircularity test, or at least it is not sufficiently clear that they do so. Perhaps they do not use any strictly semantic terms. Nevertheless, by using unanalyzed illocutionary-act terms, they thereby use terms that pose essentially the same problems as semantic terms, and hence they fail to provide the illumination we seek. Notions like suggesting that we go to the movies, and predicting that the strike will soon be over, seem to "embody content" in basically the same way as the notion of a sentence meaning that a certain strike will soon be over. In both cases we want to understand what it is that "ties" the kind of entity under discussion (in the one case, a sentence; in the other case, an action) to a certain propositional content, what gives it the capacity to convey, embody, or express, that proposition. And so rule-formulations that make use of raw illocutionary-act concepts fail to dig down into the structure of content-embodiment in such a way as to radically advance our understanding of the matter.

The above objection clearly indicates the conditions under which it can be met. We must dig down into the structure of illocutionary-act concepts and make explicit what is involved in performing such an act. This will presumably give us a basis for specifying in an illuminating way what it is that renders a sentence usable for performing such an act. (An understanding of actuality carries with it an understanding of the corresponding potentiality.) A full-dress discussion of the nature of illocutionary acts is beyond the scope of this paper. However, I shall go into the matter far enough to bring out one fundamental feature of illocutionary acts, and, correspondingly, one sort of rule that is involved in a sentence's having a certain illocutionary-act potential.

Whenever one performs an illocutionary act he "represents" certain conditions as holding, or, as I have put it previously, he "takes responsibility" for certain conditions holding. Here are some examples of conditions for the holding of which one takes responsibility in the performance of one or another sort of illocutionary act.[17]

I.   Ordering someone to run a certain engine.

---

[17] A rule of thumb (but no more than a rule of thumb) for arriving at a set of conditions for a given illocutionary-act concept is the following. Take any candidate for such a condition and subject it to the following test. Suppose that just after the speaker uttered a sentence that would normally be used to perform the illocutionary act in question, he denied that this condition holds. Would that denial show that he had not used the sentence on that occasion to perform that illocutionary act? If so, the condition belongs in our list; if not, not. Thus if someone conjoined to the sentence 'I promise to stop running the engine soon,' the denial that it was possible for him to stop running the engine soon, that addition would prevent us from supposing that he had, in any clear or straightforward way, promised his addressee to stop running the engine soon. Hence we include condition 3. On the other hand, if what he went on to say was that he didn't *want* to stop running the engine soon, that would not be sufficient to inhibit us from interpreting the original utterance as the making of the promise in question. Hence we do not include a condition to the effect that SP wants to stop running the engine soon.

1. A particular engine is contextually indicated.[18]

2. It is possible for the addressee (*A*) to operate the engine so indicated just after the time of utterance.

3. The speaker (*SP*) is in a position of authority vis-à-vis *A* (at least with respect to the operation of the engine in question).

II. Asserting that a certain man is currently operating a certain engine.

   1. Some man is contextually indicated.
   2. Some engine is contextually indicated.
   3. That man is currently operating that engine.

III. Promising someone not to run a certain engine much longer.

   1. A particular engine is contextually indicated.
   2. *SP* is now operating the engine so indicated.
   3. It is possible for *SP* to stop operating the engine shortly after the time of utterance.
   4. *A* would prefer *SP*'s ceasing to operate the engine so indicated shortly after the time of utterance to *SP*'s not doing so.
   5. *SP* intends to stop operating the engine so indicated shortly after the time of utterance.

The mode in which one "represents" a given condition as holding will vary. Sometimes one is explicitly *asserting* that the condition is satisfied as in II, 3. In other cases he is *presupposing* that the condition holds, as in the various referential presuppositions like I, 1; II, 1, 2. In the cases of nonassertive acts, like I and III, the speaker is not *asserting* anything; here the conditions that he would not be said to be presupposing, he could be described as *implying*. (I am afraid that I do not know just exactly where to draw the line between those concepts, if there is any unambiguous line to be drawn.) I have intended to use

[18] The term 'contextually indicated' is to be so interpreted that 'A particular F is contextually indicated' is equivalent to 'Something in the context can be relied on to direct an addressee's attention to one particular F.'

the terms 'take responsibility for' and 'represent' in such a way that asserting, presupposing, and implying will be specific modes thereof.

Now it seems that the simplest way to formulate a rule being governed by which would render a sentence usable to represent certain conditions as holding, would be to make the (permissible) utterance of the sentence contingent on the holding of the conditions in question. Thus, corresponding to each of the illocutionary-act types on our list we have a rule of the form: 's may be uttered if the following conditions hold', where s is some sentence that is usable to perform illocutionary acts of the type in question. Here is a list of such rules. Call them "*illocutionary rules*". In each case I have indicated parenthetically the sort of illocutionary act for which the rule fits the sentence.

I.   (Ordering someone to run a certain engine)

'Run the engine' ($S_1$) may be uttered if the following conditions hold:

A. Some engine is contextually indicated.
B. $A$ (the addressee) is not operating that engine at the time of utterance.
C. It is possible for $A$ to operate that engine just after the time of utterance.
D. $SP$ (speaker) has some interest in getting $A$ to operate that engine just after the time of utterance.
E. $SP$ is in a position of authority vis-à-vis $A$ (at least with respect to the operation of engines).

II.  (Suggesting to someone that he join with one in operating a certain engine:)

'Let's run the engine' ($S_2$) may be uttered if the following conditions hold:

A. Some engine is contextually indicated.
B. $SP$ and $A$ are not operating that engine at the time of utterance.
C. It is possible for $SP$ and $A$ to operate that engine just after the time of utterance.
D. $SP$ has some interest in $A$'s joining with him in operating that engine just after the time of utterance.

III.   (Asserting that a certain man is currently operating a certain engine:)

'He's running the engine' ($S_3$) may be uttered if the following conditions hold:

A. Some engine is contextually indicated.
B. Some man is contextually indicated.
C. That man is currently operating that engine.

IV.   (Promising someone not to operate a certain engine much longer:)

'I won't run the engine much longer' ($S_4$) may be uttered if the following conditions hold:

A. Some engine is contextually indicated.
B. *SP* is now operating that engine.
C. It is possible for *SP* to stop operating that engine shortly after the time of utterance.
D. *A* would prefer *SP*'s ceasing to operate that engine shortly after the time of utterance, to *SP*'s not doing so.
E. *SP* intends to stop operating that engine shortly after the time of utterance.

V.    (Asserting that a certain stream is still flowing:)

'It's still running' ($S_5$) may be uttered if the following conditions hold:

A. Some stream is contextually indicated.
B. That stream has been flowing prior to the time of utterance.
C. That stream is flowing at the time of utterance.

VI.   (Asserting that a certain play is still being performed in a certain locality:)

$S_5$ may be uttered if the following conditions hold:

A. Some play is contextually indicated.
B. Some locality is contextually indicated.

C. That play has been performed in that locality before the time of the utterance.

D. That play is scheduled to be performed in that locality after the time of the utterance.

VII. (Adjourning a meeting:)

'The meeting is adjourned' ($S_6$) may be uttered if the following conditions hold:

A. A certain meeting is contextually indicated.
B. That meeting is going on at the time of utterance.
C. *SP* has the authority to terminate the meeting.
D. Conditions are appropriate for the exercise of that authority.

VIII. (Reporting that a meeting has adjourned)

$S_6$ may be uttered if the following conditions hold:

A. A certain meeting is contextually indicated.
B. That meeting has been officially terminated shortly before the time of utterance.

In these formulations the conditions are stated as sufficient, but not necessary, for permissible utterance. It is the phenomenon of multivocality that prevents our adding an 'only if' to these rules. When a sentence has two or more illocutionary-act potentials, the failure of a condition associated with one of those potentials does not in and of itself render the utterance of the sentence incorrect; for the speaker may have been intending to perform one of the other illocutionary acts in the total potential of the sentence. 'The meeting is adjourned' can be used either to adjourn a meeting or to report that a meeting has been adjourned. If one is doing the former, one thereby takes responsibility for its being the case that one has the authority to determine when the meeting is terminated; and so the corresponding rule (VII) will include C. among the conditions of correct utterance. But it would be a mistake to suppose that C. is unqualifiedly a *necessary* condition of correct utterance, for one can, with perfect propriety, use the sentence to *report* that a certain meeting is adjourned, in which case one's utterance is in order provided the conditions specified in Rule VIII are satisfied. Thus a rule that corresponds to some *particular* illocutionary-act potential of a sentence will lay down only sufficient conditions of utterance. If we consider the whole array of illocutionary-act potentials of the sentence, we can envisage another rule that lays down the disjunction of these sets of conditions as a necessary condition of correct utterance.[19]

Multivocality complicates the task of seeing just how being governed by an illocutionary rule makes a sentence usable for "representing" certain conditions as holding. If every sentence were univocal, then there would be one unique set of conditions associated with it, and that set would constitute a necessary as well as sufficient condition for its correct utterance (within the literal first-order communicative use of language). In that case an addressee who is *au courant* with the language would normally take the speaker to be uttering the sentence as a sign of the holding of just those conditions. But where there is a plurality of illocutionary act-potentials it is only a disjunction of sets of conditions that is a necessary condition, and the mere fact that *this sentence* is uttered does not point to one of these sets of conditions rather than another. However, only a slight complication of the picture is required. Normally there will be something in the context of utterance to single out *one* of the illocutionary-act potentials of the sentence as the one the speaker meant to be exploiting. The addressee will normally take the speaker to be uttering his sentence as a sign of the holding of the conditions in the set corresponding to *that* illocutionary act.

I do not believe that representing certain conditions to obtain is all that is involved in performing (at least) a nonassertive illocutionary act, and hence I do not believe that being subject to a rule of the sort illustrated will be enough by itself to render a sentence usable to perform nonassertive illocutionary acts. Promising someone not to run the engine much longer is not *just* a matter of representing the conditions listed in IV to be satisfied; one might be doing that in making a complex assertion and yet not be promising anything. Hence subjection of a sentence to this rule will not distinguish between being usable to make that promise and being usable to assert that those conditions hold. (I will not have time in this paper to make explicit what else I take to be involved.) Nevertheless, even in the nonassertive cases, this is an essential part of what is involved in

---

[19] Even this disjunction is a necessary condition only within what we may call the literal, first-order communicative use of language. If I utter 'The meeting is adjourned' in order to test my voice or to give an example, or if I am using it metaphorically, none of the sets of conditions included in such a disjunction would have to obtain in order that the utterance of the sentence be allowable. This restriction of the sphere of activity within which the rule applies is quite typical. Consider the rule of tennis which specifies that in initiating play one must have his feet back of the base line. That does not hold if we are just knocking balls back and forth in order to warm up.

performing an illocutionary act, and being subject to a rule of this sort is an essential part of what gives a sentence a certain illocutionary-act potential. And if, as we have been supposing, a sentence's having a given meaning is just a matter of its being usable to perform a certain kind of illocutionary act, then being subject to a rule like this is at least part of what constitutes its having a certain meaning. To put the link between illocutionary rules and sentence meaning in a more direct manner (that is, without taking the indirect route through illocutionary-act potential) we have noted previously that linguistic meaning is what endows a linguistic expression with "content", with the capacity to express and/or communicate a certain distinctive "content". Well, illocutionary rules, by virtue of their imbedded conditions, embody that content. Thus being governed by such a rule endows a sentence with the capacity to communicate that "content". The fact that those conditions are (at least sufficient) conditions of the correct utterance of the sentence is (at least part of) what we were groping after with our initial intuitive talk of the "content" that is "tied" to the sentence by virtue of its meaning. In saying that a given sentence is governed by such a rule we have (partly) unpacked the metaphor of content that provided our initial lead.

Thus it is our hypothesis that for each distinguishable sentence-meaning we can find a rule of the form specified, such that being subject to that rule *is* (at least in part) having that meaning.

I would suggest that illocutionary rules satisfy all the requirements laid down earlier for rules that are to be used as basic illustrations of the way in which having a meaning consists in being governed by some rule. (1) They are rules in a distinctive sense of that term; they lay down conditions for the permissibility of behavior, and thereby determine particular actions as correct or incorrect, in or out of order. (2) They are translinguistic in character. Each illocutionary rule issues a license for sentence utterance that is conditional on the satisfaction of certain conditions that are nonlinguistic in character, except in those special cases where the sentence is designed for talking about language. (3) They do not contain any semantic terms except, again, in those special cases in which the sentence is used to talk about semantics. (4) They govern first-level speech; they are not confined to special areas of linguistic behavior, such as that of the linguist developing a systematic description of a language. Thus I would claim that they are unique, among the sorts of semantic rules suggested in the literature, in passing preliminary tests for being the kinds of rules that could be used at the basis of an account of linguistic meaning along the lines of the rule-theory. Whether it is actually the case that sentence meaning consists of subjection to illocutionary rules is, of course, a further question. In the above I have given some reasons for thinking so, but the issue needs much more discussion. What I would claim to have shown is that illocutionary rules cannot be ruled out in advance as the wrong kind of rule to suggest for this purpose.

## *IV*

At this point my main task in this paper is completed. However, I do want to say a few words about the place of my thesis, that sentence-meaning consists (at least in part) in subjection to illocutionary rules, in the more general enterprises of the explication of semantic concepts and the development of resources, conceptual and methodological, for the semantic description of languages.

The first part of my peroration will be a confession. Without retracting any of the claims I have made for illocutionary rules, I must admit that no such rules will figure in a semantic description of a language. There are two closely related reasons for this. First, it is impracticable to describe a language in any of its aspects—semantic, syntactic, or whatever—by assigning rules to its sentences, one by one, or by characterizing its sentences, one by one, in any way. For no limit can be placed on the number of sentences in a natural language. And even if we could justify restricting ourselves to sentences of manageable length, thus rendering the number of sentences finite, we would still be faced with an order of magnitude sufficient to discourage any such project. Second, even if practicable the procedure would not be optimal, for such an enumeration would fail to make explicit the structure of the language. Restricting ourselves to semantics, it seems abundantly clear that the meaning of a sentence is a determinate function of the meanings of the words and other meaningful constituents that compose it, together with facts about its syntactical structure. If so it seems plausible to suppose that there are general compositional principles involved in the semantics of a language, which "project" (to use the Fodor-Katz terminology) the meaning(s) of a sentence from the meanings of its constituents, plus syntactic structure. Thus, it seems clear that there is a commonality in the way in which the meanings of 'That's difficult' and 'It's satisfactory' are determined by the meanings of their constituents, and a like commonality between 'Are you swimming?' and 'Is he working?' while a member of one set is unlike a member of the other set in this respect. Again it seems that a given word, when used in the same sense (as with the word 'run' in $S_2$-$S_4$), will affect the meaning of any sentence in which it occurs in the same way, even though the total meanings of the various sentences are quite different from each other. Neither of these kinds of systematicity would be made explicit by simply specifying one or more illocutionary rules for each sentence of the language.

The two considerations are, of course, intimately related. Just because sentences are resultant rather than basic in the language (molecular rather than atomic), it is natural that there should be an infinite variety in the sentences that can be constructed. Again, where we are dealing with a type of entity that exhibits unbounded variety, a viable theory of such entities must identify more basic constituents of *limited* variety out of which, by a finite stock of principles, any entity of the former sort can be constructed.

These considerations are relevant to the questions of what is learned when a language is learned and what it is the possession of which constitutes a person a fluent speaker of a language, as well as to the question of the form an adequate description of a language would take. The numerosity of the sentences of a language inhibits us from supposing that one learns a language by attaching illocutionary rules to the sentences of the language, one by one. Again, the fact that a fluent speaker can readily understand and use sentences he has never before encountered shows that his (semantic) knowledge of the language cannot consist in having learned the meaning of some finite set of previously encountered sentences, but rather consists in the ability to construct sentences and sentence-meanings.

On the positive side, these considerations point to the conclusion that a fluent speaker's grasp of the semantics of a language consists in knowledge of the meanings of word- or morpheme-sized units, plus a mastery of principles for determining the meaning of any given sentence. And it equally points to the conclusion that an adequate semantic description of a language would feature such components. But if illocutionary rules do not figure in either of these contexts, how can we claim that our thesis about sentence-meaning can serve as the basis of an account of linguistic meaning along the lines of the rule-theory?

Though this can be made to seem, as I have been trying to make it seem, a thorny problem, I believe that the solution is actually very simple. Even though a list of sentences with their meanings is no part of the basic constitution of a language, it is nonetheless essential for the linguist to be able to characterize sentence-meaning. For it is admitted on all hands that sentence-meanings [20] constitute the major

---

[20] More generally, semantic facts about sentences, including such facts as that one sentence is a "paraphrase" of another and that a given sentence is semantically ambiguous, as well as facts about what a given sentence means.

source of data for semantics.[21] An account of the semantic constitution of a language can be looked on as a device for generating meaning assignments ("readings") for any of an infinite set of sentences. And a particular account of this sort for a particular language
can be assessed in terms of the extent to which the sentence-meanings it generates square with "semantic intuitions" at
the sentence level.[22] Hence, even though an optimal description of the
semantics of a language would not specify the meaning of any particular sentence, still the concept of sentence-meaning plays a crucial
role in semantics, just because any proposed semantic description has
to be evaluated in terms of its implications for the assignment of
meanings to sentences.[23] And so the specification of semantic rules for
sentences is not at all irrelevant to the task of explaining just how
linguistic meaning is a matter of being governed by rules.

But just *what* is its relevance? More specifically, how far does the
illocutionary rule account of sentence-meaning, by itself, take us
toward a general rule theory of linguistic meaning? And what implications, if any, does it have for the nature of word-meaning?

The first step in answering these questions is to note that, because of its crucial methodological position in semantics, any interpretation of the concept of sentence-meaning is bound to have reper-
cussions for the understanding of meaning at any linguistic level. If
we accept the above model for semantics, we are committed to the

[21] The feeling that the sentence-level is the optimal source of semantic data, that is, is
the best place at which to confront one's constructions with the fluent speaker's
knowledge of his language, is not explicitly defended by Fodor and Katz or by other
like-minded theorists. I suspect that an adequate defense of this attitude would
involve considerations similar to those we adduced in supporting the idea that the
sentence-level was the place at which to begin looking for semantic rules, especially
the point that the sentence is the minimal vehicle for a self-contained speech act.
Since this is so, it is understandable that naïve semantic intuition would be more
sensitive to the semantic properties and relations of these grosser units, than to the
properties and relations of the smaller units which make up the "fine structure" on
which the speech-act potentialities of the grosser units ultimately depend.

[22] Again these "intuitions" need not be solely made up of, and indeed need not include at
all, "intuitions" as to *what* particular sentences mean. They might consist, in whole or
in part, of pronouncements on matters more indirectly related to sentence-meaning,
for example, whether two sentences have the same meaning or whether a given
sentence has more than one meaning.

[23] This is the usual situation in science. The facts that provide the basic empirical data,
and so are prior in the order of testing, are viewed by sophisticated theories as
derivative from facts about the fine structure and micro-operations of the substances
involved, and so are posterior in the order of causality and explanation. Gross physical
properties of substances, like color and texture, and gross alterations like dissolving
and burning, provide the basic data for chemistry; but such facts are seen by developed chemical theory as derivative from facts about the micro-structure of chemical
elements and compounds, facts which are established on the basis of the gross data
they serve to explain.

view that a word-meaning, however else it is to be characterized, is at least to be construed as a certain distinctive contribution to the meanings of an indefinite number of sentences in which the word occurs. And so if a sentence's having a certain meaning consists in its being governed by an illocutionary rule, then a word-meaning, whatever else it is, is a distinctive contribution to the composition of an indefinite number of illocutionary rules. This conclusion holds regardless of the more specific characterization of word-meaning we adopt, even if it should be, for example, Katz's notion that a word's having a certain meaning is a matter of its being used as a representation of "classes of equivalent thoughts or ideas," or even if we should conclude that there is nothing more to be said on the subject except that a word's having a certain meaning is just a matter of its fitting in a certain way into a semantic system that yields certain illocutionary rules for sentences. Thus the fact that a word has a certain meaning will have *something* to do with rules holding in a society, at least at second remove.

It must be admitted, however, that this would be a relatively weak application of the rule theory to word-meaning. A more full-blooded application would involve representing each word-meaning as itself a matter of some rule governing the employment of the word in question. How might we work toward such an account from the results already set forth, and what are the prospects for the adoption of this construal of word-meaning as compared with other alternatives? Here I shall have to restrict myself to a bare hint.

Under what conditions could we expect to formulate semantic rules for words that will relate words directly to extralinguistic conditions, as well as meet our other requirements for basic semantic rules? If we recall the point that the sentence is the minimal unit of linguistic communication, it seems clear that any semantically crucial conditions on word-utterance will have to concern the utterance of words in sentences. Nevertheless we could, consistently with this principle, represent word-meanings by rules specifying extralinguistic conditions of word-utterance, if a certain specially simple state of affairs obtained. Let us remember that an illocutionary rule lays down a plurality of conditions as jointly sufficient for the permissible utterance of a given sentence. Now suppose it were the case that there were a one-one correspondence between the conditions imbedded in the rule governing $S_1$ and the minimal meaningful elements of $S_1$, so that a given element could be paired with a given condition. Furthermore, suppose it were the case that whenever a given word occurs in a sentence in a given sense, it is paired with the same condition, and whenever it or some other word is used in a different sense it is paired with a different condition. In that case we could take that condition to give the substance of the meaning of the word, and we could take the word's having that meaning to be a matter of its being governed by a rule of the form, 'W may be uttered in a sentence if condition C obtains'. In this case words as well as sentences would be related directly to extralinguistic conditions. And such a rule would provide an ideally simple and clear-cut interpretation of the notion that a word, when used with a given meaning, makes a distinctive contribution to the meaning of the sentence in which it occurs. For the word, by occurring in the sentence, would be contributing one of the conditions that make up the content of the illocutionary rule governing the sentence, which, in turn, endows the sentence with its meaning.

The illocutionary rules cited above do not meet these specifications. We do not get any one-to-one correlation between conditions and meaningful elements of the sentence. Moreover, as is clear from these examples, it is not the case that there is any particular condition(s) that is (are) present in the rule whenever the word 'run' is used in one of its senses, for example, 'operate', but not present when it is used in some other sense. The word 'run' is not, even in one of its senses, related to any unique set of extralinguistic conditions. It is related to different conditions, depending on the sentential context in which it is imbedded. (This, essentially, is why we began our account with sentence-meaning, where it is the case that a sentence, when used with a *particular* meaning, *is* related to a unique set of conditions.) Thus, in I., the fact that 'run' is used in the sentence with a given meaning affects what it is that the rule requires that the addressee not already be doing and have the capacity to do, and what it is that the rule require that the speaker have an interest in getting the addressee to do. Whereas in IV., the fact that 'run' is used in the sentence with that meaning affects what it is that the rule require the speaker to now be doing and be capable of ceasing to do shortly, and what it is that the rule requires the speaker to intend to do.

This being the case, it seems clear that any rules relating words to extralinguistic conditions will have to take into account the diversity of sentential contexts into which a given word (in a given sense) can fit. If there were a finite set of sentence-structures in a natural language, we could embark on the program of specifying for each structure a set of forms for the conditions that have to be included in the illocutionary rules that govern sentences with that structure. A given meaning of a given word might then be set out by a set of rules, each of which would govern the use of the word in a certain position in a sentence of a certain structural type. One such rule might be something like the following: 'Run' may be uttered in the blank in a sentence of the form 'Let's _____ $O$ at $t_1$' if conditions of the following correlated forms hold: (1) $SP$ and $A$ are not operating O at $t_1$; (2) It is possible for $SP$ and $A$ to operate $O$ at $t_1$; (3) $SP$ has some interest in getting $A$ to join him in operating $O$ at $t_1$. It is clear that such a rule does not enjoy the autonomy possessed by an illocutionary rule governing a sentence; it does not by itself determine any particular condition. To obtain a definite condition for any given occurrence of 'run' we have to substitute a constant for the variable '$O$', on the basis of the content of rules governing other constituents of the sentence. However, this difference in types of rules nicely mirrors the fact that sentences can be employed as autonomous units while words cannot.

The arguments put forward by Chomsky and others for the thesis that no limit can be put on the number of distinguishable sentence-structures in a language, would appear to constitute a decisive bar to the above program. An alternative approach might be made through transformational grammar. If the grammar of a language could be stratified in such a way that the base exhibits a finite variety of sentence structures, we could construct semantic rules for the use of words in the base on the model adumbrated in the previous paragraph. Provided the base is so constituted that any meaningful word (morpheme) occurs there with every meaning it exhibits in any construction, we could restrict our treatment of word-meaning to occurrences in base constructions; the meanings of other sentences would be derived transformationally from their "origins" in the base, rather than built up directly from atomic meaningful constituents.

Needless to say, the above suggestion calls for a major program of research involving a close interaction between syntactical and semantical investigations. This would seem a convenient point at which to break off these programmatic remarks about word-meaning.

Whatever the possibilities for representing word-meaning, I would submit that the illocutionary rule interpretation of sentence-meaning shows at least one crucial respect in which linguistic meaning is a matter of rules.

# 'Tensions

## DAVID LEWIS

### *Princeton University*

I have a problem for those who, like myself, admire intensional formal semantics and think it a key to understanding natural language. We can go to extremes of intensionality, if we like. Semantic rules can be stated entirely in terms of intensions, while extensions go unmentioned. But when we do, it seems for all the world as if we've gone purely *ex*tensional instead! Let me explain.

## THE INTENSIONAL LANGUAGE L₁

I begin by describing an intensional language $L_I$. There are various categories of expressions.

S is the category of sentences. A sentence takes as its extension one of the two truth values, truth or falsehood. But the truth value of a sentence may depend on facts which vary from one possible world to another; on the time, place, speaker, and other features of context; on the values assigned to any free variables that may be present; on the resolutions of various sorts of vagueness; and perhaps on other things as well. So truth in $L_I$ is a three-place relation. A sentence has a truth value as its extension relative to an *index*, that being a package of a world, a time, . . . , and whatever else (apart from meaning) might be needed to determine an extension. Equivalently, for each sentence we have a function from indices to truth values. For any possible index, the function gives the truth value of the sentence at that index. This extension-determining function is the intension (in $L_I$) of the sentence.

N is the category of names. A name takes as its extension the thing named—perhaps a concrete material object, perhaps some other sort of entity. Again, the extension may vary; so for each name we have a function from indices that gives the extension of the name at any possible index. This function is the intension (in $L_I$) of the name.

For any two categories X and Y, we have a third category X/Y of expressions which can combine with expressions of category Y to form compound expressions of category X. Examples: an S/N is something that can combine with a name to make a sentence, so it is an intransitive verb. An (S/N)/N can combine with a name to make an intransitive verb, so it is a transitive verb. An (S/S)/S can combine with a sentence to make something that in turn can combine with a sentence to make a sentence, so it is a dyadic connective or operator. There are infinitely many of these functor categories, though only finitely many are employed in $L_I$. An X/Y has no extension. Its intension is a function from appropriate intensions for members of category Y to appropriate intensions for members of category X. All the compositional semantic rules of $L_I$ are given by one simple schema, with various categories put in for X and Y:

If $\alpha$ is an X/Y with intension A and $\beta$ is a Y with intension B, then the result of combining $\alpha$ with $\beta$ is an X with intension A(B), the value of the function A for the argument B.

"Combining" may simply be concatenation; or it may be some more complicated operation, perhaps different for different functor categories or even for different members of one category. Or it may be that structures built up by many successive combinations are subsequently transformed as a whole to give the "surface" expressions of $L_I$.

I described $L_I$ as an intensional language. More precisely, (1) in any case of compounding, the intension of the compound is a function of the intensions of the constituents, but (2) the extension of the compound is not always a function of the extensions of the constituents. Part (1) follows from the given form for semantic rules; part (2) is an additional stipulation.

This completes a partial description of $L_I$, in a style that should be familiar nowadays.[1] It will be useful to give a shamelessly idealized reconstruction of the way that style evolved.

[1] I have followed the treatment in my "General Semantics," *Synthese*, XXII (1970) 18-67, stripped of such frills as many-place functors and a basic category of common nouns. The use of Ajdukiewicz's functor categories makes for brevity in stating the rules. But I could make my point just as well by discussing one of Richard Montague's well-known treatments of natural language. See his "The Proper Treatment of Quantification in Ordinary Language," in Hintikka, Moravcsik, and Suppes, eds., *Approaches to Natural Language* (Dordrecht: Reidel, 1972), or Barbara Partee's paper in this volume.

In the olden days, we knew only of extensions. We used semantic rules of this form:

(1S)  If $\alpha$ is an X with extension A, then the result of combining $\alpha$ with $\beta$ is a Z with extension f(A).

with a special rule for each $\beta$; or, when generality was possible, of this form:

(1G)  If $\alpha$ is an X with extension A and $\beta$ is a Y with extension B, then the result of combining $\alpha$ with $\beta$ is a Z with extension f(A,B).

Then we began to pay attention to languages in which extensions could depend on features of context. We relativized to various sorts of indices, but still adhered to the old dogma that the extension of the compound is a function of the extensions of the constituents. We had special and general rules of these forms:

(2S)  If $\alpha$ is an X with extension A at index i, then the result of combining $\alpha$ with $\beta$ is a Z with extension f(A,i) at index i.

(2G)  If $\alpha$ is an X with extension A at index i and $\beta$ is a Y with extension B at index i, then the result of combining $\alpha$ with $\beta$ is a Z with extension f(A,B,i) at index i.

But we knew that in a few cases, the extension of a compound at one index could depend on the extensions of the constituents not just at that index but at other indices as well. That was so for variable-binding quantifiers if we took the assignments of values to variables as indices; and for modal and tense operators, taking the indices as worlds or times. So we learned to tolerate a few special nonextensional rules of the form:

(3S)  If $\alpha$ is an X whose extension varies from index to index in manner A, then the result of combining $\alpha$ with $\beta$ is a Z with extension f(A,i) at index i.

(For example: if $\alpha$ is a sentence which takes the truth value truth at all and only the worlds in a set A, then the result of prefixing $\square$ to $\alpha$ is a sentence that takes the value truth or falsehood at world i according as A does or does not contain all worlds possible relative to i.) Often the manner of variation did not even need to be explicitly mentioned as an entity, still less stigmatized as an intension. In the case of quantification, at least, such rules were not considered a significant breach of extensionality.

But these special rules proliferated in number when we considered languages with many different modalities; and in variety when we admitted intensional predicate modifiers or intensional sentential operators that could not be handled as modalities with relations of relative possibility. Generality requires quantification over appropriate entities. Once these are at hand, it is natural to identify them with intensions, since they carry all needed information about the meanings of the corresponding expressions. Thus we progressed to rules of the form:

(3G) If $\alpha$ is an X with intension A and $\beta$ is a Y with intension B, then the result of combining $\alpha$ with $\beta$ is a Z with extension f(A,B,i) at index i.

When a rule specifies the extension at every index, it thereby specifies the extension-determining function that we have called an intension. It is only a short step, therefore, to rules of the form:

(4G) If $\alpha$ is an X with intension A and $\beta$ is a Y with intension B, then the result of combining $\alpha$ with $\beta$ is a Z with intension f(A,B).

But this short step gives us a new freedom. For intension-specifying rules, unlike any sort of extension-specifying rules, can apply even when the resulting compound belongs to a category for which there are no appropriate extensions—for instance, when it is a compound modifier or quantifier or connective. In such cases, of course, the appropriate sort of intension can no longer be an extension-determining function from indices. We have seen already, in connection with the functor categories of $L_I$, what else it might be.

When an intensional rule is needed, an extensional rule will not work. But when an extensional rule will work, an intensional rule also will work. If we need some intensional rules, then we may gain uniformity by using intensional rules throughout, even where extensional rules would have sufficed. (It is a matter of taste whether this gain outweighs the waste of using needlessly intensional rules. For me it does.) At this point, our compositional semantic rules always specify how intensions of compounds depend on the intensions of their constituents. The extensions have faded away. We have come full circle, in a way: once again expression are assigned semantic values on a single level, not two different levels. My description of $L_I$ exemplifies this final, purely intensional, stage in the evolution of formal semantics.

### The Extensional Transform $L_E$

Now I shall describe another language $L_E$; this time, an extensional language specified by purely extensional rules of the forms (1G) and (2S) above. $L_E$ and $L_I$ are obviously not identical, since one is an extensional language and the other is not. But they are closely related. All the structure of $L_I$ is mirrored in $L_E$. Following Terence Parsons (more or less), I shall call $L_E$ an *extensional transform* of $L_I$.

$L_E$ has a category of names; but we do best to divide this into two subcategories according to the sort of thing that is named. S is the first category of names; an S-name takes as its extension—that is, it names—a function from indices to truth values. After all, any old entity is entitled to bear a name; nameability is not a special privilege of concrete particulars! N is the second subcategory of names; an N-name takes as its extension a function from indices to entities of any sort. (Although S-names are not N-names, an appropriate extension for an S-name would also be an appropriate extension for an N-name.) Names, in either subcategory, have their extensions rigidly. Their extensions do not vary from one index to another. We could say that the intension of an S-name or an N-name in $L_E$ is the function which gives, for each index, the extension of the name at that index. (These are functions from indices whose values are themselves functions from indices.) But since these intensions are constant functions, they are scarcely worth mentioning.

$L_E$ also has infinitely many functor categories: for any suitable categories X and Y, there is a third category X/Y of expressions which can combine with expressions of category Y to form compound expressions of category X. The "suitable categories" are the subcategories S and N of names, and also the functor categories themselves; but *not* the two further categories of $L_E$ that we have not yet mentioned. The extension of an X/Y is a function from Y-extensions to X-extensions. All but one of the compositional semantic rules of $L_E$ are given by this general, purely extensional schema:

If $\alpha$ is an X/Y with extension A and $\beta$ is a Y with extension B, then the result of combining $\alpha$ with $\beta$ is an X with extension A(B), the value of the function A for the argument B.

Functors also have their extensions rigidly in $L_E$. We could take their intensions in $L_E$ to be the constant functions from indices to their unvarying extensions. But why bother?

Such are the lexica of noncompound expressions in $L_I$ and $L_E$, and such are the combining operations associated with functors (alternatively, the transformational apparatus) in $L_I$ and $L_E$, that $L_I$ is related as follows to the fragment of $L_E$ presented so far. Let us say that the categories S of $L_I$ and S of $L_E$ are *namesakes*; also N of $L_I$ and N of $L_E$; also X/Y of $L_I$ and X/Y of $L_E$, whenever the X's are namesakes and the Y's are namesakes. Then for every pair of namesake categories of the two languages, exactly the same expressions belong to both. Further, whenever an expression $\alpha$ has A as its *intension* in $L_I$, then also $\alpha$ has A as its *extension* in $L_E$.

So far, $L_E$ scarcely deserves to be called a language, for a language needs sentences. It would be quite wrong to think that S of $L_E$ is the category of sentences. Tradition makes clear that the extensions of sentences are supposed to be truth values; whereas the extensions of members of S in $L_E$, we recall, are functions from indices to truth values. These are appropriate *intensions*, but inappropriate *extensions*, for sentences. They are appropriate extensions only for names.

$L_E$ does have a category of genuine sentences, however; and also a category of predicates for use in forming sentences. But there is only one predicate: ϟ. That is our metalinguistic name for it; actually, it is written as a blank space and pronounced as a pause. The remaining compositional semantic rule of $L_E$, again a purely extensional rule but special to the predicate ϟ, is as follows:

If $\alpha$ is an S with extension A, then the result of prefixing ϟ to $\alpha$ is a sentence having as its extension at an index i the truth value A(i) given by the function A for the argument i.

So ϟ is a sort of truth predicate; but a safe one, since there is no way in $L_E$ to produce a paradoxical diagonalization.

We may note that whenever $\alpha$ is a sentence of $L_I$, then ϟ $\alpha$ is a sentence of $L_E$ with exactly the same truth conditions. There are no other sentences of $L_E$ besides these images of the sentences of $L_I$.

This completes my description of $L_E$. It is an extensional language, as I said it would be. Inspection of the semantic rules confirms that the extension of a compound is always a function of the extensions of the constituents.

### THE PARSONS TRANSFORM $L_P$

If we like, we can take the names and functors of $L_E$ and trade them in for predicates and quantified variables. For instance, if we have

$$\mathfrak{L}((\alpha(\beta))(\gamma))$$

as a sentence of $L_E$, where $\beta$ and $\gamma$ are in the category N and $\alpha$ is in the category $(S/N)/N$, we can replace it by

$$\exists v\,\exists w\,\exists x\,\exists y\,\exists z\;(\mathfrak{L}v\;\&\;Rvzw\;\&\;Rwyx\;\&$$
$$\bar{\alpha}x\;\&\;\bar{\beta}y\;\&\;\bar{\gamma}z)$$

where R is a predicate meaning "—is the result of operating on the argument--by the function . . ." and $\bar{\alpha}$, $\bar{\beta}$, $\bar{\gamma}$ are monadic predicates uniquely satisfied by the entities that are the extensions in $L_E$ of $\alpha\cdot\beta\cdot$ and $\gamma$, respectively. In this way we go from $L_E$ to another extensional language $L_P$ (if you consider quantifiers extensional). I shall call $L_P$ the *Parsons transform* of our original language $L_I$, since when Terence Parsons speaks of an "extensional transform" he means a language like $L_P$.[2] But $L_E$ is just as extensional as $L_P$. There is nothing anti-extensional about names and functors per se. Eliminating them is one enterprise, going extensional is another.

## THE PROBLEM

$L_I$ can be a richly intensional language, whereas $L_E$ is strictly extensional. An important difference, as we all were taught. But almost the only difference there is between the two!

Two field linguists, I and E, fully equipped to perpetrate Cartesian deviltry, go to work on a certain tribe. They investigate the dispositions to verbal behavior under a wide range of deceptive stimulation, the beliefs and desires that would rationalize that behavior, and the neural hookup and laws that would explain it materialistically. They study these things until there is nothing more to know. Then I announce my conclusion: these tribesmen use the intensional language $L_I$. My colleague E, a keen extensionalist, disagrees. He thinks it gratuitous of me to ascribe to them a language that requires the notoriously obscure apparatus of intensional semantics. After all, a better explanation lies close at hand! His opinion is that they use the extensional language $L_E$. Dumbfounded by E's perversity, I know not what to say.

## BAD REJOINDERS

I really don't know. I do know of several unsatisfactory arguments against E's opinion, and we had better clear those out of the way.

---

[2] See Parsons, *A Semantics for English* (duplicated), and "Some Problems Concerning the Logic of Predicate Modifiers," *Synthese*, XXI (1970), 327–329.

*First*, I might try arguing that E's account is worse than mine just because it is more complicated. He requires two more categories, one more lexical item, and one more rule. Besides, his extra rule departs from the standard form of his other rules.

But this argument is bad for two reasons. For one thing, extensionality itself is generally thought to be an important dimension of simplicity. E may say that it is cheap at the price. For another thing, I agree with E that a complete account should mention that speakers pause (and writers leave extra spaces) at the beginnings of their sentences. E has already covered this fact in his ascribed syntax and semantics. I have not, and I must find a place for it, at some cost in complexity, elsewhere in my total description of the tribe's use of language.

*Second*, I might try arguing that E's opinion goes against our paradigm cases of extension-bearing. "Boston" names Boston, for instance, and does not rather name some function from indices.

The paradigms, however, are cases of extension-bearing in certain particular languages: German, Polish, English, and some other familiar languages that can be translated into these by well-established procedures. We have no paradigm cases of extension-bearing in the language of these hitherto unstudied tribesmen.

Even if, in my opinion, their language does happen to be one of the familiar ones, still E cannot be expected to agree that the paradigms apply. For E and I disagree about which language is theirs.

Tarski's Convention T and its relatives will not help. Since the tribe's language is not—not uncontroversially, anyway—the same as our metalanguage for it, the only versions of these principles that apply are the ones stated in terms of translation. For instance, E and I may agree that a metalinguistic sentence of the form "—names—in their language" (or "—is a name having—as extension in their language") should be true whenever the first blank is filled with a name (in our language) of some name $\alpha$ in the tribe's language and the second blank is filled with a translation of $\alpha$ into our language. This gets us nowhere. Disagreeing as we do about what the names are and what their extensions are, E and I have no business agreeing about what the correct translations are.

*Third*, I might try arguing that their language cannot be an extensional language, as E claims, because certain inference patterns are invalid in it that are valid in any extensional language. For instance, I might point to inferences by Leibniz's Law, or by Existential Generalization, in which true premises yield false conclusions.

E should agree with me that Leibniz's Law (for example) preserves truth in any extensional language. He should also agree with me that truth is not preserved in the inferences I produce as counterexamples.[3] But he should not agree with me that those inferences are instances of Leibniz's Law. An inference by Leibniz's Law needs an identity premise, and how do we identify those? Not by looking for a stack of two or three or four horizontal lines! Semantically, an expression with two gaps expresses identity iff (1) the result of inserting names in the gaps in a sentence, and (2) the sentence so formed is true if the inserted names are coextensive, otherwise false. An identity premise is a sentence formed by thus inserting names in the gaps of an expression that expresses identity. Since E and I disagree about which are the coextensive names, we will disagree also about which are the expressions that express identity, which sentences are identity premises, and which inferences are genuine instances of Leibniz's Law. If E identifies instances of Leibniz's Law correctly according to his opinions about names and their extensions, the inferences he selects will indeed preserve truth.

*Fourth*, I might try arguing *ad hominem* that E has not really managed to escape intensionality, since the things he takes for extensions are intensional entities. Functions from indices to truth values are commonly identified with propositions (especially if the indices consist of possible worlds and little else). Functions from indices to things in general are likewise identified with individual concepts. How can *in*tensional entities be *ex*tensions?

But this is confusion. Intensionhood is relational. Intensions are things that play a certain characteristic role in semantics, not things of a special sort. E and I agree that in a suitable language (whether or not it happens in the language of this tribe) the very same thing that is the intension of one expression is also the extension of another. For instance, speaking in a fragment of technical English suited for use as the metametalanguage of a smaller fragment of English, we agree that one and the same thing is both the intension of the object-language expression "my hat" and the extension of the metalanguage expression "the intension of 'my hat'". In itself, this thing is neither an intension nor an extension.

What is true is that some things can serve only as extensions, while other things—functions from indices, for instance—can serve either as extensions or as intensions. But there is no kind of thing that is ineligible by its nature to be an extension.

---

[3] I am here ignoring our disagreement about whether an S must be preceded by ⅀ to make a sentence. Strictly speaking, if $\alpha, \beta, /\therefore \gamma$ is a non-truth-preserving inference in L$_I$, then $⅀\alpha, ⅀\beta, /\therefore ⅀\gamma$ is a non-truth-preserving inference in L$_E$. The original ⅀-less version is not any sort of inference in L$_E$, since its "premises" and "conclusion" are S-names rather than sentences.

*Fifth*, I might try arguing that E's opinion ascribes an extravagant ontology to the tribesmen. When I say that a certain word of their language names a certain concrete, material hill, E says that it names something rather more esoteric: a set-theoretic object built up from a domain of individuals that contains unactualized possibilia.

E and I, if we are consistent, believe in these esoteric entities ourselves. We do not doubt that we can have names for them. Then on what grounds can I deny E's claim that the tribesmen also have names for them? In fact, we both agree that they have names for other entities far more suspect, to wit certain far-fetched gods (according to me) or function from indices to such gods (according to E).

I might do better to argue that the ontology ascribed by E is bad not because certain esoteric things are present in it but rather because certain unesoteric things are missing from it. Saul Kripke has suggested (in conversation, 1972) that it is wrong to ascribe to someone an ontology that contains sets without their members, functions without their arguments and values, or the like.

A plausible principle. But has E really violated it in ascribing the use of $L_E$, a language in which all the names are names of functions from indices and none are names of the concrete, commonplace things that are among the values of those functions? I think not. The ascribed ontology is not the same thing as the ascribed set of name-bearers. If there is an ontology associated with our language, for instance, it includes all the real numbers; not just the countable minority of them that bear names. It is of no significance that the set of name-bearers violates Kripke's closure principle, unless it can be shown to be the whole of the ascribed ontology. But it is hard to say what ontology, if any, is ascribed in ascribing the use of $L_E$. One looks for the domain of quantification. But $L_E$ has no quantifiers! Quantifiers are sentence-makers; but the only sentence-maker in $L_E$ is $\mathbf{\Sigma}$, and that is no quantifier. So $L_E$ does not have a domain of quantification in any straightforward sense, either one that satisfies the closure principle or one that does not.

Unlike $L_E$, the Parsons transform $L_P$ does have a natural domain. More precisely, there is a set D such that we get the intended truth conditions for those sentences of $L_P$ that are transforms of sentences of $L_I$ iff D is included in the range of the quantified variables. (This assumes that the predicates of $L_P$ have their intended interpretations.) The set D, which is the same as the set of extensions of expressions in $L_E$, does violate Kripke's closure principle and so is unsuitable to be ascribed as someone's ontology. If some extensionalist claimed that our tribesmen used $L_P$, disguised by transformations, I think we would have a promising line of attack against him. But how does that affect E, whose claim is different? Perhaps there is some way to show that if it is bad to ascribe the use of L $_P$, then it is just as bad to ascribe the use of L $_E$. But so far, this looks to me like nothing better than guilt by association.

## COMMON GROUND

So I have no way to argue against E's absurd opinion. But though we certainly disagree about something, the extent of our differences should not be exaggerated. In some sense, we have given equivalent descriptions of the phenomena. (That is just what makes it so hard to build a case for one description against the other.) More precisely, if we treat our semantic jargon as theoretical vocabulary and eliminate it by Ramsey's method of existential quantification, then our disagreement will vanish. Our two accounts are equivalent in the sense that they have a common Ramsification.

We can agree on the following description in neutral terms. There is a system of categories: call them just S, N, and X/Y whenever X and Y are categories in the system. There are three relations of expressions to things: call them the 1-'tension, 2-'tension, and 3-'tension relations. The 1-'tension of an expression, but not the 2-'tension or 3-'tension, may vary from one index to another. The 1-'tension of an S at an index is a truth value; the 1-'tension of an N at an index may be anything; an expression in one of the other categories has no 1-'tension. The 2-'tension of an S or an N is the function from indices that gives the proper 1-'tension at each index. The 2-'tension of an X/Y is a function from appropriate 2-'tensions for members of Y to appropriate 2-'tensions for members of X; if $\alpha$ is an X/Y with 2-'tension A and $\beta$ is a Y with 2-'tension B, then the result of combining $\alpha$ with $\beta$ is an X with 2-'tension A(B). The 3-'tension of any expression is the constant function from indices to the unvarying 2-'tension. Finally, a tribesman speaks the truth in his language just when he utters an S preceded by a pause, and the 1-'tension of that S at the index (or set of indices) determined by the occasion of utterance is truth.

So far, so good. To complete my account, I need only add a gloss: the 1-'tensions are the extensions, the 2-'tensions are the intensions, the 3-'tensions are neither, and S is the category of sentences. To complete his contrary account, E need only add his contrary gloss: the 2-'tensions are the extensions, the 3-'tensions are the intensions, the 1-'tensions are neither, and S is a subcategory of names.

But these disputed additions do not add much. No matter which way we apply our traditional semantic vocabulary of extension, intension, naming, and sentencehood, the facts of the matter are already covered by the unglossed neutral description which is the common Ramsification of both our opinions. That is all we would need, for instance, in giving an account of the tribe's use of language as a rational activity for imparting information, or as a physical phenomenon. The questions under dispute are, so far as I can see, idle. If they are not, their import should give us a way to settle them.

## MORALS

This story has an abundance of morals. But most of them are available only if you recklessly conclude that because I have not been able to solve my problem, therefore it must be insoluble. Actually I believe nothing of the sort. Probably there is some perfectly good reason why $L_I$ and not $L_E$ is the tribe's language, and I have just overlooked it. Still, what if the problem were insoluble?

*First moral*: we would have another good example of Quine's inscrutability of reference. Different assignments of extensions would account equally well for the solid facts of the matter, and there would be nothing to choose between them. But at the same time the indeterminacy would be made to seem less formidable than we might have thought. In view of the common Ramsifications, it seems that even the semantic facts are not in dispute. E and I disagree about the proper way to describe those facts in our traditional semantic jargon. That is only a localized indeterminacy in one small region of our language. Can Quine's other alarming indeterminacies be disarmed in the same way?

*Second moral*: intension and extension would be correlative concepts. Neither would make sense except by contrast with the other. In a two-level semantic analysis, where expressions are assigned certain entities that are functions and other entities that are the values of those functions at particular indices, clearly the functions are intensions vis-à-vis the values and the values are extensions vis-à-vis the functions. But in a one-level analysis, whether we approach it by getting more and more intensional or less and less, there is no more contrast and the correlative terms might therefore be out of place.

Our *final moral* is unconditional. It stands whether or not my problem can be solved. So elusive is the difference between using an intensional language and using an extensional language that it can scarcely matter much which we do use. Those who value the superior clarity of extensional languages as such [4] are misguided. There are

[4] For instance, David Lewis when he wrote the opening lines of "Counterpart Theory and Quantified Modal Logic," *Journal of Philosophy*, LXV (1968), 113, as follows: "We can conduct formalized discourse about most topics perfectly well by means of our

differences that do matter. There is the difference between languages that can be analyzed by the methods of formal semantics and ones that (so far as we know) cannot. For any sort of ontic purist, there is the difference between languages that can be analyzed without recourse to suspect entities and ones that cannot. And there is the difference between standard first-order predicate calculus and all less familiar and less well-investigated languages. But none of these real differences between better and worse languages coincides with the difference between extensional and intensional.[5]

all-purpose extensional logic. . . . Then we introduce modal operators to create a special-purpose, nonextensional logic. Why this departure from our custom?" He proceeded to put the departure right; but his views might just as well have been presented as an intensional semantic analysis of an intensional language.

[5] I am grateful to Graham Nerlich and Max Cresswell for the conversations in which this paper had its origins, and to the National Science Foundation for research support.

# Positions for Quantifiers

## P. F. STRAWSON

### Oxford University

*I*

Tom and William play follow-my-leader. William is the leader. So Tom does whatever William does. Now, as some would ask, what is the logical form of this last statement? Or—in other words—how are we to understand our understanding of the construction it exemplifies?

Someone might too hastily say that the statement is to be understood—indeed *is* understood—as involving quantification over particular actions and has the form 'For any (action) $x$, if William performs $x$, then Tom performs $x$ too'. But if by 'particular action' here we mean what, say, Donald Davidson means, this obviously won't do. For Tom *can't* perform the particular action that William performs. The best he can do is to perform another action of the same kind. So if we are to analyze our statement as involving quantification over actions, the analysis will have to be more complicated. It might, for example, run: 'For every action-kind $K$, if there is an action $x$ such that William performs $x \, \varepsilon \, K$, then there is an action $y$, such that Tom performs $y$ and $y \, \varepsilon \, K$'. And here we quantify not only over actions, but also over action-kinds.

Now it seems undeniable that our original statement involves quantification (or something very like it). It is also undeniable that anyone who understands both our original statement and our doubly quantified analysis will acknowledge that they are, nearly enough, equivalent. But the combined force of these two truths seems insufficient to compel the conclusion that this analysis really does expose the logical form of the original. Rather, one may feel that the original statement is a good example of something for which Quine allows no place in his favored logical grammar: namely, quantification such that if we wish to represent it with the help of variables, it requires predicate-variables (or, perhaps better, a special subclass of predicate-variables). So if one were to choose a way of representing the form designed to bring out both its resemblance to, and its difference from, the kind of quantification recognized in standard logical grammar, one might write: '($\Phi$) (William $\Phi$s $\rightarrow$ Tom $\Phi$s)'.

Let us consider a comment on this from a Quinian point of view. 'There is, in this suggestion', it might be said, 'no real departure from orthodoxy, though there may well be a certain confusion—a conflation, perhaps, of two different suggestions each individually reconcilable with orthodoxy. Orthodoxy requires that all quantification be quantification over individuals (objectual, referential), *unless* it is merely substitutional. Variables of quantification can indeed genuinely fill out predicate-place; but only if they are variables of merely substitutional quantification. So if we are to take the present proposal as one according to which the variables of quantification do indeed genuinely fill out the predicate-places, then we must also take it as a proposal to view the quantification in question as merely substitutional quantification. There is, however, another alternative to the doubly quantified analysis which is also compatible with orthodoxy. We can regard our original statement as involving just one dose of quantification, and this non-substitutional quantification, if we are prepared to see the variables of quantification as ranging not over particular actions but over action-types or universals—items akin to attributes. In that case, we should make explicit in our analysis the presence of a suitable two-place predicate apt for linking the name of an actor and the name of an action-type: say 'performs' or perhaps 'exemplifies'. Indeed we might suggest that the word 'does' in our original statement has just this role. But if the proposal under consideration is to be taken in this sense, then it was confusingly presented. The presentation indeed bears all the marks of a conflation of two separately legitimate proposals.'

Now let us consider a rejoinder to this orthodox comment—or, rather, two rejoinders. The first rejoinder is to the effect that neither of the so-called legitimate alternatives is realistic, that neither, therefore, is acceptable for the purposes in hand; the second, and much more important, rejoinder is that the orthodox comment has nothing but orthodoxy to recommend it and this is no recommendation, for the orthodoxy in question is not well founded.

Is either of the two so-called legitimate alternatives realistic? What of substitutional quantification? As far as I understand the matter, the criterion of *truth* for substitutional quantification is to be found in the results of dropping the quantifier and substituting expressions of the appropriate grammatical category in the place of the variables which the quantifier binds. Thus Quine writes: "An existential substitutional quantification is counted as true if and only if there is an expression which, when substituted for the variable, makes the open sentence after the quantifier come out true"; and again "A universal quantification is counted as true if no substitution makes the open sentence come out false." [1] Now in the case of our universally quantified statement about Tom and William, what is here offered as a *criterion* of truth may well be a *consequence* of truth. But to present this consequence as a criterion seems quite bizarre. The criterion of truth for such a statement as is in question has nothing to do with expressions. Indeed, the criterion cannot be declared more clearly than it declares itself: Tom does whatever William does: however William acts, Tom acts thus too. William's behavior might be indescribable without therefore being inimitable.

Perhaps I have misunderstood Quine's explanations of substitutional quantification. Perhaps the notion of a criterion of truth is out of place or unclear. But replacing it with the perhaps looser idea of an explanation of meaning, or with the notion of explanatory paraphrase, clearly makes no change in the situation. Any paraphrase of 'Tom does whatever William does' which mentions expressions is a poor one. Substitutional quantification, if there is such a thing, must be clearly differentiated from the other sort of quantification which Quine acknowledges (quantification over individuals) without assuming the aspect of a kind of quantification of which he denies the possibility or intelligibility. But it is impossible to find in the official doctrine an account which both achieves this result and is such that our quantified statement about Tom and William can plausibly be said to be an instance of substitutional quantification. Henceforth I shall say no more about substitutional quantification.

The objection to the second proffered 'legitimate' alternative is rather subtler and more difficult to state concisely. It merges with the objection to the orthodoxy in general. If we set aside both substitutional quantification and the doubly quantified analysis, we seem to be left with two *prima facie* possibilities, one compatible with the orthodoxy and one not. Consider the two pairs of statements:

1   (a)  If Tom runs, then Tom is out of breath
    (b)  Whoever runs is out of breath

[1] *Ontological Relativity*, p. 104. Columbia University Press, New York, 1969.

2   (a)  If William hops, then Tom hops
    (b)  Tom does whatever William does.

On one view—the unorthodox view—the logical relation between 1(a)
and 1(b) is exactly paralleled by the logical relation between 2(a) and
2(b). We can say 1(b) and then go on: 'For instance, 1(a)'. We can say
2(b) and then go on: 'For instance 2(a)'. The relation in each case is
equally direct. There is a difference, of course: in the one case we are
generalizing in name- or subject-place, in the other in predicate-place
(or, perhaps better, in action-predicate-place). It is because there is the
possibility of this difference that there is the possibility of this parallel.
The orthodox view denies the possibility of this difference and hence
the possibility of this parallel. On the orthodox view the relation
between 2(a) and 2(b) cannot be direct, as is the relation between 1(a)
and 1(b). The relation between 2(a) and 2(b) is mediated, on this view: it
is mediated by something like a paraphrase [2] of 2(a) in which the
one-place predicate occurring in 2(a) is replaced by a combination of a
two-place predicate and a name. It is this paraphrase, and only this
paraphrase, which stands in as direct a relation to 2(b) as 1(a) does to
1(b). If we really want a *strict* parallel to '1(b); for instance 1(a)', then
we should say something like this: 'Tom does whatever William does;
for instance, if Tom does hopping, then William does hopping', from
which we could proceed, by paraphrase, to 'That is to say, if Tom hops,
then William hops.'

Of these two views it seems to me that, while the unorthodox view
yields a natural account of our understanding of the forms in question,
there is nothing to recommend the orthodox view except its orthodoxy.
But what is there to recommend the orthodoxy? If the orthodoxy were
merely a stipulated feature of the grammar of an artificial notation,
the question would have, in the present context, no interest. For our
present concern is with forms of natural language. So if the only merits
of the restriction in question were to be found in advantages of, say,
clarity or simplicity which it secured to the artificial notation, then it
would have, from our present point of view, no merits at all.

But it seems clear, or fairly clear, that Quine does not view the
orthodoxy in this light. When he maintains that quantification, if not
merely substitutional, is always quantification over individuals (objects), that variables of nonsubstitutional quantification can never fill
out predicative, but only referential, position, he seems to see himself
not as imposing a convenient restriction but as acknowledging a

[2] But see below, Part IV.

general truth. What are his reasons? One set of reasons can hardly
be thought compelling. It goes like this. 'Whenever we quantify,
then we can also express what we want to say by starting off with
"There is. . . ." (or its negation), followed by a phrase beginning with
"some" or "a" (for example, something, some place, some time, some
way—a thing, a place, a time, a way, etc.), followed by a relative clause.
The phrase "There is . . ." is explicitly existential, and thus explicitly
referential, directing us to objects, to things that exist. Names, too,
direct us, in their own way, to objects; but predicates do not. Predicates
are simply attached in a truth-or-falsehood-yielding way, to the referential expressions, the expressions that direct us to objects, be they
names or the "some" (or "a"-) phrases of quantification introduced by
the explicitly existential "There is". The availability of the "There
is . . ." form makes clear, as nothing else can, what we are doing when
we quantify; and *ipso facto* makes clear that, whatever the appearances, the only place for quantifiers is the referential place'.

The above is not taken from any specific page of Quine, yet seems
true to the spirit of much that he writes. It can hardly be said, however,
to be persuasive. Why should Quine, of all people, attach so much
importance to the ever-availability in English idiom, whenever we
quantify, of the "There is . . ." form? Why not rather regard this as a
trivial fact, or even as a misleading feature, of English idiom? Why not
stress rather the fact of the frequent dispensability of such constructions—with or without unnaturalness? (And often without: as, for
example, in my own sentence, above: "Whenever we quantify,
then. . . .") If we leave aside the "There is a . . ." idiom and turn to the
notion of 'object', we do not find any greater measure of clarification.
Prior, who has his own reasons for rejecting the Quinian orthodoxy,
remarks that the introduction of bindable variables in the place of
certain expressions by no means commits us to the view that these
expressions stand for or designate objects.[3] This remark would be more
helpful if we were also told how to understand the notion of an object,
or of an expression's standing for, or designating, an object. Quine, in a
way, does tell us, but only in a way which completes the deadlock:
objects (or what we take to be such) are what we quantify over, that is,
take to exist.

If we get little light on the orthodoxy by way of the notions of
existence and object, perhaps we shall get more by putting these
notions, at least temporarily, on one side. What we are left with if we
put these notions on one side is simply the notion of (singular) predi-

---

[3] Cf. *Objects of Thought*, Ch. 3, esp. pp. 35-36. Clarendon Press, Oxford, 1971.

cation, a grammatical combination into which there enter (in the simplest case) a singular term and a predicate: and along with this the notions of position for a singular term (or referential position) and predicate-position. In Quine's ideally austere language the distinction between singular terms and predicates is *identical* with the distinction between quantifiable variables and predicates. So we must obviously look outside the limits of that language if we want to ask *why* Quine holds the general doctrine that quantifiable variables can fill out only referential position and never predicate position, that is, the doctrine that there can be singular term variables and not predicate-variables. We do not have to look very far outside. It will suffice, at least for the moment, to admit the category of names. Then we have 'Fa' as the general form of predication without quantification. And we have the question: Why is it held that quantifiable variables can fill out only the a-place and not the F-place?

Quine's answer is quite explicit, and again surprising. It is that there is no way of distinguishing the parts which enter into this general combination of predication *except* as the parts one of which occupies a position accessible to quantification while the other does not. It is not a question of specifying a certain basic grammatical combination and then advancing a certain doctrine about it; rather, it is only in terms of the doctrine that we can specify the combination. Here I quote: "When we schematize a sentence in the predicative way "*Fa*" or "*a* is an *F*", our recognition of an "a" part and an "F" part turns strictly on our use of variables of quantification; the "a" represents a part of the sentence that stands where a quantifiable variable could stand, and the "F" represents the rest" [4] Again, imagining a finite universe of named objects, in which quantification lapses, as theoretically inessential, Quine adds: "And the very distinction between names and other signs lapses in turn, since the mark of a name is its admissibility in positions of variables." [5] Here the orthodox doctrine is presented as absolutely watertight; for the terms in which the doctrine is stated can only be understood if the doctrine is accepted.

But is this true? Is it true that no account can be given of the distinction between the "a" part and the "F" part of a predication (of the subject-predicate distinction, as I shall say for short), except in terms which presuppose the orthodoxy? Surely it is *not* true. For such accounts have been given, and have not been shown to be incoherent. [6]

---

[4] "Existence and Quantification" in *Ontological Relativity* p. 95; see also p. 106.
[5] *Ontological Relativity*, p. 62.
[6] Cf. Strawson "Singular Terms and Predication" and "The Asymmetry of Subject and Predicate" in *Logico-Linguistic Papers*, pp. 53-74 and 96-115. Methuen, London, 1971.

(They—or some of them—may have been framed in terms which Quine is reluctant to employ: but that is another matter altogether.)

So in default of reasons for accepting the orthodoxy, we are released from its restrictions. We can acknowledge quantification into predicate-position as a feature of the logical grammar of natural language as freely as we can acknowledge quantification into name- (or singular-subject)-position. And we can maintain the intuitively satisfactory position earlier adumbrated on our original question: that is, that "Tom does whatever William does" is as direct a predicate-generalization of "If William hops, then Tom hops" as "Whoever runs is out of breath" is a subject-generalization of "If Tom runs, then Tom is out of breath." Here are two convenient terminological decisions to accompany our recognition of our freedom. First: we will retain the familiar phrase "existential quantification" for what might otherwise be called " 'some'-quantification", whether we are quantifying into referential position or not; but, second, we will restrict the idiom of "quantifying over" to the cases where we are quantifying into referential position.

## II

Suppose we now move outside the limits of that restricted grammar which recognizes as grammatical categories just singular terms, predicates and sentences, including open sentences; and which recognizes as constructions just predication, yielding sentences from singular terms and predicates, and a small number of constructions involving either a connective or a quantifier, yielding sentences from sentences. Our purpose is to inquire where else, if anywhere, we may quantify, besides into singular-term-position and predicate-position; or, more exactly, where else, if anywhere, it is reasonable to suppose that we do in fact quantify in our natural language. Prior has one suggestion. Indeed it seems to be primarily in the interest of this suggestion that he queries the orthodoxy just discarded. He suggests that we recognize a set of constructions which, unlike any of those just mentioned, form sentences from singular terms and sentences. 'Believes that', 'says that', and so on, would be particles entering into such constructions. He then suggests that we can quantify, not only into singular-term-place and predicate-place, but also into sentence-place: the best way of representing the logical form of 'Tom believes everything that William tells him' would be '$(p)$ (William tells Tom that $p \rightarrow$ Tom believes that $p$)'. Though this freedom to quantify into sentence place is most useful in connection with constructions of this kind, it is not, of course, confined to such use. It would be suspicious if it were.

The logical form of 'Some proposition is true' is '($\exists p$) it is true that $p$', which is equivalent to '($\exists p$) $p$'. An important merit of this proposal in Prior's eyes is that it does not commit us to recognizing propositions as objects. Quantifying into sentence-place is not quantifying *over* propositions. It will be seen that though Prior rejects the Quinian orthodoxy as a whole, he accepts a part of it. Quine holds that whenever we quantify, we quantify into referential position and hence quantify over objects (or what we are committed to taking as such). Prior rejects the premise, but accepts that the conclusion follows from it. When we do indeed quantify into singular-term-position, he would agree, we are committed to the view that any specifying expression, any definite singular term, which might replace the bound variable, stands for or designates an object.

Let us put Prior's proposal on one side for a moment—I will return to it later—and turn to another class of cases. Consider the following sets of expressions: somewhere, nowhere, everywhere, anywhere, wherever; always, sometimes, never, whenever; somehow, anyhow, however. Anyone who reflects on the topic of quantification should surely be struck by the parallel between these expressions and those commonly taken to be the natural language representatives of quantification into singular-term-position: that is, something, everything, nothing, anything, whatever; and someone, everyone, no one (nobody), anyone, whoever.[7] So strong is the influence of the prevailing dogma, however, that expressions of the first class have commonly been taken, like expressions of the second, as signalizing quantification into singular-term-position: quantification, that is, *over* places, times, or occasions, and perhaps manners or means. Thus 'Holmes will meet Moriarty somewhere, sometime', will become, as a first approximation—I do not wish to saddle anyone with the suggestion that this would represent a final analysis—something like 'There is a place, $x$, and a time, $y$, such that will-meet-at-at (Holmes, Moriarty, $x$, $y$)'.

If, however, we are prepared to enrich our grammar—that is, in the present context to enrich our conception of our actual grammar—sufficiently to provide for adverbial phrases, and at the same time to make use of our new freedom with quantifiers, a quite different treatment may become possible. What the best account to give of constructions with adverbial phrases may be, is not an easy question. It is fairly certain that not all constructions traditionally classified as adverbial are to be handled in the same way. One way of handling some cases might be to recognize a construction involving a combination of predicate and adverb (or adverb phrase) which yields a complex predicate.

[7] Cf. Strawson, "Singular Terms and Predication," *Logico-Linguistics Papers*, p. 72.

We might call it the modification construction. Even this might be too close to conventional models for the sort of cases that currently concern us, and it might be better to think of some kinds of adverbial modification as yielding sentences from sentences. For our present purposes the particular solution adopted in particular types of case is indifferent, so long as it involves the recognition of certain unreduced grammatical categories of adverb-phrases, including those relating to time and place. Given that this condition is satisfied and the orthodoxy regarding quantification is abandoned, there is no obstacle in principle to recognizing quantification into adverb-phrase-place wherever we find it. And of course the suggestion is that we typically find it where we find the expressions I listed just now: that is, 'somewhere', 'always', and their kin.

Parenthetically it may be pointed out that this suggestion may throw some light on Davidson's problem about action-sentences with adverbial modification.[8] He is concerned to elucidate the understanding we have of the logical grammar of natural language, which underlies our knowledge that, for example, from the proposition that Brutus stabbed Caesar in the afternoon in the Forum there follows the proposition that Brutus stabbed Caesar or from the proposition that John kissed Mary in the garden at midnight it follows that John kissed Mary. His own solution is to regard every such sentence as involving existential quantification over actions and to treat the place- and time-specifying adverbial phrases as predicates of actions; the suggestion, in the form in which he makes it, involves displacing the apparent two-place-predicates 'stab' and 'kiss' by three-place-predicates, for which relevant triples in the given cases would consist of two persons and one action. He contrasts his solution favorably with another suggestion according to which the apparent two-place-predicates 'kiss' and 'stab' are really $n$-place predicates, for somewhat indefinite $n$, with relevant $n$-tuples including, not actions, but persons, places, times, perhaps instruments and so, somewhat vaguely, on. There is indeed little to be said for this last suggestion. But it is arguable that both it and Davidson's would seem equally unnecessary once we recognized certain categories of adverbial phrases in our logical grammar; and perhaps it would be easier to appreciate this once we recognized also the possibility of quantifying in the positions those phrases occupy. We then have 'Brutus stabbed Caesar somewhere somewhen' as a direct consequence of our original proposition; and our grasp of the fact that these quantifiers can be

[8] See Davidson, "The Logical Form of Action Sentences," in *The Logic of Decision and Action*, ed. Rescher, pp. 81-95. University of Pittsburgh Press, Pittsburgh, 1967.

added to or dropped from simple ascriptions of human action without modification of truth-value rests on nothing more recondite than our grasp of the general concept of action. 'Stab', 'kiss', and so on, retain the general formal character they appear to have, namely, that of two-place-predicates; which is surely one merit, on the score of realism, accruing to the present proposal and guaranteed on no other. (Of course this is only a sketch of a suggestion; and I do not suggest, or think, that it would be free from problems.)

### III

We have now before us a variety of proposals for recognizing 'unorthodox' quantification, that is, quantification into positions other than referential: we have, namely, quantification into predicate-place, into sentence-place and into adverbial-phrase-place. Two questions confront us, among, doubtless, many. The first is: How should we assess these proposals for realism? And here we are to remember that what we are concerned with is our understanding of the forms of natural language. For example, with reference to Prior's proposal, how are we to decide whether propositional quantification is quantification into referential position, as he says it is not, or quantification into sentence-position, as he says it is? The second question is: If we conclude in a given case that we are indeed quantifying into referential position (as the orthodoxy says we always are) what is the significance of this conclusion? What does it commit us to?

Let us take the second question first. A point on which Prior and Quine are agreed is that in general quantification into singular-term-position commits us to acknowledging a certain kind of *objects* —objects such as the attached predicates are true of, objects such as would be named or designated by any definite singular terms or specifying expressions which might occupy the place which the bound variables occupy. The commitment is said to be ontological. But is it ontological? Why should it be more than grammatical? or grammatico-logical? Quine says we are committed to a certain class of *objects*. It would be more to the point, at least at first, to say that we are committed to a certain class of *subjects*; where 'subject' is the logico-grammatical correlate of the logico-grammatical 'predicate'. Just what this logico-grammatical commitment is depends on our understanding of the significance of the correlated pair '(singular logical) subject' and 'predicate'; or 'definite referring term' and, as Quine would put it, 'general term in predicative position'. Quine, as we have seen, says that no account can be given of this correlated pair except in terms of accessibility and nonaccessibility of their respective positions to quantifiers. Prior cannot share this view. He must just think it obvious that subjects stand for objects: but since he doesn't say what he understands by 'object', it isn't obvious what he thinks obvious.

Now suppose we hold, with (presumably) Aristotle, that the base class of (singular) subject-predicate-propositions are those in which an expression designating a space-occupying, relatively enduring substantial thing (personal, animal, or merely material) is coupled with an expression signifying a general character (quality or property or kind of action or undergoing, or simply kind) of such things, in such a way as to yield truth or falsehood. The first of these expressions we call the subject; the second (which may include also the symbolism of predicative or propositional coupling), the predicate. Quite apart from the location of the coupling symbolism, this combination, as I have argued elsewhere, has a profound asymmetry about it based on the difference between what the subject-terms and the predicate-terms, respectively, signify. It can be roughly expressed by saying that general characters of substantial things intrinsically enjoy logical relations with other such characters when considered in relation to any and every substantial thing they might be assigned to; whereas it is not the case that substantial things intrinsically enjoy logical relations with other such things when considered in relation to any and every general character which they might be assigned to. (Rather, they intrinsically don't enjoy such relations.) Now this relative asymmetry condition can be generalized. It can be considered in abstraction from the types or categories we start from—those of individual substances and general characters of substances. We can form the general idea of the propositional coupling of a sentence-part A and a sentence-part B where (1) A specifies an item of X-type and B specifies an item of Y-type and (2) X-type items stand in the same asymmetrical relation to Y-type items as substances do to general characters of substances, and (3) this logical analogy is marked in a formal grammatical way by the A-part having the form which the subjects of our basic subject-predicate-sentences have, namely, the form of a noun or noun-phrase and the B-part having one or another of the forms which regularly complement a definite noun or noun-phrase to yield a sentence, for example, verb, adjective, or indefinite noun-phrase (with copula supplied in the last two cases). Then A-part and B-part stand to each other as subject to predicate. And here we have a general account of subject and predicate.

Now what of the doctrine that all subjects stand for objects and hence that all quantification into subject-position is quantification over objects? Surely 'clarity is served' by distinguishing two senses of 'object', one a merely relative, logico-grammatical sense and the other a sense which might not inaptly be called ontological. In the logico-grammatical sense some specific item is an object relative to some proposition; it is an object because some expression specifying it is propositionally coupled with another expression which, relative to the first, fulfills the conditions of being a predicate. In this sense something which is presented as object in one proposition can sometimes be presented in a quite different role in another. In this sense we quantify over objects when what the apparatus of quantification is attached to has predicate-status in relation to all the specifying expressions which might replace that apparatus. But we can and sometimes do use the word 'object' quite differently. We can and sometimes do distinguish objects from qualities, properties, relations, events, processes, species, types, and whatnot. Substances are undoubted objects in this sense. There is no grammatico-logical relativity about this sense. Rather we might say that in this sense we use the word for ontological classification or categorization; for distinguishing one ontological category from others. Never mind that it is not a particularly well-defined category. Few categories are.

Of course there is a link between the two senses of 'object'. For objects in the ontological-categorial sense are the basic objects in the logico-grammatical sense. Hard though it is to believe, it is almost impossible *not* to believe that some confusion of the two senses of 'object', or of the two ideas involved, underlies much of the persistent philosophical anxiety that goes under the name of 'ontology'. The confusion would seem too gross to be credible if it were not for the fact that in philosophy no confusion is too gross to be credible. Worries about Platonism; the talk of 'countenancing' items of this or that type or 'admitting them into our ontology'; the use of phrases like 'a grossly inflated ontology' and the rest—all of these are familiar in connection with quantification into subject-place, and the connection is very difficult to understand except on the supposition of some such confusion and quite easy to understand on that supposition.

So now back to the first of our two questions. Granted that we can ignore the bogey of ontology; granted also that we can and do quantify into places unhaunted by the bogey; how, then, should we assess such a proposal as Prior's, the proposal namely that propositional quantification should be viewed as quantification into sentence-place and not into singular-term-place?

It seems to me that the balance of realism tips against Prior and in favor of the view that propositional quantification is quantification over propositions. The language is full of what are traditionally classified as noun-phrases specifying propositions (for example, "that it is raining"; "this doctrine"; "the axiom of parallels"; "your suggestion"); it is full of what appear to be proposition-predicates (whether one-place, like "true" and "false", two-place, relating person and proposition, as "believe" "assent" "surmise", or two-place, relating proposition and proposition, as "implies" "incompatible with"): and when we quantify, the apparatus of quantification is regularly attached to these apparent predicates and replaceable by those apparent noun-phrases. Both the logical asymmetry condition and the formal grammatical conditions are satisfied for speaking of propositional subjects and propositional predicates and for saying that propositional quantification is quantification into subject-place, quantification over propositions.

These remarks may not seem to be conclusive against recognizing propositional quantification into sentence-place as well as quantification over propositions. We still have before us Prior's suggestion for parsing such sentences as 'John asserts (believes) that it is raining'; and the associated suggestion that 'the proposition that $p$ is incompatible with the proposition that $q$' is simply periphrasis for 'if $p$, then not-$q$'. Have we not similarly recognized 'If William performs an action of the hopping-kind, then Tom performs an action of the hopping-kind' as a possible periphrasis for 'If William hops, then Tom hops', and associated a double quantification over actions and action-kinds with the former as well as a quantification into action-predicate-place with the latter? So may we not recognize quantification over propositions in our language without prejudice to the recognition of Prior's kind of quantification as also in the language?

Unfortunately, the parallel is seen to break down when we turn to examples. Consider "Tom said (asserted) something incompatible with everything William said (asserted)". This is ambiguous, of course, and we can easily capture both readings in sentences in which "is incompatible with" stands in predicate-place in relation to variables of quantification in subject-place. For these readings we can equally easily find equivalents in Priorese. Thus we have '$(\exists p)$ [Tom said that $p$. $(q))$ William said that $q \rightarrow (if\ p,\ then\ \text{-}q))$]' for one reading and '$(q)$ [William said that $q \rightarrow (\exists p)$ (Tom said that $p$. if $p$, then -$q$)]' for the other. The trouble is that there just are no sentences in English which the Priorese versions, with sentential quantification, can be taken as representing in the way in which sentences with quantification over propositions can be taken as representing the two readings of the ordinary English sentence we started out with.

To say the Priorese sentences do not represent the form which English sentences actually exemplify is of course not to deny the intelligibility of Priorese. Nor is it to deny ourselves any philosophical illumination we may be able to derive from our appreciation of the equivalence of Priorese sentences and English sentences. It is not even to deny that Priorese may have certain merits or advantages which English lacks, that we may perhaps be able to express elegantly in Priorese what we may be able to express only by relatively cumbrous circumlocution in English. For example "$(p)$ (it is true that $p \leftrightarrow p$)" is well-formed in Priorese and says neatly what we cannot say very neatly in English. All that is contended is that Priorese sentential quantification is not a realistic representation of propositional quantification in our language, even though there *are* constructions in our language which do involve quantification into positions other than subject or singular-term-position.

*IV*

I should not leave the subject without attempting some explanation of the restrictive doctrine regarding quantification into predicate-place. Why should it be thought that predicate-position differs from referential position in being inaccessible to quantifiers (or variables of quantification)? I have a suggestion to make, which is best reached by bringing into prominence an accepted consequence of the doctrine.

The simple propositions

(a)  Socrates swims
(b)  Socrates is brave

yield by generalization the propositions: "Someone swims" and "Someone is brave" or "There is someone who swims" and "There is someone who is brave". According to the doctrine in question, they cannot also yield by generalization the proposition "Socrates does something" (or "There is something Socrates does") and "Socrates is something" (or "There is something Socrates is"). The proposition (a) and (b) cannot be allowed to yield these generalizations: for to allow that they did would be to allow quantification into predicate-place. However, the sentences in question are perfectly legitimate and intelligible English sentences, generalized in form, and it must be granted (and indeed *is* granted) that there are some specifying propositions to which these general propositions stand in the same relation as the general propositions "Someone swims", "Someone is brave" stand in to such specifying propositions as (a) and (b). So what sort of thing *are* the specifying propositions in these cases? Well, we are offered things like:

(A) Socrates      performs·        swimming
                  exemplifies

(B) Socrates      exhibits
                  possesses        bravery
                  exemplifies

where the nouns "swimming" and "bravery" are held to 'name attributes' or 'specify concepts' and a brand-new two-place-predicate is
introduced to couple the two names. Since these nouns occupy referential position, we can admit the generalizations and preserve the doctrine. But now, if the doctrine is to retain any substance there must be a
substantial difference between (A) and (B) on the one hand and (a) and
(b) on the other. It cannot be merely a matter of stylistic variation.

The idea, then, is that (A) or (B) *commit* us, as regards swimming
and bravery, in a way in which we aren't a bit committed by:

(a)  Socrates swims

or by:

(b)  Socrates is brave

I want to suggest to you, first, of course, that this is absurd; that this
theory of 'commitment' by noun but not by adjective or verb is about as
absolutely implausible as any philosophical view could be: that we are
every bit as 'committed' by (a) and (b) as we are by (A) and (B). By all
means say, if you like, that one who says

Socrates exemplifies bravery

thereby 'brings in' the attribute or concept, bravery, or shows himself
as recognizing or acknowledging this attribute or concept. But then
add that one who says

Socrates is brave

brings in the attribute or concept, bravery, just as much as one who says
'Socrates exemplifies bravery'.

Of course my current concern is not with the fact that the absurd
view *is* absurd, but with the question why the view should be held. And
my suggestion is that the fact that the predicate incorporates the

propositional symbolism of the *verb* makes it easier to overlook or become blind to the fact that it also specifies a concept or attribute quite as fully and completely as any noun could. It's the former fact that makes it possible to slide away from the specificatory function of the predicate by way of saying things like: predicates are just *true or false of* what subject-terms stand for. But this soothing, pacifying, deceptive phrase, if it makes any clear point at all, simply makes the point that predicate-phrases incorporate the propositional symbolism, the symbolism of the verb.

'Predicates are wanted in all sentences', says Quine (*Philosophy of Logic*, p. 28). The phrase reveals the trouble. What is wanted in all sentences is the indication of propositionality, the verb-form or whatever does its duty. It is no more necessary that sentences should contain predicates in the full sense which entails concept-specification than it is that they should contain subjects in the full sense which entails individual-specification. So 'Socrates does something' is just as good, and *just as direct* a generalization, from

Socrates swims

as 'Someone swims' is. The phrase "does something" replaces specificity with nonspecificity just as the phrase "someone" does. It also exhibits the form of the verb necessary for sentencehood (propositionality). It is the failure to see clearly that ordinary predicate-expressions *combine* the function of concept-specification with propositional indication that leads to the queer restriction on quantification.

It might be said: granted that the predicate's incorporating the propositional symbolism makes it easier to develop a kind of blindness to the concept-specificatory or attribute-specificatory function of the predicate, the explanation still seems insufficient. Why should anyone want to slide away from recognition of this function with the help of those deceptive phrases about predicates 'being true or false of what subject-terms stand for', about their being just the other parties to predication? One answer is: because of the risk of Platonism. But what is this risk? The risk of mythologizing, of taking there to exist objects which don't exist, which it perhaps doesn't make sense to suppose do exist or which, at any rate, talking too easily of gives too easy an escape from facing problems, seems to be explanatory when it isn't, and so on. But now, and finally, what has this to do with quantification? Why should generality rather than specificity in predicate-place carry any undesirable theoretical implications? Well, putting aside the triviality that "some" -quantification can always be expressed in English by

"There *is* something which . . .", I think I can make a diagnostic shot here, which returns us to a point made earlier in the paper. There is not, *in general*, much point in specifying a substantial particular ('Socrates') and then generalizing in predicate-place ('does something', 'is something') unless you have some higher-order concept or property in mind, some principle of collection which applies to those principles of collection which apply to particulars. But insofar as you have this in mind, then you are at least prepared for that grammatical shift which involves quantifying *over* what predicates specify as well as *into* predicate-position. But to have this preparedness is equivalent to having in mind the idea of specifiers of attributes or properties as fit occupants of subject-place. But the primary occupants of subject-place are particular-specifiers. So you are implicitly likening what attribute-specifiers specify to those honest spatio-temporal objects which particular-specifiers specify. The fear of Platonism is (at least in part) the fear of the reproach of this comparison. To that extent it is an unreasonable fear. For the likening is only a logical likening, the logical analogy already referred to. That it should ever have seemed more—in such a way as to inspire opposite emotions in different breasts—simply underlines the correctness of taking it that, in basic subject-predicate propositions, subjects stand for spatio-temporal objects.

# Opacity and Scope

## BARBARA H. PARTEE

*University of Massachusetts*

The purpose of this paper is to contrast two views of opacity; more specifically, two views as to how opaque contexts arise. One view, which is expressed or implicit in the work of many philosophers [1] and linguists,[2] is that opacity results from the embedding of a sentence into a construction headed by a modal (construed widely) verb, adjective, or adverb, such as *necessarily, believes that, must,* or *certain.* On this view, wherever there is an opaque context, it is a context of a sentence; grammatical relations internal to sentences such as verb plus object or adverb plus verb never create opacity. The second view, suggested by the work of Montague,[3] is that opacity is one aspect of intensionality, and that intensionality is more the norm than the exception for grammatical relations. On this view any noun phrase position is liable to be opaque, and will be unless the construction it occurs in happens to be extensional. I will describe these two views a little more explicitly, discuss some of the cases where they suggest different syntactic analyses, and compare their attractions. I will try to show that while the first view makes a stronger theoretical

---

[1] Quine, the father of opacity, is probably the primary source of this view, although he also includes the embedding of terms and other nonsentential stretches within quotation marks as a source of opacity. See Quine (1960). Most of the philosophical attention to opacity has centered on verbs of propositional attitude and modal operators.

[2] This idea can be found in Bach (1968) and is particularly clear in the work of Lakoff and McCawley, where opaque constructions are analyzed in terms of "higher predicates," that is, predicates one of whose arguments is a sentence. See Lakoff (1970), (1972), McCawley (1970), for example.

[3] This view comes out most clearly in Montague's last work, Montague (1973).

claim and would be preferable if it could be substantiated, it runs into some serious descriptive problems with constructions which the second view can handle in a straightforward way.

## 0. Some Preliminary Definitions

A context in which a term phrase can occur is an *opaque context* (or *referentially opaque context*) if substitution of a coreferential term phrase does not always preserve truth. The italicized term phrase in (1), for example, is in an opaque context:

(1)   Mary believes that *the man who lives upstairs* is insane.

A context which is not (referentially) opaque is (*referentially*) *transparent*, as, for example, the context of the italicized term phrase in (2).

(2)   The police who arrested *the man who lives upstairs* behaved badly.

Sentences in which a term phrase occurs in an opaque context are generally ambiguous; there will in general be both a *referential reading* (loosely called the "transparent reading"), on which the term phrase is used purely referentially and substitution of a coreferential term phrase does preserve truth, and a *nonreferential reading* (more accurately called a *not-purely-referential reading*; loosely called the "opaque reading"), on which substitution of a coreferential term phrase may happen to but often does not preserve truth. Thus a context is opaque if it *permits* of a not-purely-referential reading; but it will almost always permit a purely referential reading as well. The two readings of (1) are approximately paraphrased below:

(1–ref.)     Mary believes of a certain individual, namely the man who lives upstairs, that he is insane.
(1–nonref.)  Mary believes that whoever it is that lives upstairs is insane.

The opacity of sentence (1) evidently results from the verb *believes* in construction with its *that*-clause: any term phrase [4] in a *that*-clause embedded under *believes* has a nonreferential reading, while the subject of *believes*, for example, does not. As we look at

[4] If we accept the analysis of Kripke (1972), of proper names as rigid designators, then proper names are exceptions to this claim, which should then be more carefully worded in terms of term-phrase positions.

various kinds of grammatical constructions, and alternative analyses of them, we will distinguish between *extensional* and *intensional* constructions, always relative to a particular analysis. We will say, following Carnap (1947), that a grammatical construction is *extensional*, relative to a certain syntactic and semantic analysis, if the extension of the whole is a function of the extensions of the parts. And we will say that a grammatical construction is *intensional*, relative to a certain syntactic and semantic analysis, if the extension of the whole is a function of the intensions of one or more parts and the extensions of the remaining parts. Following the standard treatment of possible-world semantics,[5] we take the extension of a sentence to be a truth value, and its intension to be a function from possible worlds to truth values (the intension of a sentence is called a *proposition*); the extension of a one-place predicate is taken to be a set of individuals, and its intension, called a *property*, is taken to be a function from possible worlds to sets of individuals. On the matter of term phrases, the usual interpretation is that the extension is an individual and the intension is a function from possible worlds to individuals; but Montague suggests a different analysis which gives a uniform treatment of term phrases and quantifier phrases, which we describe briefly below before turning to the central issues.

## 1. Terms and Quantifier Phrases

On the classical view of logical structure, individual variables, proper names, and definite descriptions are grammatically treated as terms and can stand as arguments of predicates, while quantifier phrases with *all* and *some* are not treated as unitary phrases at all. Thus a representation of

(3)   John walks

in ordinary predicate logic is as in (3')

(3')   walk $(j)$

where *John* appears as a term. But in the representation of (4) as (4'):

(4)   Every man walks
(4')   $(\forall x)(\mathrm{man}(x) \rightarrow \mathrm{walk}(x))$

---

[5] See Kripke (1963) and subsequent work of Kripke, Montague, Dana Scott, David Kaplan, Richmond Thomason, and others.

there is no single constituent corresponding to *every man*; what corresponds to *every man* is the whole frame (4''):

(4'')   $(\forall x)(\text{man}(x) \rightarrow \ldots (x))$

which is not itself a well-formed formula. From the point of view of predicate logic, it is an accident that expressions like *some man* and *every man* behave as noun phrases in ordinary language. Montague (1973) proposes an analysis which treats quantifier phrases as terms, but it involves a departure from the usual semantics of terms. Instead of taking the extension of a term to be an individual, he takes it to be a set of properties. In the case of a proper name like *John*, the link between the name "John" and the individual, John, is not taken to be direct designation; rather, "John" denotes the set of all of those properties whose extension includes John. Translating English into an intensional logic which includes an individual constant $j$ which does denote John, this gives:

(5)   John: $\hat{P}{}^{\vee}P(j)$

where $P$ is a variable over properties, and $^{\vee}$ is the extension operator. Then a sentence like (3) is analyzed not as asserting simply that the individual John is in the set of entities that walk, but as asserting that the property of walking is included in John's property-set; but this is logically equivalent to the former interpretation.

(6)   *John walks*: John($^{\wedge}$walk)        ($^{\wedge}$is the intension operator)
                  $\hat{P}{}^{\vee}P(j)(^{\wedge}\text{walk})$

      $^{\vee\wedge}$walk $(j)$
      walk $(j)$

Given this analysis of terms as designating property-sets, *every man* and *some man*, as well as *the man*, can be treated as terms, since they can also be interpreted as designating sets of properties.

(7)   *every man*:   $\hat{P}(\forall x)(\text{man}(x) \rightarrow P(x))$
(8)   *some man*:    $\hat{P}(\exists x)(\text{man}(x) \wedge P(x))$
(9)   *the man*:     $\hat{P}(\exists y)[(\forall x)(\text{man}(x) \leftrightarrow x = y) \wedge {}^{\vee}P(y)]$

A sentence like *every man walks* is then analyzed as saying that the property of walking is in the property-set for *every man*, that is, is in the set of those properties which every man has. This can be shown to be equivalent to the standard interpretation:

(10)   *every man walks*:  $\widehat{P}(\forall x)(\text{man}(x) \to {}^{\vee}P(\text{x}))(^{\wedge}\text{walk})$

$(\forall x)(\text{man}(x) \to {}^{\vee\wedge}\text{walk}(x))$

$(\forall x)(\text{man}(x) \to \text{walk}(x))$

Nothing new is being said about the interpretation of the particular sentence, *every man walks*; but the treatment of *every man* as a term-phrase constituent of the sentence allows for a more direct connection between the syntax and semantics of English than is possible if *every man* is viewed as a peculiar natural-language short-hand for a complex sentential matrix. This unification of natural language noun phrases as logical term phrases is central to the alternative account of intensional constructions, as we shall see below.

One more aspect of Montague's treatment of term phrases needs to be mentioned. In the examples above, a term phrase was combined directly with a verb to form a sentence. Term phrases are introduced directly in a variety of grammatical constructions—transitive verb plus object, preposition plus object, and so on. Among the term phrases, in addition to proper names and quantifier phrases, are free variables, $x_1, x_2, \dots$. In order to represent the bound variable interpretation of pronouns and to represent scope ambiguities in sentences with more than one quantifier, there is a rule which allows a term phrase to be introduced into a sentence via substitution for a free variable. Any term phrase may be introduced in this way—not only a quantifier phrase, but also a proper noun or another free variable. The rule is given in a rough form below.

*Sentence-scope quantification*: If $\alpha$ is a term and $\varphi$ is a formula, then for any $n$, $F_n(\alpha, \varphi)$ is a formula, where $F_n$ is as illustrated in the following example:

(11)   $F_3$ (*a fish, John caught* $x_3$ *and ate* $x_3$) = *John caught a fish and ate it.*

The semantic interpretation of the rule is as follows: if $\alpha$ is interpreted as $\alpha'$, and $\varphi'$, then the interpretation of $F_n(\alpha, \varphi)$ is $\alpha'(\hat{x}_n, \varphi')$, where $\hat{x}_n$ is an intensional abstraction operator, that is, $^{\wedge}x_n$. Thus the interpretation of example (11) is as in (12) (with some parts left uninterpreted).

(12)   $\widehat{P}(\exists x)(\text{fish}(x) \wedge {}^{\vee}P(x))(\hat{x}_3(\text{John caught } x_3 \text{ and ate } x_3))$

## 2. OPAQUE CONTEXTS

Now we return to an examination of a variety of constructions
that create opaque contexts. In trying to account for the opacity of
these constructions, we will consider alternative syntactic analyses
and the alternative semantic representations they support. In each
case, at least one of the suggested analyses will follow the classical
view that attributes opacity to the embedding of a sentence under
some sort of modal operator; in a number of cases, Montague's approach allows the possibility of a more "local" analysis of opacity.

### a. That-*clauses*

The clearest and least controversial cases are those where there is
clearly an embedded sentence. Embedded *that*-clauses are almost
always opaque contexts, as the following sample illustrates.

(13)   Mary believes that the man in the raincoat is a spy.
(14)   Tom is certain that a student in my class is a spy.
(15)   That the bank president works in the bank is obvious.
(16)   That John's favorite uncle works in the bank is obvious.
(17)   It appears that a child has been writing on the walls.

The following example is transparent, but that need not contradict
the generalization that the construction it exemplifies is opaque, since
the transparency is deducible from the meaning of the word *true*, and
thus could be accounted for by a special meaning postulate for that
lexical item.

(18)   It is true that the bank president is a spy.

For opaque constructions of this sort there is general agreement
that the distinction between the referential and the nonreferential
reading is simply a matter of the scope of the quantifier of the term
phrase in question. The referential reading of (14) can be represented
as in (14a) and the nonreferential reading as in (14b).

(14a)   $(\exists x)(x$ is a student in my class $\wedge$ Tom is certain that $x$ is a
        spy)
(14b)   Tom is certain that $(\exists x)(x$ is a student in my class $\wedge x$ is a
        spy)

Such embedded constructions are generally thought of as the paradigm case of opaque contexts; controversy only arises over the question of whether all types of opacity are to be analyzed as deriving ultimately from constructions of this type.

### b. Sentence adverbs and modal auxiliaries

In sentences (19) and (20), the subject is in an opaque context even though overtly it appears to be in a simple, unembedded sentence.

(19)   Smith's murderer is probably insane.
(20)   Smith's murderer may be insane.

Since it is the sentence adverb *probably* in (19) and the modal auxiliary *may* in (20) that is responsible for the opacity, the obvious solution (and the standard one) is to treat such adverbs and auxiliaries as taking a sentence in their scope. There are at least two ways to do this. One solution, which assimilates these cases totally to the preceding type, would represent the underlying form of (19) and (20) as (19a) and (20a), with a transformational rule to delete *it is* and *true*, and move the adverb or auxiliary into what then becomes the main clause.

(19a)   It is probably true that Smith's murderer is insane.
(20a)   It may be true that Smith's murderer is insane.

However, about the only virtue of this approach is the uniformity of opaque contexts it provides. Syntactically, it leaves unanswered the question of how *probably* and *may* got into (19a) and (20a), since *it is probably true that* and *it may be true that* are presumably not unanalyzed atomic expressions, and it is hard to imagine a nonregressing source for *probably* and *may* in (19a) and (20a) that could not be invoked for (19) and (20) directly.

The second solution is more direct syntactically and departs only slightly from the model of the embedded *that*-clause. That is to treat sentence adverbs and modal auxiliaries both as sentence operators: expressions which combine with a sentence to form a new sentence, as indicated in (19b) and (20b).

(19b)   $_S$[probably$_S$[Smith's murderer is insane]]
(20b)   $_S$[may $_S$[Smith's murderer is insane]]

The only difficulty this analysis faces is in the case of the modal auxiliaries, where some kind of syntactic mechanism must be invoked to prevent iteration, since only one modal auxiliary can appear in a sentence. In either of these analyses, the distinction between the two readings can be represented as a matter of whether the quantifier has the whole sentence or only the inner sentence in its scope, so the basic mechanism is the same as in the case of *that*-clauses.

### c. Infinitives

The alternatives become a little more distinct and disputable when we consider embedded infinitive phrases, as in (21)-(23), all of which are opaque and have the usual two interpretations.

(21)   John is trying to find a gold watch.
(22)   Sam is afraid to talk to a professor in the department.
(23)   It would be wise to read an article by Russell.

On the view that seems to be most prevalent among philosophers, these infinitive phrases are to be analyzed as abbreviations of *that*-clauses:[6] for (21), for instance, the source would be (21a):

(21a)   John is trying (endeavoring) that he find a gold watch.

The advantage of such a structure is that it provides an embedded sentence which the quantifier can take as its scope on the nonreferential reading, as in (21b).

(21b)   John is endeavoring that $(\exists x)(x$ is a gold watch and he find $x)$.

From the point of view of a theory of natural language which is concerned with both syntax and semantics, the semantic neatness of such an analysis must be weighed against the fact that it leaves unexplained the syntax of English verbs like *try*, which never in fact take *that*-clause complements. It would be desirable to find an analysis which offered some explanation for the existence of a distinction between *that*-clauses and infinitives.[7]

---

[6] See Quine (1960), section 32, which is the source of this view. Bach (1968) and other linguists have argued for the inclusion of such analyses in transformational grammars.

[7] There is a spurious objection that is sometimes raised to analyses like (21b) on semantic grounds, which perhaps needs to be mentioned here. The objection usually runs something like this: "The representation (21b), unlike the original sentence (21), entails that John is endeavoring to make there exist a gold watch, so (21b) cannot possibly be a paraphrase of (21)." But this is fallacious, since the quantifier has the whole conjoined sentence as its scope, and thus the supposed entailment is invalid.

For sentence (22), the analysis is somewhat worse, since the putative source would be (22b).

(22b)   Sam is afraid that he talk to a professor in the department.

The problem here is that *afraid* does take *that*-clauses, though not normally in the subjunctive, but *afraid that* is clearly distinct in meaning from *afraid to*. It will not do to simply view the two *afraids* as homonyms, since parallel differences between the meanings of *that*-complements and *to*-complements are found with a wide range of emotive adjectives, such as *happy*, *sorry*, and so on. Perhaps the difference can be pinned on the subjunctive/indicative distinction, but that requires some analysis of the subjunctive. In the case of (23) above, a *that*-clause produces either ungrammaticality or a meaning change or both, with the added difficulty that some subject must be provided for the embedded clause, and it is not clear that there is any choice available that would not do violence to the meaning of the original sentence.

Montague's treatment, because it allows for quantifier phrases to be inserted like other term phrases directly into term-phrase positions, allows infinitive phrases to be analyzed directly as opaque contexts. A verb such as *try to* is treated as taking a verb phrase to make a new verb phrase, and semantically it is the intension of the embedded verb phrase that contributes to the extension of the whole.

In (21), the distinction between the two readings can be represented as the distinction between *a gold watch* having been introduced directly as object of the embedded transitive verb *find*, as in (21c), giving the nonreferential reading, versus substitution of *a gold watch* for a free variable at the sentence level, leading to the referential interpretation (21d).

(21c)   John ($^\wedge$ try to ($^\wedge$ find a gold watch)
(21d)   (a gold watch)($\hat{x}_1$ John ($^\wedge$ try to ($^\wedge$ find $x_1$)))

One serious difficulty encountered by Montague's analysis and not by the analysis mentioned earlier is exemplified by sentence (24).

(24)   John tried to be easy to please.

Here there is no opacity to worry about; the problem is a syntactic one. The analysis of *try to* as taking verb phrases directly is satisfactory for simple verb phrases, but *be easy to please* is a paradigm example of the sort of phrase for which transformational derivation from a full sentence (in which *easy* is the predicate and *to please* a subpart of the subject) can be very strongly argued for. For such reasons I have proposed elsewhere [8] that Montague's system be augmented by the addition of transformational rules, which can be done within the ground rules of his theory as long as it is possible to associate a unique semantic interpretation rule with each transformation. For infinitive complements, the relevant transformation is one which maps sentences having a free variable as subject into verb phrases (this rule, which I call the Derived Verb-Phrase Rule, has no direct counterpart in standard transformational grammar because there transformations always convert sentences [with their associated structure] into sentences). The rule is illustrated in (25).

> (25)(a)  $x$ finds a gold watch $\Rightarrow$ find a gold watch
> (25)(b)  $x$ is easy to please $\Rightarrow$ be easy to please

The semantic interpretation is simply predicate abstraction: if the sentence $\varphi$ is interpreted as $\varphi'$, the derived verb phrase is interpreted as $\hat{x}_i\ \varphi'$, where $x_i$ is the deleted variable. Then given an ordinary transformational derivation of the sentence "$x$ is easy to please," we have a derivation and an interpretation of the verb phrase "be easy to please." We can then insert such a verb phrase as the complement of *try to*. In fact, if we like, we can require that all infinitives be derived via abstraction using the derived verb-phrase rule, and if we did that, we would have the advantages of both the two preceding analyses: infinitives would be kept syntactically distinct from *that*-clauses, but would be derived from sentential forms. The distinction between nonreferential and referential readings would then still be representable as a difference in quantifier scope: the scope would be the embedded sentence or the whole sentence, as in (21e) and (21f).

> (21e)   John ($^\wedge$ try to ($\hat{y}$ ($\exists x$)($x$ is a gold watch $\wedge$ $y$ finds $x$)))
> (21f)   ($\exists x$)($x$ is a gold watch $\wedge$ John ($^\wedge$ try to ($\hat{y}$ ($y$ finds $x$))))

This analysis is very similar syntactically to the usual transformational analysis of infinitive complements, except that it makes use of the derived verb-phrase rule, with its interpretation as abstraction over a free variable, in place of the usual Equi-Noun-Phrase Deletion Rule. Semantically it is equivalent to Montague's analysis. As for the account of opacity, the analysis I have ended up with here supports both of the views that I am comparing: the verb-plus-infinitive phrase

---

[8] Partee (1972a), Partee (1972b).

construction is intensional, but it is also possible to view all infinitive phrases as deriving from sentences, although the underlying sentences must be open sentences and hence not full sentences semantically. Thus, although several accounts of opacity in infinitives are possible, the one that seems most adequate is neutral on the central issue.

### d. Verb phrase adverbs

Assuming that we can, at least in clear cases, make a distinction between sentence adverbs and verb-phrase adverbs,[9] we find that verb-phrase adverbs can create opaque contexts in the verb phrases they modify, though not in subject position (this being one of the distinguishing criteria between the two types of adverbs). For example, the term phrases in the verb phrases of the following examples have both a purely referential and a not purely referential[10] reading.

(26)    Big Mack intentionally shot a student.
(27)    Mary reluctantly bet on the best horse.
(28)    Sam willingly invited the robber into his house.

The major alternatives in representing the construction so as to account for its opacity are, as in the preceding case, either to find an appropriate underlying structure in which a whole sentence falls under the scope of the adverb, or to represent the construction directly as modification of a verb phrase by an adverb, but bring the intension of the verb phrase into the corresponding semantic interpretation.

On the first alternative, the problem is to find a suitable paraphrase to serve as a plausible underlying form. The most promising line seems to be to make use of the corresponding adjectives, *intentional, willing,* and so on, since many of the adverbs of this category which create opacity are of the *Adj-ly* form (though not all: *on pur-*

---

[9] See Thomason and Stalnaker (1973).
[10] Since all these adverbs are "standard" in the sense that the entailment (a) below holds for them,

(a) $a$ $\beta$-ly VP'ed $\rightarrow$ $a$ VP'ed

the distinction between "not purely referential" and "nonreferential" is particularly important here. In each of sentences (26)-(28), the term phrase in question has a particular referent if the sentence is true, even on the not-purely-referential reading, but the substitution of another description of the same referent will not necessarily preserve truth on that reading.

*pose, with malice aforethought,* and so on). I am convinced that no such suitable paraphrases exist, but it is virtually impossible to argue conclusively for such a point. The following might seem to be appropriate first tries, but note that not only are they not good paraphrases, but they involve infinitives which in turn would have to be reanalyzed as sentences to maintain the first view.

> (26a)   It was intentional of Big Mack to shoot a student.
> (27a)   Mary was reluctant to bet on the best horse.
> (28a)   Sam was willing to invite the robber into his house.

A considerably closer paraphrase can be gotten by conjoining such sentences with the original sentences minus their adverbs, since part of what is missing in the (a) paraphrases is the factivity of the originals. (26a) does appear to be factive as it stands; it would be more parallel to the others if we used the verb *intend*.

> (26b)   Big Mack intended to shoot a student, and Big Mack shot
> a student.
> (27b)   Mary was reluctant to bet on the best horse, and Mary
> bet on the best horse.
> (28b)   Sam was willing to invite the robber into his house, and
> Sam invited the robber into his house.

Now the (b) sentences do seem to be implied by the original sentences, and in an informal way help elucidate the dual referential and nonreferential role played by the term phrases in the verb phrases of the originals. But for the implication to go the other way it would be necessary to establish identity of some appropriate sort between the verb phrases in the two conjuncts in each (b) sentence. And since in each case the first conjunct has an intensional construction and the second conjunct an extensional one, it is hard to imagine what an appropriate sort of identity would be; perhaps it is with good reason that the verb-phrase adverb constructions of the originals manage to make double use of a single occurrence of the verb phrase.

As I indicated above, I don't take my argument as conclusive refutation of an embedded-sentence analysis of verb-phrase adverbs, since all I have done is point out problems for what seems to me the most plausible approach to such an analysis. I am sure, in fact, that such an analysis can be maintained by invoking abstract predicates whose meanings are appropriate by fiat and which trigger obligatory transformations to insure that·they end up as verb-phrase adverbs.[11] But let me turn instead to the analysis suggested by Montague, in which verb-phrase adverbs are analyzed as verb-phrase adverbs. Montague's analysis agrees semantically with the proposal of Thomason and Stalnaker (1973).

On the Montague analysis, a verb-phrase adverb combines with a verb phrase to give a new verb phrase; as with the verbs like *try to*, in the semantic interpretation the adverb is interpreted as a function which takes the intension of the verb phrase as its argument. Also as in the *try to* case, the transformational extensions that I mentioned earlier make it possible for verb-phrase adverbs to be applied to sententially derived verb phrases as well as to basic ones. For the case of (26), the two readings can be represented as (26c) and (26d) if we apply Montague's system directly. If we were to require that verb-phrase adverbs apply only to verb phrases derived via abstraction, we would end up with (26e) and (26f) instead; but these are logically equivalent to (26c) and (26d), respectively, though that may not be apparent from my loose notation.

(26c)　Big Mack ($^\wedge$ intentionally ($^\wedge$ shoot ($^\wedge$ a student)))

(26d)　$(\exists x)(x$ is a student and Big Mack ($^\wedge$ intentionally ($^\wedge$ shoot $(x)$))))

(26e)　Big Mack ($^\wedge$ intentionally ($\hat{y}((\exists x)(x$ is a student and $y$ ($^\wedge$ shoot$(x))))))$)

(26f)　$(\exists x)(x$ is a student and Big Mack ($^\wedge$ intentionally ($\hat{y}(y(^\wedge$ shoot$(x))))))$)

On the analysis which is like Montague's with the addition of the derived verb-phrase rule, the generalizations that emerge are the same as for the infinitive complement case. On the one hand, we have an intensional construction of adverb plus verb phrase; on the other

---

[11] Lakoff, in fact, proposed something of this sort in Lakoff (1970), where he suggests structures such as:

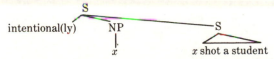

This gives verb-phrase adverbs like *intentionally* the same underlying structure as verbs like *try*, with the differences between them represented as differences in the rules they undergo: *try* triggers infinitive formation and ends up as the main verb of the sentence, whereas *intentionally* undergoes "adverb-lowering" and ends up embedded in the lower sentence. The same structure would, with different transformations, yield sentences like "It was intentional of John to shoot a student."

hand, the verb phrase can be taken to be derivative from a sentence, though again it is necessarily an open sentence. Note that in both of the last two constructions examined, it is only the transformationally complex verb phrases that need to be derived via the derived verb-phrase rule; there is no syntactic reason to require all verb phrases entering these constructions to be derived via that rule, and the only reason for doing so would be to preserve the generalization that all opaque contexts be contexts of sentences. In the next section, I will turn to the class of constructions for which the two approaches have the most sharply divergent consequences.

## 3. The opacity of look for

There are a few verbs whose direct objects can be interpreted nonreferentially.

(29)   John is looking for a unicorn.
(30)   You owe me a Coke.
(31)   Mary offered John a cigar.
(32)   Janice advertised for a cook.

On Montague's approach these are analyzed directly as transitive verb plus object; semantically, the verb is analyzed as a function from intensions of term phrases to extensions of verb phrases. They thus fall under the generalization that grammatical relations in general are to be interpreted in a function-argument way, with the argument in general an intension. This generalization can be shown most naturally with the notation of categorial grammar: taking t as sentence, T as term phrase, IV as verb phrase, and CN as common noun phrase, the major grammatical relations can be sketched as follows (see Partee, 1972b, for a fuller explication).

(33)(a)   Subject-Predicate:

$$t$$
$$t/IV \qquad\qquad IV$$

Term = t/IV

(b)   Verb-Object:

$$IV$$
$$IV/T \qquad\qquad T$$

Transitive Verb = IV/T

(c)   Adjective-Noun:

$$CN$$
$$CN/CN \qquad\qquad CN$$

Adjective = CN/CN

(d)   Adverb-Verb Phrase

$$IV$$
$$IV/IV \qquad\qquad IV$$

Verb-Phrase Adverb = IV/IV

(e)   Adverb-Sentence:

$$t$$
$$t/t \qquad\qquad t$$

Sentence Adverb = t/t

(f)   Verb-Sentential Complement

$$IV$$
$$IV/t \qquad\qquad t$$

Believe that, etc. = IV/t

In each case, if the semantic interpretation of the $A/B$ constituent is $\alpha$ and the interpretation of the $B$ constituent is $\beta$, the semantic interpretation of the resulting $A$-phrase is taken to be $\alpha(^\wedge\beta)$. Thus in each case it is the intension of the $B$ constituent which enters into the semantic interpretation of the result.

Of the constructions listed above, only the subject-predicate construction appears to be always extensional;[12] the other constructions turn out to be sometimes intensional and sometimes extensional, depending on which lexical items of the $A/B$ classes are involved. Since the extension can be determined from the intension (plus the way the world is) but not vice versa, Montague takes the intensional case as fundamental and adds meaning postulates for the lexical items whose associated functions are extensional. Among the adjectives, for example, *good*, *alleged*, *famous*, and *large* are intensional, while *blue*, *oval*, *dead*, and *four-footed* are extensional, so a meaning postulate would be added for the adjectives of the latter class. For the subject-predicate construction, either a meaning postulate can be added for the construction as a whole, or it can be reanalyzed to start with as $\alpha(\beta)$ rather than $\alpha(^\wedge\beta)$.

Looking at this range of constructions, it is the extensionality of the subject-predicate construction rather than the intensionality of (some cases of) the verb-object construction which appears to be exceptional. It is not surprising that the opposite has generally been assumed, since (a) the subject-predicate construction is a central one, and in the simplest sentences is the only one; it has been canonized in

---

[12] Montague (1973) regards even some subject-predicate constructions as intensional, for example, sentence (a) below, because of the invalidity of inferences like that from (a) and (b) to (c).

    (a)   The temperature is rising.
    (b)   The temperature is ninety.
    (c)   Ninety is rising.

But the "intensionality" of verbs like *rise*, *change*, *increase* relates only to the time coordinate of the $<$time, world$>$ pairs in Montague's semantics, and not to opacity of the usual sort. Furthermore, his analysis of the (b) sentence as a simple equational sentence is open to question.

There are other sentences which appear on the surface to be instances of a nonextensional subject-predicate construction, such as (d) below.

    (d)   A unicorn appears to be approaching.

Montague suggests that such a sentence should not be generated directly, but treated "indirectly as a paraphrase," which agrees with the common transformational view that (d) should be derived from (e) which in turn derives from (f).

    (e)   It appears that a unicorn is approaching.
    (f)   *That a unicorn is approaching appears.

the $P(a)$ notation of logic; (b) logicians have been concerned primarily with "scientific discourse," which can be restricted to extensional constructions with very little loss, and have been concerned with intensional constructions only when they bear on matters of philosophical relevance, as *necessarily* and *believe* do but *look for* and such cases presumably do not; (c) a direct analysis of verb-object constructions is not feasible without something like Montague's treatment of quantifiers as term phrases.

The two interpretations of (29) in Montague's system can be represented grossly as (29a), the nonreferential reading, and (29b), the referential reading.

(29a)   [John ($^\wedge$ look for ($^\wedge$ a unicorn))]
(29b)   [(a unicorn)($\hat{x}$(John($^\wedge$ look for($x$))))]

Expanding the interpretation of *a unicorn* into its analysis as the set of all properties which some unicorn has, that is, the union of the sets of properties of individual unicorns, (29a) and (29b) become (29c) and (29d), respectively.

(29c)   [John ($^\wedge$ look for ($^\wedge\overline{P}$ ($\exists y$)(unicorn ($y$) $\wedge^\vee$ $P(y)$)))]
(29d)   [($\overline{P}$ ($\exists y$)(unicorn (y) $\wedge^\vee$ $P(y)$))($\hat{x}$(John($^\wedge$ look for ($x$))))]

(29d) is equivalent in turn to (29e).

(29e)   ($\exists y$)(unicorn($y$)$\wedge$ John ($^\wedge$ look for ($y$)))

In the nonreferential interpretation, *look for* is a relation between John and the property of being a property of a unicorn; in the referential interpretation, *look for* is a relation between John and an individual unicorn. The same kind of analysis applies to *owe, offer, advertise for, hunt for, guard against, listen for, need, demand* (although probably not to *worship* or *conceive*, for which Montague also intended it).

Now let us consider the approach which tries to preserve the generalization that opacity is a property of sentence contexts. On this approach, a transitive verb like *look for* cannot be regarded as lexically basic, but must be viewed as lexically decomposable into a complex expression like *try to find*, where the infinitive in turn is derived from a sentence. The decomposition of *look for* into *try to find* was first proposed by Quine (1960), was argued for linguistically by Bach (1968), and has become generally accepted within the generative semantics framework.

Support for this view can be found in the existence of a considerable range of verbs which can be used either as transitive verbs or with embedded complements; *need, want, demand, ask for, insist on, wish for, hope for* and *expect*, for example. In their use as transitive verbs, furthermore, a good paraphrase can almost always be found by forming a complement with the verb *have*, so that the transitive verb use can be regarded as resulting from *have*-deletion.

(34)   John needs a winter coat.
(35)   John needs to have a winter coat.

*Expect* does not always have paraphrases with *have*; with *company* or *a letter* or *a train*, a more suitable candidate for deletion might be *arrive*. *Offer* and *promise* when used as two-object verbs generally have paraphrases with *give*.

But a number of verbs which can have nonreferential objects do not double as complement-taking verbs, and for such verbs, including *look for*, an underlying complement form must be specified individually for each one. This would not be a very heavy price to pay if a good paraphrase could be found for each such verb, since it would allow the generalization of opacity as a property of sentence contexts to be maintained.

But there are at least two serious problems in trying to maintain the lexical decomposition view for *look for* and related verbs. The first problem is that *look for, search for, seek, hunt for, hunt, ransack ... for, rummage about for*, and several other expressions all share *try to find* as a part of their meaning, but they are not synonymous with each other, and so *try to find* can be the lexical decomposition for at most one of them; it is doubtful that it is a fully adequate paraphrase for any of them. This problem is central to the lexical decomposition approach; if there are no perfect paraphrases which have the appropriate complement structure and which consist entirely of actual English lexical items, then the decomposition analysis must posit abstract (one is tempted to say fictitious) lexical items in the underlying structure, for example, *try-to-find-LOOKINGLY, try-to-find-SEARCHINGLY*, or the like. In this kind of case, unlike the somewhat stronger arguments for abstract CAUSE, DO, and the like (see Lakoff [1970], Ross [1972]), there is no independent evidence, either syntactic or semantic, for the elements in question; they are simply an unexplained semantic residue that must be invoked to maintain the analysis, in this case to maintain the generalization that opacity always involves sentence embedding.

The second problem with the decomposition analysis of such

items as *look for* is a syntactic one. This problem is similar to one of the objections raised by Fodor (1970) to the analysis of *kill* as *CAUSE to die*.

Consider first the verbs like *need, want, demand, promise*, which double as transitive verbs and complement-taking verbs. There is some fairly strong syntactic evidence that the transitive use of these verbs *is* derived from the complement use, and I will show below that this same type of evidence can be turned against the decomposition analysis of *look for*, and the like.[13] This evidence concerns the occurrence of various types of adverbial modifiers with transitive verbs.

(36)   John wanted my car until next Tuesday.
(37)   The foundation has demanded a report by next month.
(38)   I expected you tomorrow.
(39)   Sally asked for the typewriter for two hours.

Sentences (36)-(38) are well formed, and sentence (39) is ambiguous, whereas similarly constructed sentences with other transitive verbs are not; cf. (40)-(43).

(40)   *John washed my car until next Tuesday.
(41)   *The foundation has written a report by next month.
(42)   *I saw you tomorrow.
(43)   Sally used the typewriter for two hours. (unambiguous)

The differences are predictable on the hypothesis that (36)-(39) are derived from (44)-(47), respectively.

(44)   John wanted to have my car until next Tuesday.
(45)   The foundation has demanded to have a report by next month.
(46)   I expected you to arrive (come) tomorrow.
(47)   Sally asked to have the typewriter for two hours.

The adverbs in the first three examples must be analyzed as associated with the embedded verb phrases; the last one can be as-

---

[13] This argument emerged during informal conversation with some invited speakers at the University of Massachusetts in April, 1973, and was not included in the oral presentation of this paper. Unfortunately, I no longer remember whether the idea was mine or was developed jointly, and I am not sure who I was talking with, though I suspect it was Richmond Thomason and/or Lauri Karttunen, whom I hereby tentatively thank.

sociated with either verb. A simple lexically governed transformation which deletes the embedded *to have* (or *to arrive*, with *expect*), can then produce (36)–(39).

Other constructions which are peculiar to *have*, or nearly so, can show up with transitive *want*, *need*, and the like, further bolstering their derivation from complement structures. For instance, corresponding to the construction *have it ready* is sentence (48):

(48)   I want it ready by 5.

If (48) were not derived from a source containing "to have", it would be necessary to add another kind of basic structure for *want*, namely object plus adjectival complement. Such examples can be proliferated, strongly supporting the contention that the infinitival complement construction underlies the superficially transitive verb-plus-object construction with the verbs like *want*, *need*, *expect*, which occur in both types of construction.

But such tests give negative results for the putative derivation of *look for*, *hunt for*, and so on, from *try to find* (with or without an added abstract element like *LOOKINGLY* or the like). Corresponding to (49), we would expect (50) to be well formed, but it is not.

(49)   Martha is trying to find an apartment by Saturday.
(50)   *Martha is looking for an apartment by Saturday.

Similarly, since *alone* is an acceptable complement to *find*, (51) is ambiguous, but (52) does not share the ambiguity.

(51)   I tried to find you alone.
(52)   I looked for you alone.

Sentence (53) is likewise ambiguous, and again the corresponding sentence with *look for* does not share the ambiguity.

(53)   Fred was trying to find the minutes before the meeting began.
(54)   Fred was looking for the minutes before the meeting began.

This kind of evidence seems to me particularly strong, since it discriminates among transitive verbs, supporting a decompositional analysis for some and arguing against it for others.[14] And while it supports the idea that the opacity of sentences like (55) is traceable to a sentential context (or at least to an embedded verb phrase), it disconfirms that idea for sentences like (56) with *look for* and other similar verbs.

(55)   John wants a paper that's classified "Top Secret".
(56)   John is looking for a paper that's classified "Top Secret".

It seems to me both surprising and unfortunate that the choice between two such large-scale hypotheses about the nature of opacity should come down to the fine-grained analysis of a handful of verbs. As far as I know, there aren't more than one or two dozen verbs like *look for*; I have only been able to find *look for, search for, seek, hunt for, hunt, ransack . . . for, rummage about for, advertise for, listen for, guard against,* and *owe*. If these verbs were missing from the language, or if their syntax were slightly different, then there would seem to be no empirical difference between the theory that all opacity results from sentence-embedding and the theory that intensions are centrally involved in the semantic interpretation of all or most grammatical relations. Since these two hypotheses are linked with very different views about the degree of abstractness needed in syntax for natural languages, basic questions about the relation between syntax and semantics in natural language are at issue. Although I believe I have shown that the balance of the available evidence goes against the hypothesis that all opaque contexts are sentential contexts and in favor of basic grammatical relations being intensional, it is certainly to be hoped that clearer kinds of evidence on the question will eventually be discovered.

[14] Incidentally, some of the verbs for which such tests support a decompositional analysis require a considerably more abstract decomposition than just an added "to have" or the like; Lakoff pointed out in a La Jolla English syntax conference some years ago such evidence for decomposition of *lend, borrow,* and similar verbs, with sentences such as (i) and (ii).

(i)   I lent John my bicycle until next Saturday.
(ii)  I have rented this house until September.

What the underlying forms should be is much less clear for these examples. It is still not out of the question that these examples do not in fact force a decompositional analysis; it is possible that adverbs such as *until September* can co-occur not only with certain tenses, whatever the verb, but also with certain verbs, whatever the tense. For example, *last* is a verb that clearly seems to co-occur with durative adverbs, so perhaps *lend, rent,* and so on also have an inherently durative feature that would be sufficient to account for (i) and (ii). That is in part why I have included above evidence from complements like *have NP ready, find NP above,* and the like, as well as from time adverbials.

## Bibliography

Bach, Emmon (1968). "Nouns and Noun Phrases," in E. Bach and R. Harms, eds., *Universals in Linguistic Theory*. New York: Holt, Rinehart and Winston.

Carnap, Rudolph (1947). *Meaning and Necessity: A Study in Semantics and Modal Logic*. Chicago: University of Chicago, Phoenix Books (paper, 1967).

Fodor, Jerry (1970). "Three Reasons for Not Deriving 'Kill' from 'Cause to Die'," *Linguistic Inquiry*, 1.4, 429–438.

Kripke, Saul (1963). "Semantical Considerations on Modal Logic," *Acta Philosophica Fennica*, Fasc. 16, 83–94.

——— (1972). "Naming and Necessity," in D. Davidson and G. Harman, eds., *Semantics of Natural Language*. Dordrecht: Reidel.

Lakoff, George (1970). *Irregularity in Syntax*. New York: Holt, Rinehart and Winston.

——— (1972). "Linguistics and Natural Logic," in Davidson and Harman (1972) (*op. cit.*)

McCawley, James D. (1970). "Where Do Noun Phrases Come From?," in R. Jacobs and P. Rosenbaum, eds., *Readings in English Transformational Grammar*. Waltham, Mass.: Ginn and Co.

Montague, Richard (1973). "The proper treatment of quantification in ordinary English," in K. J. J. Hintikka, J. M. E. Moravcsik, and P. Suppes, eds., *Approaches to Natural Language: Proceedings of the 1970 Stanford Workshop on Grammar and Semantics*. Dordrecht: Reidel.

Partee, Barbara H. (1972a). "Some transformational extensions of Montague grammar," in R. Rodman, ed., *Papers in Montague Grammar*. UCLA Occasional Papers in Linguistics #2, Los Angeles.

——— (1972b). "Montague Grammar and Transformational Grammar" (draft).

Quine, Willard V. O. (1960). *Word and Object*. Cambridge, Mass.: MIT Press.

Ross, John Robert (1972). "Act," in Davidson and Harman (1972) (*op. cit.*).

Thomason, Richmond, and R. C. Stalnaker (1973). "A Semantic Theory of Adverbs," *Linguistic Inquiry*, 4.2, 195–220.

# Questions about Questions

## JAAKKO HINTIKKA

### *Academy of Finland*

## 1. The State of the Subject

There exists a respectable-sized body of work on the logic of questions ('erotetic logic') among logicians.[1] There also exist a fair number of papers by linguists on the grammar of interrogatives.[2] A kind of connecting link between these two bodies of literature is constituted by the attempt of J. J. Katz to show how a kind of logic of questions can be based on recent linguistic theories.[3]

Although I do not propose to carry out a detailed survey of this whole body of literature here, I would nevertheless like to begin by registering my disappointment with it. With one exception, logicians have failed to come to grips with the most important aspects of the logic of questions, it seems to me.[4] Whatever the merits of linguists' work on questions may be on the level of syntax, I do not see that they

---

[1] See, e.g., Åqvist (1965), (1969), (1971), (1972); Belnap (1963), (1969); Belnap and Cresswell (1968); Cresswell (1965), Harrah (1961), (1963), (1969); Kubinski (1961), (1968); Pawlovski (1969); Petrov (1969); Prior and Prior (1955); Tondl (1969).

[2] See, e.g., Bach (1970); Baker (1970); Koutsoudas (1968); Kuno and Robinson (1972); Langacker (1965). The grammar of questions is also discussed, e.g., in Jacobs and Rosenbaum (1968) and Katz and Postal (1964).

[3] See Katz (1968), and cf. Katz (1972), Katz and Postal (1964). Somewhat similar attempts have been made by others to extract logical and philosophical conceptualizations from recent grammatical theories; see Bromberger (1966a), (1966b); Brown (1970).

[4] This exception is Åqvist. See Åqvist (1965), (1969), (1971), (1972), and compare below sections 10-11.

103

have even come close to doing justice to the semantics of questions.[5]
As to Katz, he is simply wrong in most of his specific claims. These
charges will be documented to some extent in the body of this work.[6]

## 2. QUESTIONS ARE REQUESTS FOR INFORMATION.
## THE DESIDERATUM OF A QUESTION

In spite of this somewhat gloomy view of the current scene, I
believe that the key to the logic of questions is fairly straightforward.
In a way, nothing could be simpler. If there is anything here that
virtually all parties agree on, it is the idea that a question is a request
for information. The questioner asks his listener to supply a certain
item of information, to make him know a certain thing. Thus all that
there is to the logic of questions is a combination of the logic of
knowledge with the logic of requests (optatives, imperatives). Now
the logic of knowledge, known as epistemic logic, is a relatively
well-known subject. A sketch of its semantics is presented in my book,
*Knowledge and Belief* (1962). Moreover, the epistemic aspect of questions is clearly the more interesting and more problematic one of the
two ingredients in the logic of questions. Once it is specified what
information a questioner wants, all that remains is for him to ask for
it.

I propose to dub a description of the (epistemic) state of affairs a
questioner ostensibly wants to have brought about the *desideratum*
of his question. In the formalization soon to be presented, it is the
statement comprising the scope of the initial optative or imperative
operator. It has to be distinguished sharply from the *presuppositions*
of the question and from (potential) *answers* to it.

What I just said amounts to suggesting that the logical properties of a question are mainly determined by its desideratum.

Admittedly a number of results are also available concerning the
logic of requests and commands. But we scarcely need this logic here.
The contribution of the imperative or optative element to the complicated problems of the logic of questions is a rather small one, as is
shown, for example, by the fact that questions about indirect (imbedded) questions are scarcely any simpler than those about direct
ones, although there does not seem to be any imperative or optative
operator actually present in them (not even in their deep structure).

The close relationship between questions and imperatives was

---

[5] Cf. below sections 15-24.
[6] See below, especially sections 20, 25, 32.

acknowledged by Katz (1968, p. 467, n. 6), but he neither exploits the idea systematically nor mentions that it had been pointed out and employed already in Åqvist (1965).

## 3. The Nature of the Imperative Element

One problem in formulating the imperative operator nevertheless has to be mentioned. Any satisfactory formulation has to bring out the fact that an honest questioner not only wants to be informed but also wants the information to be supplied by the person to whom the question is addressed.[7] This is analogous with the fact that an imperative is normally addressed to a specific person and concerns what *he* is to do or to refrain from doing. It is neither quite obvious how this relativization to a person (respondent) is to be expressed nor how integral a part it is of the concept of a question. (For one thing, operators relativized in this way have not been studied very successfully by logicians, one of the most important exceptions being Hilpinen, 1969.)

Fortunately, it seems to me that these problems do not affect the rest of what I want to say, for it seems to me that most features of the logical and grammatical behavior of a question depend only on its desideratum. (Cf. section 12 below, however.)

A related point that has to be made concerning the imperative operator is that the imperative in question is not an absolute one but conditional on the truth of the presupposition of the question. Thus to paraphrase

(1)   Who will kill Cock Robin?

as

(2)   Bring it about that I know who will kill Cock Robin

is inaccurate, and the reason for the inaccuracy is clear enough. Normally, the questioner does not want to bring about the murder of Cock Robin. Yet the desideratum of (2)—the description of the state of affairs the questioner ostensibly wants to be brought about—is

(3)   I know who will kill Cock Robin

---

[7] There is clearly no implication that this information has to be conveyed to the questioner verbally, however, contrary to what Belnap seems to think. Thus a nod is a perfectly legitimate answer to a yes-or-no question.

which may be thought to imply [8]

(4)   Someone will kill Cock Robin

which need not be a part of what the questioner wants. A more accurate paraphrase will therefore be something like

(5)   Assuming that Cock Robin will be killed, bring it about that I know who will kill Cock Robin.

We shall return to this whole problem of the presuppositions of questions later. (See below, sections 6 and 24.) This will lead me to amplify in certain respects what was just said of the conditional nature of questions.

### 4. Åqvist's Approach

In view of the fact that the analysis of questions just outlined has already been used (and defended) by Lennart Åqvist (see Åqvist, 1965, 1969, 1971, and 1972), it might seem that all that can be done here has already been done by him. Åqvist has indeed written at some length on the logic of questions. Åqvist bases his whole discussion on the very idea just mentioned, namely, that a question is a kind of imperative or optative, requiring the addressee to add to the speaker's knowledge in a certain way. It is true that this idea is in my view the key to the whole logic of questions. In this sense, Åqvist is entirely right. However, this insight can be pushed further in several directions into which Åqvist himself does not venture.

For one thing, the kind of approach he uses can be applied so as to discuss the role of questions in natural languages. Furthermore, in epistemic logic itself Åqvist fails to understand fully the interplay of quantifiers with epistemic operators, thereby depriving himself of interesting further insights. By this failure I mean a failure to appreciate the finer points of the logical semantics (in the sense of Tarski and Carnap) of quantification into epistemic contexts. We shall return to this point in sections 9–10 below. (It is nevertheless only fair to add that the most recent treatment by Åqvist (1973) of quantification into epistemic contexts is not subject to some of the objections to be made against his earlier views.)

---

[8] This implication is not unproblematic, however, for reasons which will not be discussed here.

## 5. Different Kinds of Questions

Before discussing these problems, a couple of important distinctions are in order. In terms of epistemic logic, we can easily distinguish between what has been called nexus-questions and WH-questions (the latter have also been called $x$-questions). These two different kinds of questions differ with respect to the logical form of their respective desiderata. Since the desideratum describes my epistemic status such as I would like it to be made, the desideratum will have to contain at least one phrase 'I know'. Since the other constructions with 'knows' can be shown to reduce to that-constructions, it will have to be tantamount to a sentence containing one or several occurrences of 'I know that'. Now the desideratum of a nexus-question begins with this operator, or is a truth-function of propositions beginning with it. This is not so for WH-questions, which involve quantification into a context governed by 'I know that'. In other words, in the desideratum of a WH-question 'I know that' occurs within the scope of at least one quantifier. By WH-questions I shall thus mean the same as Katz means by $x$-questions. They include, as we shall see, who-, what-, where-, and when-questions. A logician would say that the alternatives we typically envisage in such questions have the logical type of an individual. (More generally speaking, answers to such questions are values of a quantified variable, which does not have to be an individual variable.) WH-questions are to be distinguished from such questions as present us with propositional alternatives. They are called by Katz nexus-questions. Notice that whether-questions are propositional questions, not WH-questions, the presence of the operative letters notwithstanding.

One advantage we can already claim for our of analysis of questions and which these distinctions illustrate is that this analysis avoids the kind of multiplication of operators without necessity which is characteristic of certain current theories of the logic of questions. The only operators we need are epistemic and imperative (optative) operators which we have to use and to study anyway, independently of any logic of questions.

It is also to be noted that initially I shall assume in this work that the WH-questions we are dealing with are questions which do not presume exhaustiveness, that is, that they are 'for instance' questions. Thus 'Who is my next-door neighbor?' will be assumed to have the force 'Who for instance is my next-door neighbor?' Hence an answer to such a question does not imply that there are not other, equally acceptable answers.

This assumption may have to be revised in a more comprehensive study of the different kinds of questions. (See Hintikka, 1974.) However, in this study we shall make this assumption.

Another distinction will also be helpful. Among WH-questions we distinguish *simple* questions from *multiple* and *iterated* ones. Iterated questions involve subordinate questions. In multiple WH-questions, more than one quantifier binds variables inside the epistemic operator 'I know' in the desideratum of the question in question. In English, such questions typically involve several WH-words (other than 'whether') in the same clause.

We shall in this work study mostly the problems connected with simple WH-questions, and only indicate some of the main problems connected with multiple and iterated WH-questions (see sections 16-23 below). A further discussion of problems connected with them is given in Hintikka (1974).

## 6. Some Basic Concepts

Although we are mainly interested in WH-questions, the main facts about nexus-questions will nevertheless have to be registered first. The general logical form of such questions may be taken to be

(6)   Bring it about that I know whether $p_1, p_2, \ldots,$ or $p_k$

or, analyzing the 'whether' clause in the obvious way,[9]

(7)   Bring it about that (I know that $p_1 \vee$ I know that $p_2 \vee \ldots \vee$ I know that $p_k$)

Here the desideratum is the bracketed disjunction

(8)   I know that $p_1 \vee$ I know that $p_2 \vee \ldots \vee$ I know that $p_k$

more idiomatically

(9)   I know whether $p_1, p_2, \ldots,$ or $p_k$.

The *presupposition* of (6) is the disjunction

(9)(a) $p_1 \vee p^2 \vee \ldots \vee p_k$.

---

[9] See Hintikka (1962), Ch. 1.

If it is false, no true (direct) answer can be given to (6). The *potential* (direct) *answers* to (6) are clearly $p_1$, $p_2$, ..., and $p_k$. (By a potential answer, I mean a reply which would be an acceptable direct answer if it were true.)

By calling (9)(a) the presupposition of (9) I of course don't mean that this kind of presupposition cannot be canceled by pragmatic (contextual) factors. Whoever doubts this might well ponder on the fate of the logically minded immigrant who after due deliberation answered the question, "Do you advocate the overthrow of the U.S. government by violence or by force?", "By force."

A part of my undertaking in this work is to see how these notions of presupposition and answerhood can be extended to WH-questions. A good clue is here offered by the formal logical relationships between an explicitly formulated question (in our analysis), its desideratum, and its presupposition. The desideratum is obtained from the fully analyzed question by omitting the optative operator 'bring it about that', and the presupposition results from the desideratum by omitting the epistemic operator 'I know that'.

Yes-or-no questions, typified by

(10)   Is it the case that $p$?

can be accommodated in (6) as the special case where $k = 2, p_1 = p, p_2 = \sim p$. Thus the analysis of (10) is

(11)   Bring it about that I know whether $p$ or $\sim p$

or, more fully,

(12)   Bring it about that I know that $p$ or I know that $\sim p$.

The desideratum of (10) is

(13)   I know that $p$ or I know that $\sim p$

while the presupposition of (6) is the tautology $(p \lor \sim p)$.

## 7. EPISTEMIC LOGIC AND IMBEDDED WH-QUESTIONS

It follows from our definition of WH-questions that the main problems concerning them are likely to be questions concerning the interplay of quantifiers and epistemic operators. These questions have in fact been one of the central concerns of epistemic logic (cf.

sections 16–20 below). How important the problem of 'quantifying in' is for the logic of questions can perhaps be partly seen already from the obvious fact that a large class of indirect (imbedded) WH-questions involve (logically speaking) quantification into an epistemic context. Sentences of the form

(14)   *a* knows who ...

are logically speaking of the form

(15)   (*Ex*)(*a* knows that *x* ...)

with the range of the bound variable '*x*' restricted to persons, and analogous remarks pertain to the different sentences beginning with

(16)   *a* knows what ...
        *a* knows where ...
        *a* knows when ...
        *a* knows why ...
        etc.

These translations are obvious enough, it seems to me.[10] What else can possibly be meant by knowing who *b* is except knowing of some one person *x* that *b* is that person *x*? It also seems to me that this point is strongly reinforced when the semantics which I am about to sketch is appreciated.

### 8. ON THE SEMANTICS OF EPISTEMIC LOGIC. CROSS-IDENTIFICATION

Elsewhere (especially Hintikka, 1962, 1969) I have presented the main features of an explicit semantics (model theory) for epistemic logic. Hence it suffices here to indicate only the main ideas. This logical semantics uses the notion of a possible world as a primitive. Another primitive idea is a relation which to a possible world *W*, a person *a*, and a time *t* associates a set of possible worlds, the *epistemic a-alternatives to W at time t.*[11] They may be thought of intuitively as all the worlds compatible with everything *a* knows in *W* at time *t*. Hence an expression of the form

---

[10] Cf., for instance, Hintikka (1962), (1969). For a major qualification, see Hintikka (1974). There the objections of George Lakoff (1972, pp. 654–655, note 8) are refuted in detail.

[11] In this work, I am taking the liberty of treating such *placeholders* for singular terms as '*a*', '*b*', ... as if they were themselves particular singular terms, and likewise for expressions for entities of other logical types.

(17)   $a$ knows that $p$

is true in $W$ iff $p$ is true in all the epistemic $a$-alternatives to $W$. (I am dropping the reference to time here and in the sequel since it is an element in which we are not primarily interested in this study.)

As a consequence, (15) is true in $W$ if and only if there is some person—call him '$x$'—such that in all the epistemic $a$-alternatives to $W$ it is the case that $x$ . . . . In particular,

(18)   $(Ex)$ $a$ knows that $(b = x)$

is true in $W$ if there is an individual, say $x$, such that in each epistemic $a$-alternative to $W$ the singular term '$b$' picks out that one and the same individual. This of course means that $a$ *knows* in $W$ that '$b$' picks out that particular individual, and (18) therefore clearly amounts to saying that $a$ knows (in $W$) who $b$ is.

This semantics of course works satisfactorily only if the right assumptions are made concerning the behavior of our individuals in the different possible worlds we have to consider. For instance, I have repeatedly pointed out that different individuals must be allowed to exist in different possible worlds, so that not all actually existing individuals need to exist in epistemic alternatives to the actual world. Trivial though this point is, it is still being missed by some linguists who accordingly fail to see how neatly our semantics captures, for example, the difference between

(19) $a$ knows who stole the book

which has the form

(20)   $(Ex)$ $a$ knows that $x$ stole the book

and

(21)   $a$ knows that someone stole the book

which is of the form

(22)   $a$ knows that $(Ex)(x$ stole the book).

However, my semantics is also subject to subtler presuppositions. Among other things, it presupposes (as such formulations as [18] show) that we can *cross-identify* between possible worlds, in the case of (18) between the epistemic $a$-alternatives to $W$. By cross-identification I mean telling (in principle) of an inhabitant of one world whether or not it is identical with a given individual in another. This is just what happened in interpreting (18). We had to say there that the individuals '$b$' picks out from the different epistemic $a$-alternatives to $W$ are identical.

## 9. WORLD LINES AND THEIR LIMITATIONS

The natural semantical counterpart to cross-identification is (I have argued elsewhere) to postulate the existence of an objectively given set of 'world lines', each of them connecting the several manifestations of one and the same individual in different possible worlds. I have also argued elsewhere that these world lines cannot always be continued from a world to others.

What is especially important to realize that world lines may fail to be extendable to a new world $W'$ not just in the sense that the individual in question does not happen to exist in $W'$, but also in the subtler sense that it may be impossible to tell what it would mean for this individual to exist in $W'$, and hence impossible to tell whether it exists in $W'$ or not.

Furthermore, on different occasions we are in effect quantifying over longer or shorter bits of the world lines. This depends on the class of possible worlds as members of which we are considering the values of our different quantified variables. This is in turn shown by the sequence of epistemic operators within the scopes of which each of these variables occurs in a sentence. (The reason is that what forces us to consider more worlds than this one actual world of ours are epistemic and other modal operators, as shown by the truth-conditions of 'knows that' statement formulated above. It is precisely these truth-conditions that force us to extend our horizon from a given world to its alternatives. *A fortiori*, iterated epistemic operators lead us to consider alternatives to these alternatives, and so on.) The same holds for an individual constant '$a$'. If it occurs only outside epistemic operators, we are considering $a$ as a member of that actual world only. If '$a$' occurs also within the scope of '$b$ knows that', we are considering $a$ also as a member of the several epistemic $b$-alternatives to the actual world. If '$a$' occurs simultaneously within the scope of '$b$ knows that' and '$d$ knows that' (in this order), we are considering $a$ as a member of all the $d$-alternatives to the different $b$-alternatives to the actual world; and so on.

These different modes of a singular term's occurring in a sentence '$p$' may be summed up by the *modal profile* of '$a$' with respect to '$p$'. My point may now be expressed succinctly by saying that what we are quantifying over in '$(Ex)p$' depends on the modal profile of '$x$' in '$p$'. The modal profile shows what the worlds are as a member of which our individuals are being considered, and the values of '$x$' are in a sense those world lines, or bits of world lines, that span all these worlds. Thus '$(Ex)p$' is true iff there is a world line connecting all those worlds as a member of which $x$ is considered in '$p$', as indicated by the modal profile of $p$ with respect to '$x$', such that the individual which goes together with that world line satisfies '$p$'.

The necessity of following this course can almost be seen from what has already been said. The truth-conditions of statements involving such locutions as knowing who someone (say $b$) is, have been seen to involve the question whether the individuals which the term '$b$' picks out in certain class of possible worlds are the same, that is to say, whether they are connected by one and the same 'world line'. What this class is, that is, how long world lines have to be considered here, depends obviously on whose knowledge (or whose knowledge of whose knowledge, etc.) we are talking about. This is just what the modal profile of a sentence shows.

Since quantifiers range (on their normal, 'objectual' interpretation) over genuine individuals which can in principle be reidentified in different worlds, quantifiers will have to go together with world lines or bits and pieces of such lines. But since the selection of these 'bits' (restrictions to a given class of worlds) of world lines varies together with the class of worlds involved, quantifiers too must exhibit a kind of systematic ambiguity depending on the modal profile of '$p$' with respect to '$x$' in '$(Ex)p$' and '$(x)p$'. This systematic ambiguity cannot be avoided by quantifying over world lines spanning *all* possible worlds. There are two main reasons for this.

(i) The class $C_1$ of all world lines spanning a given set of worlds $\Omega_1$ cannot be obtained from the class $C_2$ of all world lines spanning a wider class $\Omega_2$ of possible worlds, $\Omega_2 \supset \Omega_1$, by restricting those lines to $\Omega_1$. (Here we are of course especially interested in the case in which $\Omega_2$ is the class of *all* possible worlds.) Why? As was already indicated, there may be world lines in $C_1$ (that is, world lines spanning all the worlds in $\Omega_1$) that cannot be continued to the rest of $\Omega_2$ and hence cannot be obtained from any member of $C_2$ by restriction. This failure of world lines to be indefinitely extendable thus makes it impossible to recapture all shorter bits of world lines from longer ones by restricting them to smaller sets of possible worlds.

(ii) There are good reasons to believe that *no* world line can extend to *all* possible worlds, at least not the world line of any concrete empirically given individual (as distinguished from such abstract entities as numbers). I have argued briefly for the impossibility of extending world lines arbitrarily far, in Hintikka (1972a).

In order to avoid having a different pair of quantifiers for each different modal profile, we must thus allow the kind of systematic variation or, better, dependence of quantifiers on modal profile which we have just described.

## 10. THE SHORTCOMINGS OF ÅQVIST'S QUANTIFIED EPISTEMIC LOGIC

These brief hints at my semantical theory will have to suffice here. They are intended to be supplemented by the fuller accounts which I have given elsewhere and below.[12] It is also illustrated nicely by what we find in Åqvist's account of the semantics of quantified epistemic logic. In his latest and hence presumably his most fully considered discussion of the subject (Åqvist, 1971), he defines all sorts of so-called quantifiers, but none such as would to the whole job required here. His $(Ex)$, $(Ux)$, $(E_+ x)$, $(U_+ x)$ are quantifiers in name only. In them, we are not quantifying over individuals at all, as defined by world lines, but rather over any old functions which may pick out different individuals from different possible worlds. As a consequence these so-called quantifiers are useless for the purpose of capturing the meaning of who- and what-expressions. For instance,

(23)   $(Ex)$ $a$ knows that $(b = x)$

is analytically true, and hence cannot translate (or paraphrase) a who- or what-statement. Moreover,

(24)   $(E_+ x)$ $a$ *knows* that $(b = x)$

is true as soon as $a$ knows that $b$ exists, and hence equally useless for explicating who- or what-expressions.

Åqvist's other quantifiers

$(E_{ws}x)$, $(U_{ws}x)$, $(E_s x)$, $(U_s x)$

are genuine quantifiers all right. Apart from certain questions of existence which I am here disregarding, they are the quantifiers which in my approach take in such bits of world lines for their values as span *one world together with its alternatives*, but no longer seg-

---

[12] See Hintikka (1969, chapters 6 and 7; 1972a.

ments of world lines. It is immediately obvious that they are entirely inadequate whenever we are dealing with nested epistemic operators, for a sentence with iterated operators forces us to consider alternatives to alternatives to a given world and/or alternatives to such alternatives, and so on. In such cases, we are considering an individual as a member of a given world $W$ and as a member of alternatives to alternatives to ... to $W$. In such circumstances, quantifiers will have to rely on world lines binding together worlds which are more distant from each other than the alternatives to a given world are from it. Åqvist's quantifiers fail to do so.

Examples are in fact easily produced to show that Åqvist's semantics goes haywire in the case of iterated epistemic operators. Among other bad things, we lose the possibility of capturing the sense of certain slightly more complicated 'knows who' locutions by means of expressions of the form (1) above.

For instance, one tries in vain to express the following in Åqvist's language:

(25)   I know who is known by the FBI to be a spy.

For instance, the following straightforward 'translation' does not work:

(26)   $(E_{ws}x)$ (I know that FBI knows that $x$ is a spy).

For from Åqvist's semantics it follows, if you work it out, that it is trivially (although not logically) true, whereas in actual fact it need not be. The triviality follows from the fact that you can surely find a function to serve as Åqvist's '$V$' such that its several values in the epistemic FBI-alternatives to my epistemic alternatives are all spies. Such a function can be found as soon as I know that the FBI knows that there exist spies—a requirement considerably more trivial than the displayed statement. (Knowing this ensures that in each of the FBI-alternatives to my epistemic alternatives there is at least one spy. All we therefore have to do is to choose a function that in each such world picks out a spy.)

It does not help Åqvist to introduce a new pair of quantifiers which require uniqueness not only in a given world and its alternatives, but in the alternatives to these alternatives as well. (Let us call them two-step quantifiers.) For one thing, we can have longer sequences of nested operators than those consisting of two epistemic ones. For the same reason as in the preceding example, the two-step quantifiers are unable to handle three-step sequences of operators (or longer ones). What is even more important, two-step quantifiers cannot do the job of the one-step quantifiers. For instance, consider a statement of the form

(27)   I know who $b$ is.

We cannot express this by means of two-step quantifiers by

(28)   $(E_2x)$ I know that $(b = x)$

This will be true in a world $W$, as you can calculate on the basis of the kind of truth-conditions Åqvist is using, only if there is a valuation which for each epistemic alternative $W'$ to $W$ *as well as* for each alternative $W''$ to such a $W'$ picks out one and the same individual and which satisfies 'I know that $(b = x)$'.

When these alternatives to alternatives are with respect to another person (or the same person's other attitudes, such as perception or memory), this requirement is of course stronger than that of the truth of '$a$ knows who (or what) $b$ is'.

What this means can be illustrated as follows: if a name, say '$c$', picks out the same individuals as this function, '$c$' picks out one and the same individual in $W$, in all the alternatives $W'$ to $W$, *and* in all the alternatives $W''$ to such alternatives. This implies, if the standard connection between 'knows who' and possible-worlds semantics (which was mentioned above) is assumed (and if it is assumed that these other alternatives can be with respect to other persons) that I know that everyone knows who $c$ is.[13] This illustrates the fact the quantifier in (28) ranges over individuals of which I know that everyone knows who or what they are, and that (28) therefore is true only if I not only know who (or what) $b$ is but also know that everyone knows who $b$ is (under some guise or other). This means that the truth-conditions of (28) are stricter than those of plain 'knowing who $b$ is' statements: (28) cannot express 'I know who $b$ is'.

This illustrates the fact, mentioned above, that one cannot obtain briefer bits of world lines from longer ones by restricting the class of possible worlds one is considering.

More generally, examples of this kind show that Åqvist needs a separate pair of quantifiers for each different sequence of epistemic operators and in general for each different modal profile. Since he

---

[13] If these alternatives are with respect to the same person $a$ but relative to his memory rather than his knowledge, (28) is likewise true only if $a$ knows that he remembers who $b$ is—over and above knowing who $b$ is.

actually has (apart from the question of existential presupposition) only two pairs of quantifiers, his semantics of quantified epistemic logic is seriously inadequate.

This lack of a satisfactory theoretical foundation is also reflected by Åqvist's surprising suggestion that interpretational problems in this area can be resolved simply by introducing different kinds of quantifiers. There is no positive harm in trying to do so, but as was already indicated one cannot in the last analysis help ending up with a separate quantifier with each modal profile. This comes pretty close to a *reductio ad absurdum* of Åqvist's suggestion. Åqvist speaks of "Hintikka's different modes of quantification," but in reality he will himself be forced to multiply quantifiers beyond necessity. It is precisely a recognition of the dependence of quantifiers on modal profile that enabled me to get along with just one pair of quantifiers. Åqvist's formulation thus turns the actual situation neatly upside down.

Thus the shortcomings of Åqvist's account in interpreting natural-language statements by its means illustrate strikingly the need of building up our semantics of quantified epistemic logic in the way I have proposed, that is to say, so as to let such quantifiers as '$(Ex)$' in '$(Ex)p$' range over those parts of world lines which span precisely the set of worlds we are considering $x$ in '$p$'.

## 11. WIDER HORIZONS

Lest it seem that we are dealing with matters of merely semantical and hence possibly merely grammatical detail, it may be in order to recall the thesis of an earlier paper (see Hintikka, 1972a). There it was argued that the failure of world lines to be extendable arbitrarily far—which was seen to cause the kind of systematic relating of quantification as shown by the dependence of substitutivity conditions on modal profiles—is closely related to Quine's notion of ontological relativity, and perhaps serves to bring out one valid element in the latter notion. Hence the semantical questions we are dealing with here are closely tied to large-scale philosophical problems.

Apart from the problems connected with quantification, however, Åqvist is generally on the right track, and deserves a great deal of credit for his pioneering work. It may in fact be not only more constructive but more interesting to try to indicate some of the previously unexamined applications of this approach than to criticize its details.

## 12. Nonstandard Questions.
## Subordinate Questions in a Performatory Context

A word of caution may be in order at this stage of our discussion. There are many uses of questions which *prima facie* do not fall within the scope of our treatment. A case in point is an examination-question. There the questioner is not asking to be better informed, but is rather checking whether the addressee of the question knows the subject matter.

It is not too difficult to show how such uses of questions can be related to the basic ideas of the approach advocated here. (We could of course also appeal instead to the fairly obvious fact that an examination situation involves secondary use of language anyway. However, it is more illuminating to try to spell out precisely how such derived uses are derived.) What happens in an examination situation is that the questioner wants the addressee to demonstrate *his* knowledge. An approximate analysis of such a question, say, will therefore be something like this:

(29)   Who did $X$?
(30)   Please tell me who did $X$.

Hence an examination-question like (29) can be thought of as an elliptical form of the corresponding request (30). This ellipsis is made especially tempting by the fact that the desired responses to (29) and (30) are the same.

Although there thus does not seem to be any major problem with examination questions, the remarks just made may seem inadequate because I have not indicated how to treat subordinate questions with such words as 'asks', 'tells', 'wonders', and so on, as the main verb. (My treatment has so far been restricted to epistemic verbs like 'knows', 'believes', 'perceives', 'remembers', and the like.) There is nevertheless no major problem as to the semantics of such verbs as 'asks', 'tells', or 'wonders'. The main additional ingredient involved is a reference to a speech- or thought-act. Its content can be analyzed as of old. Thus for instance

(31)   $a$ asked $b$ who $d$ is

has roughly the semantical analysis

(32)  $a$ addressed to $b$ an optative to the effect that $b$ bring it
      about that he knows who $d$ is.

Likewise,

(33)  $a$ wondered whether $p$

may perhaps be analyzed (as the first approximation) as

(34)  $a$ expressed his uncertainty whether $p$.

Thus there do not seem to be any special problems about such verbs.

One of the main features of my analysis of questions may be said
to be the relative detachment of the imperative or optative element
from the rest of the question. This may perhaps be taken as a partial
explanation why it is relatively easy to turn a question into an entirely different kind of sentence by the use of so-called parenthetical
verbs. A case in point is

(35)  Did John get to school on time, I wonder?

Here 'I wonder' has the effect of replacing the optative operator
by another.

I will not inquire here into the grammatical problems connected
with these semantical analyses. Needless to say, analyses like (32) and
(34) are not offered as anything like a syntactically relevant 'deep
structure' of (31) or (33), respectively.

There is no difficulty in accounting for some of the other familiar
cases in which a question in the grammatical sense of the word is
doing duty for some other kind of utterance, for example,

(36)  Can you help me?

as having essentially the same force as

(37)  Please help me, if you can.

Any reasonable theory of conversational implications and conversational forces should easily account for such cases.

### 13. STATEMENTS DE DICTO AND DE RE

The phenomenon of nonstandard questions thus does not reduce the interest of an Åqvist-type approach to the logic of questions. I want to suggest that on the basis of an improved Åqvist-type approach we can build an account of the logic of questions which is much more satisfactory than anything else that is found in the literature. To defend this claim, I have to discuss several different problems that come up in this area and which we can partially elucidate.

One general point which we can make in terms of our epistemic logic is to reconstruct the important distinction between *de dicto* and *de re* interpretations of certain expressions. I have discussed this point earlier (see Hintikka, 1969, pp. 103-104, 120-121, and 1973). Hence a short summary will have to suffice. Suppose that we are given an expression of natural language containing a singular term (noun phrase) '*b*' occurring within the scope of an intensional operator. Suppose further that its *prima facie* translation in our symbolism is of the form '$F(b)$'. Then we have a choice between understanding it to be about *b*, whoever or whatever *b* is (*de dicto* reading), and understanding it to be about the individual, who in fact is *b* (*de re* reading). This distinction can be spelled out as being between

$$(38) \quad F(b) \qquad\qquad\qquad (de\ dicto)$$

and

$$(39) \quad (Ex)(x = b\ \&\ F(x)) \qquad\qquad (de\ re)$$

for it is bindable variables like '$x$' that range over well-defined individuals.

We can see here also why the *de dicto-de re* distinction is relevant only in certain types of contexts. For only when several possible worlds are considered together can the individuals that '*b*' picks out from different possible worlds fail to be connected by one and the same world line. (If only one world is considered, this kind of discrepancy cannot come about.) For it is seen that if the several references of '*b*' in the different worlds as a member of which *x* is considered in '$F(x)$' are connected by one and the same world line, the *de dicto-de re* distinction disappears. Thus the possibility of reconstructing the *de dicto-de re* distinction is already something of a vindication of our possible-worlds semantics for epistemic logic.

A similar distinction can of course also be made between the different ways in which a bindable variable, say '$v$', can enter into a context governed by the operator 'knows that' or into any other intensional context, in one case directly (as in, say, '$F(y)$' where '$v$' occurs within the scope of intensional operators) and in the other as mediated by another existential quantifier, as in

(40)  $(Ex) (x = y \& F(x))$,

or perhaps by a universal quantifier, as in

(41)  $(x)(x = y \supset F(x))$.

It would be highly interesting to study the manifestations of the *de dicto-de re* contrast in natural languages. No such study will be attempted here, however. Let me only remark that in the case of quantifiers ordinary discourse seems to exhibit a fairly strong preference for the *de re* construction.

## 14. EPISTEMIC LOGIC VERSUS NATURAL LANGUAGE

Next, something must be said of the relation of my approach to discussions of questions in linguistics. The situation here seems to be as follows. According to the approach I am considering, the logical form of a WH-question is in the simplest (but not atypical) case something like this:

(42)  Bring it about that $[(Ex)$ I know that --- $x$ ---].

As was already hinted at, the logical properties of (42) are pretty well determined by the bracketed part of (42), that is, from its desideratum. Which WH-question we have, and how it is to be translated into a natural language, will have to be read from this part of (42).

Here we have in fact a highly interesting field open for case studies of the relations between logic and grammar and to some extent also between semantics and syntax. The key problem in both cases is the translation between our symbolic language and the natural language whose grammar we are studying. If we could have a set of hard-and-fast rules for such translation, our epistemic logic would yield as a by-product a grammatical theory of questions. (In such a theory, the translation rules themselves would presumably also play a major part.) It would accordingly be highly interesting to find such rules and also to know whether there is any hope in principle of formulating them. An impossibility result would be as interesting as a positive solution here, it seems to me. No set of such rules will be attempted here, although it is not difficult to translate individual questions back and forth in a large number of cases.

## 15. Epistemic Logic and Linguistics

We can say more than this, however. The semantical distinctions which can be based on the analysis of the desiderata of different questions are of such a nature that they would have to be incorporated in *any* satisfactory semantics of questions, including semantics constructed for the purpose of linguistics. Examples will be given later to bring home this truth. A skeptical reader is invited to study the readings (43.1)-(43.2) and (43.3)*-(43.5)* of the single English question (43) (below, sections 17-18). He will then see that those readings do represent, in a down-to-earth sense, different meanings which (43) can have. For instance, what counts as an answer to them varies with the reading, as will be indicated later (in sections 17 and 30). Surely any grammatical theory which fails to account for the differences between these readings will be seriously inadequate.

Thus the problem of translating between the language of our combined imperative and epistemic logic and a natural language like English or Finnish will also be highly relevant to the question of the interrelations of syntax and semantics. For instance, even without claiming that the structure of questions uncovered by our epistemic logic is what some grammarians are trying to get at in terms of their 'deep structures' or 'semantical representations', there apparently has to be a close connection between the two if the deep structure or semantic representation is to serve as the bearer of meanings in the way often assumed. In fact, we may tentatively think of our epistemic logic as providing a kind of a peculiar 'deep structure' or perhaps rather 'semantical representation' of questions. Then the problem of translating between the language of epistemic logic and natural languages will become very much like the problem of finding the appropriate transformations (in the sense of transformational grammar) to carry us from the deep structure to the various surface structures. Thus any specific result (positive or negative) concerning the possibility of such transformations from our epistemic 'deep structure' into actual grammatical surface structures would be rather interesting.

Here we shall only indicate somewhat more clearly what some of the different possible structures are in terms of our epistemic logic. Although we shall not discuss systematically the 'transformations' which would carry us from a logical 'deep structure' to the surface forms of natural language, the resulting insights can be used to discuss some of the competing semantical representations and deep structures postulated by linguists and logicians.

For these reasons, our observations possess a great deal of potential relevance to the enterprise of a linguist. Since they bring out certain unmistakable features of the semantical situation, they will serve as a set of 'adequacy conditions' for any linguistic semantics and *a fortiori* for any semantical representation of interrogatives as well as for any deep structure of questions which is claimed to be sufficient for their semantical interpretation.

### 16. The Structure of Questions Is Determined by the Interplay of Quantifiers and Intensional Operators

In trying to give a more detailed account of the situation, it is advisable to begin with a general point. Although (42) is a typical form of a WH-question, several variations are possible here. In indirect questions, the imperative operator ('bring it about that') is missing. Hence we are in effect left only with the interplay of epistemic operators and quantifiers as the whole basis of our analysis of questions. This basis may seem exceedingly narrow. However, this impression of narrowness can arise only if one does not realize how subtle and multifarious such interplay in fact is and how difficult it often is to capture in ordinary language. In fact, the symbolic paraphrases of an ordinary-language question may contain several quantifiers, not all of them existential, in the place of the single $(Ex)$ of (42). In nested questions, there often are choices as to where the quantifier is to be located which (from our point of view) goes together with a given WH-phrase. All this creates a rich variety of different (but easily distinguishable) symbolic expressions which clearly have a different meaning but whose ordinary-language counterparts are apparently not obtained by an equally neat set of rules.

### 17. Examples

Examples may bring home some of these phenomena to you. Consider, for instance, the following question (borrowed from Bach, 1970, and Baker, 1970).

(43)   Who remembers where she bought what?

This is multiply ambiguous, as a moment's thought will show. As a crude approximation, we may say that the state of affairs the speaker wants to have brought about may be any of the following:

(43.1)   $(Ex)(Ey)(Ez)$(I know that $x$ remembers that she bought $y$ at $z$).

(43.2)   $(Ex)$(I know that $(Ey)(Ez)(x$ remembers that she bought $y$ at $z$)).

(43.3)   $(Ex)$(I know that $(y)(Ez)(x$ remembers that she bought $y$ at $z$)).

(43.4)   $(y)(Ex)$(I know that $(Ez)(x$ remembers that she bought $y$ at $z$)).

(43.5)   $(y)(Ex)(Ez)$(I know that $x$ remembers that she bought $y$ at $z$).

In section 30 below it will be pointed out that in most cases the answers to (43.1)-(43.5) even have a different form. In order to convey the reader some feeling for the difference between (43.1)-(43.5), I will give sample answers (potential answers, if you prefer the term) to them.

(43.1)(a)   John remembers that she bought the hat at Filene's.

(43.2)(a)-(43.3)(a)   John remembers where she bought what.

(43.4)(a)   John remembers where she bought the hat, Sally remembers where she bought the mink stole, and Bill remembers where she bought the dress.

(43.5)(a)   John remembers that she bought the hat at Filene's, Sally remembers that she bought the mink stole at Saks, and Bill remembers that she bought the dress at the Co-op.

A moment's thought also shows that, for reasons which that are largely implicit in what has already been said in this paper—and in common sense—(43.3)-(43.5) should really be written in a slightly different form:

(43.3)*   $(Ex)$[I know that $(y)$ $(Ez)$(she bought $y$ at $z$) $\supset$ $(Eu)(y = u$ & $(Ez)(x$ remembers that she bought $u$ at $z$)) )]

(43.4)*   $(y)$[$(Ez)$(she bought $y$ at $z$) $\supset$ $(Ex)(Eu)(y = u$ & I know that $(Ez)(x$ remembers that she bought $u$ at $z$))]

(43.5)*   $(y)$[$(Ez)$(she bought $y$ at $z$) $\supset$ $(Ex)(Ez)(Eu)(y = u$ & I know that $x$ remembers that she bought $u$ at $z$)]

An explanation why we·have to move from (43.3)-(43.5) to (43.3)*-(43.5)* may be formulated as follows:

Clearly, what is involved in (43) on any reading are only the things she actually bought and the places where she actually bought something. This explains the antecedent added in (43.3)*-(43.5)*. However, these things and places have to be considered independently of whether they are known to the people involved. This explains the added quantifier which ensures that the initial universal quantifier ranges over actual objects, not objects known to someone, i.e. it explains the added existential quantifier in the consequent.

## 18. A GENERALIZATION

Our example in fact enables us to characterize a large class of WH-questions (with nonexclusive answers). Their desiderata are of the form obtained by iterating the following structure:

(44)  $(y_1)(y_2)$ .... $(y_i)(Ex_1)(Ex_2)$ .... $(Ex_j)(Eu_1)$ $(Eu_2)$ ....
$(Eu_{i+k})$ $[G(y_1, y_2, \ldots, y_i)$ $\supset$ $(u_1 = y_1$ & $u_2 = y_2$ &
... & $u_i = y_i$ & $u_{i+1} = w_{m+1}$ & $u_{i+2} = w_{m+2}$ & ... &
$u_{i+k} = w_{m+k}$ & $z$ knows (remembers, believes, perceives, sees, ...) that $F(x_1, x_2, \ldots, x_j, z, u_1, u_2, \ldots, u_{i+k}, w_1, w_2, \ldots, w_m))]$

Here $z, w_1, w_2, \ldots, w_{m+k}$ are either bound to outer quantifiers or replaced by constants, and $F$ may have the same structure or be simply a first-order sentence. I shall not try to specify the list of all verbs that can enter into this characterization. It must be the case, however, that the outmost verb is 'know' in 'I know'.

It is readily seen that (43.1)-(43.2) and (43.3)*-(43.5)* are, apart from trivial transformations (in the logical sense of the word), of the form (44). In (44) '$w_1$', '$w_2$', ..., '$w_m$' are those outside variables with respect to which the structure in question is *de dicto* and '$w_{m+1}$', ..., '$w_{m+k}$' those with respect to which it is *de re*.

This shows that there is room for some further variation (of a minor sort) in (43.1) and in (43.4)*-(43.5)* in that inmost epistemic ('remembers that') context in (43.4)* may be taken to be *de re* with respect to '$u$' and that the same context in (43.1) and in (43.5)* may be taken to be *de re* with respect to '$u$' or '$z$' or both. As was already mentioned, in ordinary discourse these *de re* constructions seem to come more naturally than (43.4)*-(43.5)* as they stand. One may even wonder whether in (44) we should consider *de re* constructions only and hence put $m = 0$.

These more natural forms (43.1) and (43.4)*-(43.5)* will clearly be, respectively,

(43.1)** $(Ex)(Ey)(Ez)$ [I know that $(Eu)(Ew)(y = u$ & $z = w$ & $x$ remembers that she bought $u$ at $w$)],

(43.4)** $(y)$ [$(Ez)$(she bought $y$ at $z$) $\supset$ $(Ex)(Eu)(y = u$ & I know that $(Ez)(Ew)(u = w$ & $x$ remembers that she bought $w$ at $z$))],

and

(43.5)** $(y)[(Ez)$ (she bought $y$ at $z$) $\supset$ $(Ex)(Ez)(Eu)(y = u$ & I know that $(Ew)(Et)(z = w$ & $t = u$ & $x$ remembers that she bought $t$ at $z$))].

It is perhaps not especially remarkable that the underlying logic of the apparent simple question (43) can be as complicated as this. What seems to me remarkable is that we are led to uncover this complexity as naturally, not to say inevitably, as we have in fact done.

### 19. ADEQUACY CONDITIONS ON GRAMMATICAL THEORIES OF QUESTIONS

Returning to our example (43), it may be noted that of the above readings, only (43.2) and (43.4)* were mentioned by Emmon Bach when he recently discussed (43). Without wanting to be impolite, I may perhaps air my dissatisfaction with current linguistic discussion of questions by recalling that Bach and Baker find it a virtue of their theory that it predicts *two* meanings for (43), which apparently has at least five of them. Even if some of these readings are not actually accepted in normal discourse, a linguist must be able to represent and to discuss them, if only to explain why they are not acceptable.

This point may be generalized. As was already pointed out our logic of questions may be compared, at least for heuristic purposes, with those deep structures of questions which linguists have postulated. Insofar as it is claimed that these deep structures are what determine the meanings of different questions, they are in the same ballpark with my epistemic logic of questions which is supposed to do just that (when given the intended semantical interpretation). But if so, linguists' deep structures of questions all seem to be inadequate. For what is needed to specify the meaning of a WH-question? We have seen that each of its WH-phrases corresponds to a quantifier. The following things (at least) have to be specified about these quantifiers in order for the meaning of the question to be fixed:

(i)     their order;
(ii)    between which epistemic operators each of them is located;
(iii)   which of them are existential and which ones universal.

Of course a full answer to (ii) partly prejudges the answer to (i). However, it still leaves open the order of quantifiers which are located between the same epistemic operators. It is also to be noted that the order of (adjacent) quantifiers of the same sort (both existential or both universal) does not matter.

## 20. Adequacy Conditions Applied to Linguistic Theories of Questions

Of those deep structures which linguists have postulated and with which I happen to be familiar, none have a combinatorial multiplicitly equal to all the three tasks (i)-(iii). Katz and Postal (1964) operate with a question morpheme Q and a WH-morpheme. The function of the latter is said to indicate the scope of Q. It is not clear what is meant by 'scope' here, however. Since they postulate a Q-operator only for direct (nonimbedded) questions the scope of their Q (in a logician's sense of 'scope') is in any case irrelevant to the structure of the desideratum into which their Q does not enter at all. Moreover, I do not see that the scheme of Katz and Postal offers us any way whatsoever of answering questions (ii)-(iii). Nor do they say anything that would throw light on how questions (i) are to be answered in the case of ordinary-language questions.

It appears in fact that Katz and Postal are overlooking completely the problem (iii) and not just failing to solve it. Katz (1968) suggests that the noun phrases to which the WH can attach "are proforms such as 'someone', 'something', 'sometime', 'someplace', 'someway', etc." (p. 468). This amounts to claiming that only existential quantifiers can occur in the desideratum of a question as the counterpart of a WH-phrase. There are plenty of examples (besides the ones we already have) to show that this is simply false.

In an interesting paper, C. L. Baker (1970) proposes a deep structure for questions which is "of the form Q(i,j,...)S where S contains one or more occurrences of each of noun phrases NP(i), NP(j), . . . ." Here 'i', 'j', . . . are cross-referential indices.

This is clearly a more flexible scheme than the Katz-Postal one. An essential part of the rationale of Baker's improvement over Katz and Postal can in fact be said (in my terminology, not Baker's) to be able to answer questions of type (ii). This Baker can do by assuming that a similar question operator occurs also in indirect questions, for example, in the ones imbedded in (43). Thus the position of the operator to which a noun phrase NP(i) is tied 'i' shows between which epistemic operators the corresponding quantifier is located. However, there is no element in Baker's scheme to indicate whether we are dealing with a universal or an existential quantifier. (Cf. my question (iii).) Hence even Baker's deep structure is insufficient for the relevant semantical purposes.

This can be spelled out more fully. Baker (1970) and Bach (1970) explain the ambiguity of (43) essentially by pointing out that its surface structure does not enable us to answer questions of the type (ii). As Bach puts it (p. 159), we cannot see from (6) whether 'what' is "interrogative with respect to the sentence governed by *remember* or with respect to the top sentence" governed by what Bach surmises to be "an abstract performative verb" and which we can think of as our 'I know that'. However, we can have an ambiguity in questions where there is no imbedding and hence only one main verb. Thus the desideratum of the question

Where did she buy what?

can be (in a first approximation) either

(45)   $(Ex)(Ey)$(I know that she bought $y$ at $x$)

or

(46)   $(y)(Ex)$(I know that she bought $y$ at $x$).

This ambiguity is impossible to explain by means of the methods used by Bach and Baker, for it is due to the possibility of taking 'what' to represent either an existential or a universal quantifier.

## 21. Do We Need a Question Operator in Subordinate Questions?

A possible objection to Baker's deep structure of questions is perhaps the absence of any performative interpretation when his question-morpheme occurs in indirect questions. Almost the whole force of Baker's operator Q(i, j, . . .) is to enable us to answer questions of type (ii).[14] There is nothing questionable in such occurrences of the question morpheme, one is tempted to say. The 'interrogative char-

---

[14] Baker does use the question operator for another main purpose, too, viz., to explain why only one questioned constituent may be moved to a clause-initial position. This phenomenon admits of other explanations, however.

acter' of indirect questions will simply mean that one quantifies in them into an epistemic context (or into certain other types of referentially opaque context). Hence the only role that a question morpheme retains from the viewpoint of an epistemic logic is to serve as a counterpart of our imperative or optative operator in linguists' deep structure.

This point can perhaps be generalized. If I am right, the logic of questions is to a large extent the logic of the interplay of epistemic operators and quantifiers. If so, the logic of questions is linguistically speaking related to the more general problem of how quantifiers, especially their order and their scope, are expressed or indicated in natural languages, and should be studied in connection with this larger problem. Small wonder, therefore, that "interrogative words and indefinite pronouns are often morphologically related or even identical in a wide variety of genetically unconnected languages," as Emmon Bach notes (1970, p. 158), for indefinite pronouns typically do also duty for quantifiers, especially existential ones.

As a reminder of this close relationship between quantifiers and the WH-element, we may use the observation that one of them can occasionally do the same job in one language as the other in another. A case in point is the English question

(47)   Where is each of you coming from?

It may be translated into Finnish as follows:

(48)   *Mistä kukin teistä tulee?*

Here the job of the 'quantifier' *each* is taken over by the interrogative *kukin*.

It is customary to say, as is done for instance by Bach (1970), that the question word embodies the feature specification [– Definite]. We have seen, however, that an occurrence of the question word can represent a universal quantifier and not an existential one. Hence the correctness of Bach's point will depend on whether we take such words as 'every' and 'everyone' to be [ + Definite] or [– Definite]. All the usual tests fail to distinguish between those alternatives, however. (For instance, we have the nondeviant sentences

Everyone else was at the party.
As big as each python was it did not scare me.
I hereby christen every kid John.
Fuck everyone!

confounding all of Bach's tests in *op. cit.*, p. 157.) To my mind, this casts serious doubts on the adequacy of the very notion of definiteness. And, even apart from these doubts, the claim that a question word embodies the feature specification [− Definite] is suspect somewhat in the same way as Katz's claims critized above.

## 22. INTERROGATIVES AND QUANTIFYING IN

In fact, if I had to suggest a general characterization of interrogative pronouns (albeit one which needs certain qualifications), it would be to say that an interrogative pronoun is an ordinary-language counterpart to a quantifier which binds (from the outside) variables occurring within the scope of an epistemic (or certain other opaque) operator (in a wide sense which comprises not only knowing that but, for example, remembering that and perceiving that). The logic of interrogative pronouns is the logic of quantifying into epistemic contexts. This is the reason, incidentally, why those semantical problems of quantifying into propositional-attitude contexts which were discussed in the first part of this paper with reference to Åqvist are absolutely vital to any serious semantical study of interrogatives. Here we can therefore see a belated justification for spending so much time on the problem of quantifying in (which is to a large extent equivalent with the problem of cross-identification) in sections 8-10 above.

This suggestion has a considerable grammatical interest. If it is correct, then interrogatives can be characterized as counterparts of quantifiers binding (from the outside) variables in an epistemic (or otherwise opaque) context.

Interrogative (uses of such) pronouns (as) 'who', 'what', 'when', and so on, are then separated from the corresponding relative (uses of the same) pronouns 'who', 'what', 'when', and so on, by their grammatical context, in that the latter involve (perhaps) a kind of quantificational cross-reference but not quantification *into* an epistemic context (or into a similar opaque context). But if so, it not only becomes redundant to postulate any question-morpheme for indirect questions. It begins to look as if there is no need of countenancing any irreducible distinction between interrogative pronouns and relative pronouns. They are both surface-structure counterparts to deep structures involving quantifiers, and they are distinguished from each other simply by the construction in which these quantifiers occur.

## 23. THE ORDER OF QUANTIFIERS

So far I have not said anything about the problem (i) (section 19 above) concerning the order of quantifiers in the desideratum of a question. It is clear, however, that the order of the WH-phrases in a natural-language question is often highly relevant here as an indication of what the deep structure of the question in a question is. For instance, there are expressions which are, as it were, mirror images of (43.3)*-(43.5)*:

(49.3)*   $(Ex)$[I know that $(z)((Ey)$(she bought $y$ at $z) \supset (Eu)(z = u$ & $(Ey)(x$ remembers that she bought $y$ at $u))$]

(49.4)*   $(z)[(Ey)$(she bought $y$ at $z) \supset (Ex)(Eu)(z = u$ & I know that $(Ey)(x$ remembers that she bought $y$ at $u))$]

(49.5)*   $(z)$ $[(Ey)$(she bought $y$ at $z) \supset (Ex)(Ey)(Eu)(z = u$ & (I know that $x$ remembers that she bought $y$ at $u)$]

If my intuitions are sharp enough in this area, however, these are possible desiderata of an ambiguous question different from (43), namely:

(49)   Who remembers what she bought where?

Notice, incidentally, that (43.1) and (43.2)—we may rename them (49.1) and (49.2) for the purpose—can also be desiderata of (49).

This does not solve all the problems in this department, but rather poses new ones. Elsewhere, the order of quantifiers in the deep structure often mirrors their order in the surface structure. For instance, the difference between

(50)   every man loves some woman

and

(51)   some woman is loved by every man

is essentially that between $(x)(Ey)(---)$ and $(Ey)(x)(---)$. In the case of questions, however, the order of quantifiers in our 'deep structure' of desiderata is the reverse of the order of the corresponding WH-phrases in sentences (43) and (49). An explanation of this fact might be interesting, for it seems to be connected with the transformation which moves a questioned constituent to a clause-initial position, which occurs in several languages, and which appears to have features which are 'linguistically universal' (see Bach, 1970).

## 24. PRESUPPOSITIONS OF QUESTIONS

Our analysis of the different readings of (43) shows that more has to be said of the presuppositions of questions than Katz and others have so far said. Katz uses in effect the presupposition as a step in the derivation of the question. For instance, the presupposition of (43) would for him be something like

(52)    Someone remembers that she bought something somewhere

This view is belied by our observations above. Katz's (52) can be the presupposition of (43) only on one of the several readings of (43). Hence Katz's theory cannot apply to the presuppositions of all questions.

What the presupposition of a question is is nevertheless easy to see in terms of our epistemic logic. In the case of the question whose desiderata are (43.1)-(43.2), (43.3*-(43.5)*, they are obtained by dropping the operator 'I know that' from these desiderata—a procedure which can be applied generally to yield the presupposition of a question. What is not at all clear is how these presuppositions are supposed to be connected with the generation of the ambiguous question (43). Of course, this generation itself is highly problematic, being an instance of the problem of the relation of the surface forms of ordinary language to the 'deep structures' exhibited by our epistemic logic. Presuppositions of questions are closely connected with their deep structure (semantic structure) and are not any easier to get hold of by starting from the surface structure than the rest of the deep structures.

## 25. WHAT IS AN ANSWER? KATZ CRITICIZED

Our theory also enables us to solve several systematic problems which have been discussed in the logic of questions. Our answers of course apply to natural languages only insofar as they can be translated into our semi-symbolic language. However, several competing current answers can be seen to be mistaken already when applied to the latter.

One of the most important questions in this department is: What counts as a (possible) direct *answer* to a given question? (I understand the notion of a possible answer in the same way as Katz: a possible answer is one which would satisfy the questioner if it were true.)

Another is: When is a question trivial so as to be self-answering (in the sense of Katz's (1968) ill-named notion of being *linguistically answered*)?

The former problem is not a formidable one in the case of nexus-question. For WH-questions, however, it is more problematic. It is ironical that the one recent writer (namely, Åqvist) who (as it seems to me) is in the position to give a satisfactory solution to the answerhood problem has disregarded it, while those who have considered the question-answer relationship have failed to explain its true nature.

In order to indicate what I mean, let me note that Belnap (1963) simply restricted his discussion to question-and-answer situations "where both questioner and respondent know in advance exactly what should count as an answer" (p. 5). This neatly severs Belnap's discussion from a large class of interesting problems.

Katz, in contrast, offers a detailed answer to the question of what constitutes a possible (that is, acceptable if true) answer to given WH-question $q$. His answer, soon to be explained, is as follows: $S$ is a possible answer to $q$ iff it results from the presupposition $p$ of $q$ by a replacement of the following kind: (i) what is being replaced are those noun phrases $NP_i$ of $p$ which correspond to the different WH-ed noun phrases of $q$; (ii) each such $NP_i$ is replaced by a noun phrase $NP_j$ such that the reading for $NP_j$ has more semantical markers than the reading for $NP_i$. Speaking of semantical markers presupposes of course that the replacement is thought of as taking place in the semantically interpreted underlying phrase marker.

I cannot here define all the concepts used in this attempted definition. Fortunately, doing so is not necessary, either. What is essentially involved is that an answer to a question $q$ is a substitution-instance of the desideratum of $q$, with the (first) epistemic operator 'I know that' omitted, provided that the substituting noun phrases are more informative than the individual variables (including the specification of their respective ranges) for which they are substituted. This requirement of additional information is interpreted by Katz as requiring that the substituting noun phrases have more semantical markers than the NP (which is of the nature of a variable or of a specification of a variable by means of a proform) for which it is substituted in the presupposition.

There is no reason to think that this interpretation is appropriate, however. There is no evidence that the kind of 'added information' which is manifested by the extra semantic markers is the kind of information the questioner wants to have by way of an answer, or that it even represents information in any reasonable sense of the word. Counterexamples are in fact easily forthcoming.

The following 'answers' pass Katz's muster but are nevertheless unlikely to be accepted as answers by anyone:

(53)(a)    Who is a spy around here?
(53)(b)    The tallest spy around here.
(54)(a)    Who is August married to?
(54)(b)    To his loving and beloved wife, the mother of his chil-
           dren.

(For explanatory comments on these sample counterexamples, see
below section 26, last paragraph.) The 'answers' (53)(b) and (54)(b) are
likely to draw such further responses as

(55)    But who *is* the tallest spy?

or

(56)    But who *is* she?

The insufficiency of Katz's answer can also be seen in other ways.
For one thing, a very natural class of answers to who-questions use
proper names as substituting terms (for the purposes of Katz's
attempted definition). They cannot always be said to be characterized
by additional semantical markers in the sense Katz is presupposing,
and hence are not captured by his characterization of (possible)
answers.

Katz's own examples (56) and (57) (1968, p. 476) use the proper
names 'Lyndon Johnson' and 'Paul Goodman' as substitution values in
possible answers. This can be squared with his characterization only
by noting that the particular proper names in question import the
semantic marker [+ male] to the answer, for otherwise such a proper
name does not have any more semantic markers than the corresponding quantifier, for example, 'someone'. To rely on this additional
marker is clearly beside the point, however. Surely the status of a
proper name as a potential answer to a question like 'Who is president
of the U.S.A.?' does not depend on whether or not it specifies the sex of
the person in question. 'Pat Brown' or 'Gail Goodrich' are surely as
good (potential) answers here as Katz's examples.

For another thing, Katz is again overlooking the possibility that
some of the initial quantifiers of the desideratum might be universal
ones. Then a single substitution-instance is insufficient, for an answer
will have to specify a class of substitution-instances. For instance, an
answer to a question whose desideratum (43.4)* will have to specify,

for each of the relevant values of '$y$' (that is, for each place where she bought something), who remembers what she bought there. Katz's characterization is powerless to handle such cases. His attempted solution of the answerhood problem is therefore mistaken. As far as I can see, no answers better than his can be found in the literature.

### 26. THE QUESTION OF ANSWERHOOD ANSWERED

Yet a very simple argument shows what the right answer to the question of answerhood is. Let us consider first a simple question of the (somewhat schematically represented form)

(57)  'Who is such that $F$(he)?'

Its desideratum is

(58)  $(Ex)$[I know that $F(x)$].

Suppose that someone tries to answer such a question by a suitable noun phrase, say '$a$', as one can do quite idiomatically.[15] We shall assume that this is a *direct* answer, that is, neither a paraphrase of an answer nor a circumlocution of one nor a response which equals an answer only in virtue of tacit background information and conversational implications. In order to see when '$a$' could serve as a possible answer, let us assume the circumstance in which this 'potentially' as it were would be realized: let us assume that the answer is correct and that the questioner understands and believes it.

What the reply brings about under these assumptions is that the questioner can now say, truly,

(59)  I know that $F(a)$.

This is not yet the desideratum (58) of our original question, however. The problem therefore becomes: When does (59) imply (58)? What we are asking in when the response '$a$' or '$F(a)$' satisfies the questioner, and *per definitionem* it does that if and only if it brings about the state of affairs described by the desideratum.

What we have to ask is thus: When does (59) imply (58)? Now I have argued at length on earlier occasions [16] that this implication

---

[15] 'Suitable' normally means here at least [+ Animate], [+ Human]. There are exceptions to this, however, as noted below in section 23.

[16] See Hintikka (1962), Ch. 6, and Hintikka (1969).

obtains if and only if the following additional premiss is available to the questioner:

(60)   $(Ex)$ I know that $(a = x)$.

In view of what was said in the beginning of this paper, this has pretty much the same force as

(61)   I know who $a$ is.

Thus a possible answer to a simple question of the form 'Who is such that $F$(he)?' is of the form '$a$' or '$F(a)$' *where the questioner must know who (or what, or where, etc.) a is.*

That the italicized requirement has a great deal of explanatory force should be obvious to the most casual observer of people's actual linguistic behavior. Answers to who-questions are apt to be rejected by the questioner if he does not know what the noun phrases refer to that are proffered as answers.

Other services performed by this criterion of answerhood include the ruling out of the counterexamples which were mentioned above and which bother Katz's definition of an answer. For whoever seriously asks (53)(a) does not know who the tallest spy around here is. Nor is one who asks (54)(a) likely to know who John's wife is. Hence (53)(b) and (54)(b) are not likely to be potential answers to (53)(a) and (54)(a), respectively, according to our lights.

## 27. The Contextual Character of Our Answer

It is nevertheless clear that much of the evidence that can be evoked in favor of my definition of answerhood is softer than the kind of evidence which linguists apparently like to play with in these days and which typically deals with people's intuitions about (say) the interrelations of linguistic expressions and about their grammaticality rather than with such contextual and apparently nonlinguistic matters as the extent of the speaker's knowledge. Some writers seem to think that almost anything can in suitable circumstances be made to pass as a reply to a question. But by any token a distinction is needed between a *reply* to a question and an *answer* to it. There is reason to believe that more attention should be paid by linguists and by logicians to contextual factors than they have devoted to such factors of late. Elsewhere,[17] I have also tried to give some reasons for thinking that such an enterprise might discover logically interesting

---

[17] Hintikka (1969), Ch. 1.

general structures quite as easily as an examination of linguists' 'surface' evidence.

## 28. FURTHER QUESTIONS ABOUT ANSWERS

Many reasonable replies (responses to questions) can be shown to be irrelevant to our present concerns here by pointing out that they might equally well be expressed by prefacing the reply by 'I do not know, but ...'. Thus the chief of police might ask of a detective: 'Who robbed the bank last night?' and receive the perfectly reasonable reply 'Obviously the same man who robbed two banks the day before' even though neither the chief nor the detective knows who that robber is. This might even look like a counterexample to my analysis until it is pointed out that the detective could have said equally well 'I don't know, but it is obviously the same man ...'. (I owe this point to a suggestion by Barbara Hall Partee.)

Certain types of inconclusive responses to questions would nevertheless merit a detailed discussion, although we cannot devote one to them here. They are responses of the same form (that of a singular term, or, in the language of the linguists, a noun phrase) as possible answers without being such answers. Examples are offered by the kinds of replies discussed in the preceding paragraph. Why are many such replies accepted virtually in the same way as genuine answers? They are so accepted when they provide information which narrows down the range of remaining alternative answers. Such replies may be called *partial* (possible) *answers*. An essential part of their theory will be to show how this information can be measured. The greater this information is, the better the partial answer. Measures of semantical information developed for first-order languages may be hoped to be helpful here. However, it would take us too far to develop a theory of partial answers in this paper. Suffice it to say that the theory of partial answers appears useful for the study of question-and-answer sequences sequences (cf. Åqvist, 1969; Belnap, 1969; Harrah, 1961) and for the theory of scientific explanation (better or worse answers to certain why-questions), among other things.

There is nothing in my analysis to rule out that some weaker notion of possible answerhood could be characterized in context-independent logical and semantical terms, unlike the characterization given above. The latter being context-dependent in the sense of being relative to what the questioner knows at the time the question is being asked. It looks to me very unlikely, in the light of cases like our counterexamples to Katz, that a satisfactory noncontextual notion of (possible) answerhood can be found.

Notice, furthermore, that there is a strong theoretical reason for this conjecture. The logical and linguistic nature of answers to a question is essentially connected with their function as providing information of the sort specified by the question. Conditions of answerhood which merely turns on the status of potential answers as substitution-instances to certain schemata related to the original question do not yet guarantee 'answers' meeting such conditions perform this function, as shown by our observations above. Even Katz puts in the requirement that the substitution-value must import new semantic markers, obviously in order to guarantee the informativeness of his 'answers'. What we have seen shows that characterizations along such lines just do not work. Rather, an application of the informativeness requirement leads directly to my condition of answerhood.

An additional remark may help to prevent misunderstandings here. It is worth emphasizing that the quantifiers which correspond to 'who' do not always range over persons and that the ranges of other quantifiers may likewise vary from one context and one use to another. For instance, assume that someone asks

(62)    Who administers the oath to a new president?

The force of this question might be (and would naturally be taken to be) such that the quantifier corresponding to 'who' ranges over different officials (offices), not over individual persons. Then possible answers might include, say, 'The Chief Justice' or 'The Secretary of State'. Thus we can explain why they can count as full-fledged answers here, although they need not specify a unique person.

This account is corroborated by observing what conditions possible answers now have to satisfy. It is not required any longer that the questioner must know who (which person) is the Chief Justice or the Secretary of State. What he must know is what offices these are—thereby showing that we are quantifying over officials (offices) and not over persons.

This kind of switch in the criteria of knowing who is neither unusual nor disconcerting. It is beautifully reflected by the familiar reference-book title *Who's Who*. It marks neither a break with the syntax (inferential relationships included) we have sketched for who-constructions nor with our semantics for them. The former remain unchanged as long as one and the same set of criteria of knowing who are applied. And these criteria can be thought of as changing in the way our semantics presupposes, namely, insofar as one's ideas change as to when one has located one and the same person in the different possible worlds one is considering.[18]

Certain systematic changes in these methods of cross-identification nevertheless call for special discussion, which will be attempted in section 36 below.

In other cases a 'what' question may be intended as being answered, not by the specification of a unique individual, but by a specification of what *kind of* thing is in question.

We can now also see what is essential and what is inessential in our own counterexamples (53)–(54) to Katz above. The main point was not that the desired 'who' is described in tautologous terms, as the case nearly is in (53)(b) and (54)(b). Rather, what is essential is that they are described in a way of which it is not known by the questioner whom it applies to. The easiest context-independent examples of this phenomenon are of course such almost or completely empty descriptions as are illustrated by (53)(b) and (54)(b). However, context-dependent examples are likely to be more realistic and much more frequent. (By 'context' I mean here the circumstances of utterance, not the linguistic context.) Unfortunately, their very dependence on the circumstances of utterance is likely to make them less persuasive as a part of a general argument like my present one.

### 29. SOME IMPLICATIONS OF OUR ANSWER TO THE QUESTION OF ANSWERHOOD

The implications of my solution to the answerhood problem are illustrated further by some of its consequences. It follows from it that although the presupposition of a WH-question is satisfied, there need not exist any true (possible) answer to it. That the presuppositions of a simple who-question, say, of

(63)    Who killed Cock Robin?

are satisfied means that the following is true:

(64)    Someone killed Cock Robin.

[18] The same point is illustrated by the (rather male chauvinist) saying quoted in Evelyn Vaugh's diaries:

"Always be polite to girls. You never know who they may become."

The principles of cross-identifying (knowing who) employed here are embarrassingly obvious. (A girl may become Mrs. So-and-So; *that's* how you place girls later on socially.)

However, there may not exist any way of referring to Cock Robin's killer such that the questioner would know who is being referred to. Hence there need not exist a true answer to the question for all speakers and for all occasions, even if its presuppositions are fulfilled. It seems to me that this consequence of my theory is as it should be. On some occasions, it is just impossible to satisfy a questioner without first imparting fresh background information to him.

In fact, this conclusion seems to be highly pertinent to any systematic theory of the pragmatics of questions. It shows the interesting fact that responses to WH-questions, even to a simple one like 'Who is such that $F$(he)?', may have two different functions. Over and above providing the questioner with a substitution-value, say '$a$', which makes (if the answer is true) a substitution-instance '$F(a)$' of the presupposition true, a response may have to serve the additional purpose of supplying enough background information to enable the questioner to know who is being referred to by '$a$'.

This throws some light on people's actual responses to WH-questions. Often, the reply '$a$' to our simple question draws the rejoinder, 'But who is he?', namely, when the questioner does not know who $a$ is. Thus the respondent is apt to try to anticipate this and to reply straightaway somewhat as follows: '$F(a)$—and $a$ is such-and-such a person', where the appended explanation is calculated to provide the questioner with further information which hopefully will enable him to recognize (that is, know) who $a$ is. The predicament is illustrated by the following exchange from Anthony Powell's *At Lady Molly's*:

> "Who is he?"
> "He is called Kenneth Widmerpool. I was at school with him as a matter of fact. He is in the City."
> "I know his name of course. And that he is in the City. But what is he like?" [19]

---

[19] Witness also Inspector Maigret interviewing a witness:

> "Who is Lise?"
> "Her maid."
> "I know. I mean what kind of person is she?"

(Georges Simenon, *Maigret hesite*, 1969, Ch. 3.)

Here, too, a reply which gives the questioner a true substitution-instance of the presupposition is not accepted as an answer, but leads to further questions, which are not any longer who-questions but are calculated to elicit further facts about the person in question.

Here, too, a reply which gives the questioner a true substitution-instance of the presupposition is not accepted as an answer, but leads to an attempt to elicit further facts about the person in question.

Note that supplying this background information is not extrinsic to the essential function of questions. It is often part and parcel of making the questioner know what he wants to know, that is, of making the desideratum of the question true.

Someone might try to improve on the account given above and define a (possible) answer to a question as an answer which possibly could serve as a (possible) answer, that is, would be a (possible) answer for some speaker under some conceivable circumstances. It seems to me, however, that on this definition any substitution-instance of the matrix (that is, the unquantified part) of the presupposition of a WH-question which is not already implied by the presupposition is a possible answer. Thus (54)(b) might be a possible answer to a questioner who knows who August has lived together with, and had children by, while (53)(b) is entailed by the presupposition of (53)(a), that is, by 'someone is a spy around here'. (It is of course presupposed here that no two spies are equally tall and that there is an upper bound to their size.) Thus no interesting results on the notion of answerhood are obtained, and instead we still face all the old problems connected with answers to more complicated questions (for example, answers to (43)).

## 30. DIFFERENT KINDS OF ANSWERS

What answers to more complicated questions will look like at this stage of my discussion can be almost gathered from what has already been said. Examples will perhaps convey the gist of the matter. Consider, for the purpose, the different readings (43.1)-(43.2), (43.3)*-(43.5)* of the ambiguous WH-question (43). Answers to them will be, as was already noted, of the following respective forms:

(65.1)          $a$ remembers that she bought $b$ at $c$

(65.2)-(65.3)   $a$ remembers where she bought what

(65.4)          ($a_1$ remembers where she bought $b_1$) &
                ($a_2$ remembers where she bought $b_2$) &
                . . .

(65.5)          ($a_1$ remembers that she bought $b_1$ at $c_1$) &
                ($a_2$ remembers that she bought $b_2$ at $c_2$) &
                . . .

These deserve—and require—certain comments. First, the difference between them shows vividly that there is in fact a clear difference between the different readings. The only reason why (65.2) and (65.3) are run together is that the imbedded question is ambiguous in the same way as (43).

In (65.1), the questioner must know who $a$ is. If the desideratum is formulated as in (43.1), it looks as if he would also have to know that $a$ remembers what $b$ is *and* where $c$ is. This requirement can be relaxed by replacing the desideratum (43.1) by (43.1)** as was already shown to be natural to do in any case. Then it very nearly suffices for the questioner himself knows what $b$ is and where $c$ is, as shown by the fact that the variables (bound to the initial quantifiers) whose substitution-values $b$ and $c$ are intended to be occur in (43.1)** only within the scope of the operator 'I know that'. At most, the questioner must know that $a$ remembers what $b$ is and where $c$ is under some description or other. In (65.2)-(65.3), the questioner has to know who $a$ is.

In (65.4)-(65.5) $b_1$, $b_2$, ... have to be all the different things she bought. Moreover, the questioner has to know of each $a_i$ who he is. Certain further requirements have also to be satisfied, but they will be largely eliminated when their desiderata are reformulated somewhat in the same way as in (43.1)**, that is, when they are interpreted as (43.4)** and (43.5)**.

For instance, in (65.4) the questioner must either know that each $a_i$ remembers what $b_i$ is or else (if (43.4)** is presupposed so that the 'remembers that' context becomes *de re* with respect to '$a$') just to know himself what each $b_i$ is.

These examples show how answers to more complicated questions depend on their desiderata. They also show that there obtains a considerable complexity in the question-answer relationships. This complexity is largely due to the possibility of an interplay of existential and universal quantifiers and to the interplay of quantifiers and epistemic operators in the desideratum of a question. Its contextual nature (due to the fact that what counts as an answer depends on what the questioner knows) and its dependence of the choice between different kinds of quantifiers in the desideratum of the question yields an important conclusion. It is that Åqvist is entirely right in rejecting as inadequate all the approaches to the logic of questions which use the question-answer relationship as such as a basic, unanalyzed idea. This relationship is itself highly derivative and cannot sustain a heavy theoretical load such as has been put on it by Belnap and others. The logicians who take this question-answer relationship for granted are perhaps wrong for even stronger reason than those Åqvist gives in so many words. Our observations put their approach in a sharp critical light.

## 31. DIFFERENT KINDS OF QUESTIONS

Admittedly, several earlier students of the logic of questions have made distinctions between different types of questions requiring different kinds of answers. They have usually left these distinctions unanalyzed, however, failing to notice that many of the relevant differences are due simply to different epistemic and/or quantificational structures of the desiderata of questions. These distinctions therefore do not give rise to any need to postulate irreducible different types of questions. For instance, some questions require the presentation of an exhaustive list of entities satisfying a certain condition. A case in point is

(66)   Who are the members of the Brazilian national soccer team?

With the help of the analytical truth that a soccer team had precisely eleven members, we can readily see that the desideratum of (66) is

(67)   $(Ex_1)(Ex_2)\ldots(Ex_{11})((x_1 \neq x_2) \& (x_1 \neq x_3) \& \ldots \& (x_{10} \neq x_{11}) \&$ I know that $[(y)(y$ is a member of the Brazilian national soccer team $= ((x_1 = y)^\vee (x_2 = y)^\vee \ldots ^\vee (x_{11} = y))])$

Further types of questions are easily defined in our framework, and the nature of (possible) answers to such questions can likewise be characterized. Thus all need of postulating irreducibly different types of questions disappears, and we are merely left with differences as to what the epistemic state of affairs is that the questioner requests to be brought about.

For instance, Belnap's (1963) distinctions between unique-alternative, complete-list, and nonexclusive which-questions are derivative, and can be defined in terms of the structure of the desiderata of different questions. Furthermore, in Hintikka (1974) it will be argued that many of the apparently different kinds of questions are in fact easily obtained by means of a unified procedure as natural different readings of questions of one and the same form.

## 32. SELF-ANSWERING QUESTIONS: KATZ CRITICIZED

Another important problem here is when a WH-question is trivially answerable. Katz (1968) calls such questions 'linguistically answered', but I prefer the term '*self-answering*'.

Katz proposes the following solution to this problem: A WH-question "is linguistically answered just in case its semantically interpreted underlying phrase marker contains a matrix-structure which has the form of an underlying phrase marker for a question $q'$ and a constituent-structure which has the form of an underlying phrase marker for a possible answer to the question $q'$ ".

The concepts employed by Katz would require lengthy definitions. Fortunately the main idea can be made clear by means of an example. The characterization Katz offers is intended to cover questions like

(68)   Who is buried in the tomb in which Smith is buried?

The semantically interpreted phrase marker of (68) contains (as its matrix-structure in the sense of Katz) the phrase marker of the question

(69)   Who is buried in the tomb?

It also contains (as its constituent-structure in the sense of Katz) the phrase marker of the sentence

(70)   Smith is buried in the tomb.

According to Katz's lights, (70) is always a potential answer to (69), as it of course *can* be. Hence his definition of 'being linguistically answered' (in our terminology, being self-answering) applies to (68).

Katz's definition admits of a neat counterexample. Remember that we are here dealing with 'for instance'-questions, not requiring unique answers or exhaustive lists of alternatives as their answers. Keeping this in mind, we can see that the following question is surely linguistically answered:

(71)   Who is buried in the tomb in which Smith and Jones are buried?

The semantically interpreted phrase marker of (71) contains as a

matrix-structure that of (69). It also contains as constituent-structures the underlying phrase markers of (70) and of

(72)   Jones is buried in the tomb.

This in fact suffices to show that (71) is linguistically answered according to Katz's definition. In fact, there seems to obtain a rare
(comparative) unanimity among linguists that the deep structure of
(71) contains those of (70) and (72) as its (nonoverlapping) parts. Even
the doubts expressed in Partee (1970) do not touch this case. The 'and'
in (71) is a typical conjunctive 'and'.

But if so, by the same token the underlying phrase markers of
(70) and (72) must be contained as constituent-structures in the semantically interpreted underlying phrase marker of

(73)   Who is buried in the tomb in which Smith or Jones is
       buried?

By Katz's definition, (73) should therefore be self-answering
(linguistically answered) which it of course is not.

Notice, incidentally, that this counterexample is doubly insured
against criticism. Even if it could be claimed that the underlying
phrase markers of (70) and (72) are not contained in that of (71), some
explanation of (71)'s being self-answering (linguistically answered)
must be given by Katz. The only reasonable alternative seems to be to
say that (71) is self-answering because its semantically interpreted
underlying phrase marker contains as a constituent structure the
phrase marker of

(74)   Smith and Jones are buried in the tomb.

But if this is acceptable as a possible answer to (69), then surely (75)
will also be, according to Katz's definitions:

(75)   Smith or Jones is buried in the tomb.

This also destroys the difference between (71) and (73) vis-à-vis their
being self-answering.

This counterexample illustrates a general shortcoming of Katz's
definition. Its main flaw is that no satisfactory analysis is given in it
as to *how* the underlying phrase markers of possible answers to $q'$
occur in that of the original question. There is nothing to exclude the
possibility that they occur there so to speak in roles altogether differ-

ent from that of being underlying phrase markers of answers to $q'$, even if they occur there as constituent-structures. Katz's characterization is thus mistaken, even apart from the difficulties caused by his mistaken solution to the answerhood problem.[20]

## 33. FURTHER PROBLEMS ABOUT SELF-ANSWERING QUESTIONS

There are further difficulties attaching to Katz's characterization of being self-answering (linguistically answered) which can be illustrated by the following example. The paradigm cases which his characterization is supposed to cover include

(76)   Who is buried in Grant's tomb?

However, the similar question,

(77)   Who is buried in the unknown soldier's tomb?

is not self-answering, for 'the unknown soldier' clearly is not a satisfactory answer to (77). Katz seems to dismiss such problematic cases by saying that questions like (76) (or (77)) are ambiguous in that (76) can also mean, roughly,

Who is buried in the so-called Grant's tomb?

as distinguished from the literal reading

Who (for instance) is buried in the place where Grant is buried?

(and analogously for (77)). This does not work with (77), however, for the literally interpreted question

(78)   Who is buried in the place where the unknown soldier is buried?

is not self-answering, either.

---

[20] I would also like to see how Katz handles the following questions:

Who is buried in the tomb where Jones is also buried?
Who won the tournament Sam Snead won repeatedly?

This example points to a further reason why Katz's characterization of a question's being self-answering is mistaken. It is true that a question like (77) or (78) itself provides us with a true substitution-instance of the nonepistemic part of the desideratum of (78). This desideratum is

(79)  (*Ex*) I know that $x$ is buried in the place where the unknown soldier is buried,

and the true substitution-instance is of course

(80)  The unknown soldier is buried in the place where the unknown soldier is buried.

As pointed out in my discussion of answerhood, (80) implies (79) only if

(81)  (*Ex*) I know that (the unknown soldier $= x$)

is true, which it often (always?) is not.

What Katz unsuccessfully tries to do with his characterization is to specify when a question (including its presupposition) provides us with a true substitution-instance of the nonepistemic part of the desideratum of the question, that is, a substitution-instance implying the presupposition of the question. His attempt was earlier seen to be unsuccessful. Now it is also seen to be misguided. It overlooks the possibility that the questioner does not know who or what the substituting term refers to. (It also overlooks the fact that one substitution-instance may be insufficient.) If the phrase 'the unknown soldier' is felt to be too much of an idiom, we may consider such questions as

(82)  Who (for instance) is buried in the tomb where the last three Grand Dukes of Ruritania are buried?

If the questioner does not know who the last three Grand Dukes are, the question makes perfectly good sense. It is nevertheless linguistically answered according to Katz's criterion.

We also have questions of the type

(83)  Who is buried in the tomb in which John believes Buffalo Bill is buried?

The status of such examples vis-à-vis Katz's thesis depends on his analysis of belief-clauses. I do not find anything, however, that would rule out

(84)    Buffalo Bill is buried in the tomb

as a constituent-structure of the semantically interpreted underlying phrase marker of the question.

Another problem for Katz will be to explain why the question

(85)    Who is buried in the tomb where nobody is buried?

is self-answering.

## 34. QUESTIONS AND LOGICALLY PROPER NAMES

All this leads to interesting further observations. We have seen that the problem of characterizing a question's being self-answering falls into two parts. First, we want to define a class of substitution-instances, or conjunctions of such instances, of certain parts of the desideratum as being possible answers. What we have seen suggests that the only interesting answers to this question are in terms of what the questioner knows, more specifically, what he knows about the identity of persons, things, times, places, and so on. In other words, a purely grammatical characterization (in the sense of context-independent characterization) is not likely to be interesting.

Such a definition might become interesting, however, if we had a class of singular terms (noun phrases) such that they would pick out one and the same individual (in the logician's sense of the word) in all the worlds we are considering in the semantics of epistemic logic. The question whether such singular terms exist is closely related to the question whether there are so called *logically proper names*, that is to say singular terms that cannot possibly refer to any individual other than the one to which they in fact refer. This idea of a logically proper name has led to a great deal of interesting discussion. Without pretending that there are no major unsolved problems here, we can nevertheless say that our epistemic logic strongly suggests that in some sense the notion of a logically proper name is an illusion. For there does not seem to be any guarantee that for some singular term '$b$' the identity of $b$ is necessarily known to every rational being who understands '$b$'. This suggests, furthermore, that the notion of being linguistically answered cannot be defined in a context-independent way.

Be these suggestions as they may, we can in any case see that there obtains an interesting connection between the problem of linguistically founded answers and philosophers' problem of logically proper names. This is one of the several directions in which the logic of questions leads us to highly interesting further problems. Several others fall outside the (somewhat arbitrarily drawn) scope of my discussion here.

## 35. QUESTIONS WITH IMBEDDED INTENTIONAL VERBS

There is a class of questions to which my theory might *prima facie* seem not to apply very naturally. They are certain questions which contain an imbedded intentional verb, like 'wants' or 'searches for', for instance

(86)   What does John want (to have)?

This question can be construed along the same lines as we have followed above so as to have as its desideratum something like

(87)   $(Ex)$ I know that John wants that John has $x$.

This is in fact one natural way of understanding (86). Then it might have as a (possible) answer, say, 'The Myth of Malham' or in general any other noun phrase of which the questioner knows what it refers to. There is no reason not to assume, it seems to me, that (87) is basically what the logical form of (86) is.

Of course, in the case of (87), as in the case of most other WH-questions, we may get responses which do not specify a unique individual but nevertheless narrow down the class of eligible individuals somewhat. A sample response might be, say, 'a sloop'. Earlier, I have said that such responses can be conceived of as a kind of partial answers, which can be prefixed by 'I do not know, but'. The new feature that we encounter in the case of questions containing an imbedded intentional verb is that this strategy will not work equally naturally here—or so it seems. There need not be any answer definite down to the level of a single individual, for propositional attitudes like wants and intentions need not have a definite individual as their object. In fact, the most specific answer to (86) that one can give may be, say, 'a sloop'. (As Quine puts it, John may merely want relief from slooplessness.) Then it will perhaps not seem very natural to call such a response a 'partial answer', for no fuller answer will be forthcoming, or to preface it with 'I do not know, but', for there will not be anything further to know.

I nevertheless want to insist that, in the interest of conceptual clarity, we should nevertheless think of (87) as having a desideratum of the form (86). What happens here, for the reason of the indeterminacy just mentioned, is that the natural-language question (86) is easily understood as having the force of

(88)   What kind of thing does John want (to own)?

More specifically, since the fullest available answer to (86) will often be an answer to (88), (86) is easily assimilated to (88)—or perhaps we should say that (88) becomes as natural a reading of (86) as the one on which it has (87) as its desideratum. (In some languages, these two readings of a question like (86) will have a different grammatical form.) There is nothing here that violates my theory, however. On the contrary, we can understand in terms of my theory why it is precisely questions like (86) which contain an imbedded intentional verb (in the sense of a question having (87) as its desideratum) that give rise to this somewhat confusing situation, including the ambiguity of (86) between (87) and (88).

In terms of answers, it is perhaps tempting to suggest here that a response like 'a sloop' should be acceptable as a possible answer to (86). It seems to me happier to say, however, that (86) is ambiguous and that 'a sloop' is an acceptable answer to (86) only when it is understood as (88). The desideratum of (88), incidentally, is also easy to spell out:

(89)   (*EA*) I know that John wants that
        (*Ex*)(John has $x$ & $Ax$)

where '*A*' ranges over kinds (predicates of a certain sort).

This point is strengthened by the general observation that 'what'-questions can involve two different kinds of quantification even apart from any problems about questions with imbedded intentional verbs. In the one type of case, a 'what'-question has as its answer the name of a physical object (or some other noun phrase specifying a physical object). In the other type of case, the variable of quantification ranges over sets, kinds, or species of individuals or over some other entities of a higher logical type than individuals—or perhaps over values of a different sort altogether. Then the relevant answers are not names of individual objects but of some other form, for instance 'a X', where 'X' is a common noun, or perhaps a mass term.

These uses of 'what' questions do not seem to present any new problems, however. Thus no violation of my theory is forthcoming here.

## 36. QUESTIONS RELYING ON INDIVIDUATION BY ACQUAINTANCE

In earlier works, for instance in Hintikka (1969, ch. 8), and in Hintikka (1972b), I have shown that, in circumstances where a person has firsthand cognitive relations to his environment, not one set of trans world heir lines of cross-identification but two such sets are involved. One, called descriptive, is what we have so far been dealing with in this study. It is what goes together with the normal WH-constructions with such verbs as 'perceives', 'remembers', 'knows', and so on. In other words, descriptive world lines are what is involved in the truth-conditions of such sentences as (16) or (18).

The other mode of cross-identification may be said to rely on acquaintance. Sometimes it may also be called demonstrative cross-identification. It identifies those members or different possible worlds whose firsthand cognitive relations to the subject (person) in question are the same. The simplest case in point is visual perception, where this means identifying those objects (members of different states of affairs compatible with what someone, say $a$ sees) which occupy the same position in $a$'s visual space. Likewise, one can cross-identify 'by acquaintance' those individuals which play the same role in $a$'s personally remembered past, even if $a$ does not remember who they were.

I have also shown that cross-identification by acquaintance plays essentially the same role in the truth-conditions of direct-object constructions with such verbs as 'sees', 'perceives', 'remembers', and 'knows' as descriptive cross-identification plays in the truth-conditions of WH-constructions with these verbs. If we use $(Ex)$, $(x)$, $(Ey)$, $(y)$, etc., as quantifiers relying on descriptive world lines and $(\exists x)$, $(\forall x)$, $(\exists y)$, $(\forall y)$, etc., as quantifiers relying on acquaintance, we may therefore say that while

(90)   $a$ perceives who $b$ is

can be rendered as

(91)   $(Ex)$ $a$ perceives that $(x = b)$

where '$x$' ranges over persons,

(92)   *a* perceives *b*

is of the 'logical form'

(93)   $(\exists x)$ *a* perceives that $(x = b)$

or, more likely, of the corresponding *de re* form

(94)   $(\exists x)(x = b \ \& \ (\exists y)$ *a* perceives that $(x = y))$

The same applies, *mutatis mutandis*, to those other epistemic verbs which have a similar direct-object construction in English.

The parallelism between the two kinds of quantifiers so explained applies in the first place only to those simple cases in which the general form of WH-constructions

|        | (95) | knows that |        |
|--------|------|------------|--------|
| $(Ex)$ *a* |   | remembers  | $F(x)$ |
|        |      | perceives  |        |

is narrowed down to the forms where $F(x)$ is an identity $(x = b)$. It extends partly to other cases through locutions like

(96)   *a* saw someone robbing the bank.

If 'someone' is here subjected to the *de re* reading, (96) may be taken to be of the form

(97)   $(\exists x)$ *a* saw that *x* robbed the bank).

Since world lines based on acquaintance and the corresponding quantifiers are not normally connected with WH-words, it might seem that they have little to do with questions in English. On second thought one can nevertheless easily see why the borderline between the two kinds of world lines and between the two kinds of quantifiers is not likely to be impenetrable in English. Surely one often wants to be informed of the identity of persons or objects, cross-identified perceptually or more generally by acquaintance, and wants to express this desire of his. The only grammatical device he has available for him in English is the familiar WH-question, which he is therefore likely to use (or misuse) for the purpose. It may thus be expected that in actual English usage WH-questions and other WH-constructions often rely on perceptual or demonstrative cross-identification rather than descriptive individuation, quite apart from the kind of variation in the criteria of 'knowing who' which was discussed above in section 28. One is thus virtually led to suspect that many WH-constructions are in practice ambiguous in that they can express either descriptive individuation or perceptual (demonstrative) individuation.

This expectation is amply confirmed by examples. It explains the curious duality there is in our use of questions. Someone can walk into a room full of people, point to a man, ask, "Who is that man over there?", and draw the reply, "Why, he is John Jones". Someone else can walk into the same room, ask, "Who is John Jones?", and prompt the response, "Why, that man over there" (pointing to him). Now we can express succinctly what is going on here and what the difference between the two questions is. The latter inquirer is clearly presupposing as the desideratum of his question

(98)   $(\exists x)$ I know that (John Jones = $x$).

An acceptable (direct potential) answer '$b$' must therefore satisfy here the condition

(99)   $(\exists x)$ I know that ($b = x$)

naturally with the same sort of quantifier as in (98). Since this quantifier, '$(\exists x)$', relies on demonstrative cross-identification, 'that man over there' is apt to satisfy (99) in the role of '$b$'.

Notice that 'John Jones' will not do here as an answer, for although the questioner presumably knows who John Jones is (descriptively individuated), it will not initially true for him to say

(100)   $(\exists x)$ I know that (John Jones = $x$)

for this is just what he wants to be brought about, that is, he wants to be able to recognize John Jones also perceptually (demonstratively).

The former questioner's desideratum is by the same token

(101)   $(Ex)$ I know that (that man over there = $x$).

Here an acceptable (potential direct) answer '$d$' will have to satisfy

(102)   $(Ex)$ I know that ($d = x$)

which presumably rules out 'that man over there' but not 'John Jones'.

It is instructive to note here the close semantical relationship of the question "Who is John Jones?" whose desideratum is (98) to the direct-object construction. For the questioner could almost have asked instead, "Do you see John Jones?".

Notice also how naturally the criteria of answerhood applied here follow from my earlier, general characterization of (potential direct) answers to a given WH-question. A criteria of answerhood which merely turns on the status of a singular term (noun phrase) as a substitution-value of the presupposition of a question will be incapable of accounting for the difference between the two questions with (98) and (101) as their respective desiderata.

Specific examples of WH-questions and other WH-expressions relying on demonstrative cross-identification are likewise easy to find. In Hintikka (1972b) it was already pointed out that Russell in his famous essay on knowledge by acquaintance (Russell 1918) uses 'knowing who' for the kind of acquaintance which is more properly expressed by a direct-object construction. Russell defines "merely descriptive" knowledge (that is, knowledge which is not by acquaintance) to be of 'so-and-so' when we do not know "who or what the so-and-so is". Yet Russell uses as his prime examples of such merely descriptive knowledge his knowledge of Caesar and of Bismarck. Russell knew of course perfectly well *who* these gentlemen were. His point was, rather, that he was not acquainted with them, that he did not know *them*.

Similar examples of the use of WH-constructions in connection with perceptual cross-identification (individuation by acquaintance) can be multiplied *ad libidum*.

It is somewhat more interesting to note that demonstrative cross-identification can be involved in the use of all the different WH-words. Thus there is a use of 'where' which refers to locations in one's perceptual space rather than in an impersonal frame of reference and hence relies on perceptual cross-identification. Again the connection with the direct-object is unmistakable. For in this use of 'where' 'seeing $b$' and 'seeing where $b$ is' are very close in meaning. (Notice that one can see where $b$ is in one's visual space without seeing where it is in the physical space, namely, when one does not see where in the latter one is located oneself.)

The demonstrative individuation of time-instants is amusingly illustrated by the following quotation.

"The present 'I am eating' cannot raise the question 'when?' since it means 'now'." (A. C. Lloyd, *Activity and Description in Aristotle and the Stoa*, Dawes Hicks Lecture, British Academy [1970]. London: Oxford University Press, 1971.)

That this is not the only possible use of 'when' will be made clear by asking (in the same logical breath as Lloyd), "What time is it?" Here the expected answer can scarcely be, "Now."

The success of my two-kinds-of-quantifiers analysis in dealing with questions which call for a demonstrative answer provides further evidence for this analysis.

## BIBLIOGRAPHY

Åqvist, Lennart. *A New Approach to the Logical Theory of Interrogatives*, Mimeographed. Uppsala: Filosofiska Föreningen, 1965.

———. "Scattered Topics in Interrogative Logic," in J. W. Davis, D. J. Hockney, and W. K. Wilson, eds., *Philosophical Logic*. Dordrecht: Reidel, 1969. Pp. 114-121.

———. "Revised Foundations for Imperative-Epistemic and Interrogative Logic," *Theoria*, XXXVII (1971), 33-73.

———. "On the Analysis and Logic of Questions," in Raymond E. Olson and Anthony M. Paul, eds., *Contemporary Philosophy in Scandinavia*. Baltimore: Johns Hopkins University Press, 1972. Pp. 27-39.

———. "Modal Logic with Subjunctive Conditionals and Dispositional Predicates," *Journal of Philosophical Logic*, II (1973), 1-76.

Bach, E. "Questions," *Linguistic Inquiry*, I (1970), 153-166.

Baker, C. L. "Notes on the Description of English Questions: the Role of an Abstract Question Morpheme," *Foundations of Language*, XI (1970), 197-217.

Belnap, Nuel D., Jr. *An Analysis of Questions: Preliminary Report*, Technical Memorandum TM 1287 1000/00. System Development Corporation, Santa Monica, California, 1963. 160 pp.

———. "Questions: Their Presuppositions, and How They Can Fail to Arise," in Karel Lambert, ed., *The Logical Way of Doing Things*. New Haven and London: Yale University Press, 1969. Pp. 23-37.

——— and Sylvain Bromberger. "Questions," *Journal of Philosophy*, LXVIII (1966), 597-606. (1966a).

Bromberger, Sylvain. "Why-Questions," in Robert G. Colodny, ed., *Mind and Cosmos*. Pittsburgh: Pittsburgh University Press, 1966. (1966b).

Brown, D. G. "Knowing How and Knowing That, What," in Oscar P. Wood and George Pitcher, eds., *Ryle: A Collection of Critical Essays*. Garden City, New York: Modern Studies in Philosophy, Anchor Books, Doubleday, 1970. Pp. 213-248.

Chomsky, N. *Syntactic Structures*. The Hague: Mouton, 1957.

———. "Current Issues in Linguistics," in J. Fodor and J. J. Katz, eds., *The Structure of Language*. Englewood Cliffs, N.J.: Prentice-Hall, 1964.

———. *Aspects of the Theory of Syntax*. Cambridge, Mass.: MIT Press, 1965.

Cresswell, M. J. "The Logic of Interrogatives," in J. N. Crossley and M. A. E. Dummett, eds., *Formal Systems and Recursive Functions*. Amsterdam: North-Holland Publishing Company, 1965. Pp. 7-11.

Hamblin, C. L. "Questions," *The Australasian Journal of Philosophy*, XXXVI (1958), 159-168.

———. "Questions aren't statements," *Philosophy of Science*, XXX (1963), 62-63.

———. "Questions in Montague English," *Foundations of Language*, X (1973), 41-53.

Hansson, Bengt. "An Analysis of Some Deontic Logics," *Nous*, III (1969), 373-398.

Harrah, David. "A Logic of Questions and Answers," *Philosophy of Science*, XXVIII (1961), 40-46.

———. *Communication: A Logical Model*. Cambridge, Mass.: MIT Press, 1963.

———. "Erotetic Logistics," in Karel Lambert, ed., *The Logical Way of Doing Things*. New Haven and London: Yale University Press, 1969. Pp. 3-21.

Hilpinen, Risto. "An Analysis of Relativized Modalities," in J. W. David, D. J. Hockney, and W. K. Wilson, eds., *Philosophical Logic*. Dordrecht: Reidel, 1969. Pp. 181-193.

Hintikka, Jaakko. *Knowledge and Belief*. Ithaca, New York: Cornell University Press, 1962.

———. *Models for Modalities: Selected Essays*. Dordrecht: Reidel, 1969.

———. "The Semantics of Modal Notions and the Indeterminacy of Ontology," in Donald Davidson and Gilbert Harman, eds., *Semantics of Natural Language*. Dordrecht: Reidel, 1972. Pp. 398-414. (1972a).

———. "Knowledge by Acquaintance—Individuation by Acquaintance," in D. F. Pears, ed., *Bertrand Russell: A Collection of Critical Essays*. Garden City, New York: Doubleday, 1972. Pp. 52-79. (1972b).

———. "Grammar and Logic: Some Borderline Issues," in Jaakko Hintikka, Julius M. E. Moravcsik, and Patrick Suppes, eds., *Approaches to Natural Languages: Proceedings of the 1970 Stanford Workshop on Grammar and Semantics*. Synthese Library. Dordrecht: Reidel, 1973. Pp. 197-214.

———. "The Semantics of Questions and the Questions of Semantics" (forthcoming, probably in 1974).

Hiz, Henry. "Questions and Answers," *Journal of Philosophy*, LIX (1962), 253–265.

Jacobs, Roderick A., and Peter S. Rosenbaum. *English Transformational Grammar*. Waltham, Mass.: Blaisdell, 1968.

Katz, J. J. "The Logic of Questions," in B. van Rootselaar and J. F. Staal, eds., *Logic, Methodology and Philosophy of Science III, Proceedings of the Third International Congress for Logic, Methodology, and Philosophy of Science, Amsterdam, 1967*, Studies in Logic and the Foundations of Mathematics. Amsterdam: North-Holland Publishing Company, 1968. Pp. 463–493.

———. *Semantic Theory*. New York: Harper & Row, 1972. (See Ch. 5.)

Katz, J. J. and Paul M. Postal. *An Integrated Theory of Linguistic Descriptions*, Research Monograph No. 26. Cambridge, Mass.: MIT Press, 1964.

Koutsoudas, Andreas. "On wh-words in English," *Journal of Linguistics*, IV (1968), 267–273.

Kubinski, Tadeuz. "An Essay in the Logic of Questions," in *Atti del XII Congresso Internazionale di Filosofia* V. Florence, 1961. Pp. 315–322.

———. "The Logic of Questions," in Raymond Klibansky, ed., *Contemporary Philosophy—La Philosophie contemporaine* I, Florence: La Nuova Italia Editrice, 1968. Pp. 185–189.

Kuno, Susumo, and Jane J. Robinson. "Multiple WH-Questions," *Linguistic Inquiry*, III (1972), 463–487.

Lakoff, George. "Linguistics and Natural Logic," in Donald Davidson and Gilbert Harman, eds., *Semantics of Natural Language*. Dordrecht: Reidel, 1972. Pp. 545–665.

Lakoff, Robin. "Answerable Questions and Questionable Answers" (forthcoming).

Langacker, Ronald W. "French Interrogatives: A Transformational Description," *Language*, XLI, 4 (1965).

Leonard, Henry S. *Principles of Right Reason*. New York: Henry Holt, 1957.

Mackay, Donald M. "The Informational Aspects of Questions and Commands," London Symposium on Information Theory, pp. 469–476.

Moritz, Manfred. "Zur Logik der Frage," *Theoria*, VI (1940), 123–149.

Partee, Barbara Hall. "Negation, Conjunction, and Quantifiers: Syntax vs. Semantics," *Foundations of Language*, VI (1970), 153–165.

Pawlowski, Tadeusz. "Theory of Questions and Its Applications in the Social Sciences," *The Polish Sociological Bulletin* No. 2 (20), 1969, pp. 95-109.

Petrov, Yuri A. "Version of Erotetic Logic," in *Akten des XIV Internationalen Kongresses für Philosophie* III. Vienna: Herder, 1969. Pp. 23-24.

Prior, M., and A. N. Prior. "Erotetic Logic," *Philosophical Review*, LXIV (1955), 43-59.

Quine, W. V. *Word and Object*. Cambridge, Mass.: MIT Press, 1960.

———. *Ontological Relativity*. New York: Columbia University Press, 1970.

Russell, Bertrand. "Knowledge by Acquaintance and Knowledge by Description," in *Mysticism and Logic*. London: Longmans, Green, 1918. Pp. 209-232.

Tondl, Ladislav. "Logical-Semantical Analysis of the Question and the Problem of Scientific Explanation," in *Akten des XIV Internationalen Kongresses für Philosophie* III. Vienna: Herder, 1969. Pp. 23-24.

———. "Semantics of the Question in a Problem-solving Situation," in *Problems of the Science of Science: Special Issue of the Quarterly*. Warsaw: Zagadnienia Naukoznawsta, 1970. Pp. 79-101.

# Attributives and Interrogatives

## DENNIS W. STAMPE

### University of Wisconsin

*I.*

**1** On a simple view of such a sentence as

(1)    The cat on the mat has got fleas

there is a subject expression, in that sentence, which refers or is used to refer to something—properly to some particular cat—and a predicate expression which says or is used to say something about the thing referred to. The two expressions are of course related by dint of their being the subject and the predicate of the same sentence; they are constituents of the same construction, and that they should be parts of such a construction is necessary for the expressions to have such referring or predicating functions as they do have. But beyond that, there is no obvious reason why the two expressions should be in any *other* way connected or significantly related, for their functions are distinct and in other respects independent: thus nothing I might want to say about the cat requires me to refer to it, or prevents me from referring to it, in any particular way, and vice versa. And if there must be a reference made in order that a predication should be made—or vice versa—it is not necessary that the reference be made *correctly* for the predication to be *true*, nor that the predication be true in order for the reference to have been correct.

    **2** I shall be concerned in this paper with certain deviations from this simple paradigm. Deviations include, notoriously, such sentences as (1) *as* they occur within certain sentential structures—so-called opaque contexts—that is, *complex* sentences such as

(2) Oedipus thought that his mother would make him an unsuitable wife,

and also apparently *simple* sentences involving "attributive" definite descriptions,[1] such as

(3) The inventor of the miniskirt deserves our thanks.

It is with these *attributives* that I shall be mainly concerned; I shall try to understand how it is that such sentences both refer to and predicate something of a particular subject, *by and while therein* expressing a connection between certain properties of that subject. Thus in (3), under one natural interpretation, one takes the subject expression ('the inventor of the miniskirt') to indicate not only *who* is being said to deserve our thanks, but also the speaker's *basis* for saying, of the person to whom he refers, that he deserves our thanks. His reason is taken to be that that person is the inventor of the miniskirt.[2] By contrast, it is not supposed that the reason that the cat on the mat is being said to have fleas is that it is the cat that is on the mat, or that the cat is on the mat. No such connection between the subject and predicate of sentence (1) is *suggested*. But immediately it occurs to one that (given, for example, a badly flea-infested mat) such a connection, and thus such an interpretation, is perfectly possible.

   3 I shall treat the availability of the two interpretations as owing to an ambiguity in the meaning of the sentence (though the claim that it is such is controversial), and I shall represent the ambiguity as *syntactic* in nature. That is to say, I shall represent it as arising not

---

[1] As they have been named by Keith Donnellan, in his "Reference and Definite Descriptions," *The Philosophical Review*, LXXV, 3 (July, 1966). Throughout, references to Donnellan are to this article.

[2] While it is attributive descriptions that will mainly occupy me, it does seem that sentences like (2) also, though in a different way, express a connection between subject and predicate. That sentence is ambiguous as between a reading on which it is presumably true and one on which it is presumably false. (The false one being equally well expressed where the name 'Jocasta' is substituted for 'his mother'.) Consider the true proposition it expresses. The attempt to express this truth about Oedipus constrains the selection of the subject of the embedded sentence: it must be, e.g., 'his mother' and cannot be 'Jocasta'. Here too it appears necessary to give expression to a certain connection between the subject and the predicate expression or the properties expressed thereby—the property of being (thought by Oedipus to be) unsuitable for marriage and the property of being (thought by Oedipus to be) the mother of Oedipus: it is as if the woman was thought to have the former property because she had the latter.

from any ambiguity in any of the words in the sentence, but rather from an ambiguity in the relationships among them—as owing to the fact that the constituents of the sentence may be interpreted as standing in either of two systems of syntactic relationships, each of which give rise to a distinct interpretation. My motive in advancing this syntactic hypothesis is only incidentally to account for the possibility of the two interpretations. That can perhaps be done in other ways. My principal motive is rather to understand, by devising an appropriate theoretical representation of sentences containing them, the duality of function displayed by attributive definite descriptions, as they at once refer to some certain thing and also express a connection between the property in terms of which the thing is being referred to, and that property being predicated of it. Accordingly, I suggest that we may attribute certain of the characteristics of attributive sentences to their "surface structure", while ascribing certain others to the "deep" or "underlying" syntactic structure. Occurring as it does as the surface subject of the sentence, the definite description ('the such and such') does *refer* to that thing or person about which something is being said. But I shall offer some evidence that in the underlying structure of these sentences, the *surface* subject occupies the position of a *predicate*. Supposing that properties are expressed by predicates, I hope by this means to identify the basis—a basis in the syntactic structure of the sentence—of the fact that attributive sentences express a connection of properties, that basis being, I submit, that the sentence is in fact a structure connecting two predicates, in a certain way. More specifically, my conjecture is that attributive sentences have a structure which may be represented as a configuration of these clauses:

(4)   wh.ever it may be
                    wh. is THE *F*
                              I say that
                                        THE *F* is *g*

Particular clauses and features of this representation will be explained in due course. But here it may be noted that the definite description (THE F) which occurs (preceeding the copula) as the *subject* nominal of the lowest clause also occurs (following the copula) as the *predicate* nominal of a higher clause.

  **4** The implication of a connection between the property of being the *f* and the property of being *g*, then, will come about as follows. One says something having the form of (4), either covertly (like (3), under its attributive interpretation) or overtly, like

(5)    Whoever it may be who is the inventor of the miniskirt, I say
       that the inventor of the miniskirt deserves our thanks.

In saying such a thing, one says something about the *f* in implicit or
explicit disregard of what the answer may be to the *question* which is
represented by the second clause in (4), sc. *wh. is THE F*—that is,
whatever the answer may be to the question Who is the *f*?, What is the
*f*?, Where is the *f*?, etc.

One who says that the *f* is *g* gives it to be understood that he
thinks or knows that the *f* is *g*. But if he therein also gives it to be
understood that he says that without regard to who the *f* may be—for
example, that he does not know, or would say the same thing even if
he did not know, the answer to the appropriate question, wh. is the
*f*?—then the question arises, What *reason* might he have for thinking,
and saying, that the *f* is *g*? Presuming that he does have some reason
for saying what he says, we infer that his reason is just that one and
only thing we may presume that the speaker *does* know, or thinks it
necessary to know, about the *f*: the fact that the *f*, wh.ever it may be,
is the *f*. We infer that his reason for saying that the inventor of the
miniskirt deserves our thanks is just that one thing that someone who
doesn't know who invented the miniskirt nonetheless *does* know about
that person: to wit, that that person invented the miniskirt. (Our
speaker is prepared to assert that the *f* is *g* whatever the answer to the
question, Who is it who is the *f*? The answer to that question may be
virtually anything: but it may not be such as to imply that the *f* is not
the *f*.)

**5** On my view the distinctive interpretation of sentences involving attributive definite descriptions is a function of the distinctive
relationship of that description (the *f*) to a certain *question* (wh. is it
that is the *f*?): its occurrence in the context of the implicit or explicit
understanding that having the answer to that question is irrelevant
to the making of the predication. In an effort to indicate that this talk
of a *question* associated with the description is something more than a
conceit, and to provide background to what follows, I devote the next
section to some phenomena related, some intimately but some rather
tangentially, to the subject of attributives. This effort to anchor the
apparatus to some neighboring territory interrupts the discussion of
attributives themselves, the thread of which the reader may recover,
at his pleasure, below at §16.

## *II*. Questions, Definite Phrases, and Identities

**6** To suggest that attributives have a crucial formal relationship with interrogative clauses is not to suggest that they are a unique or isolated phenomenon among the species of definite descriptions. Consider for instance such (ambiguous) sentences as

(6)   I know the current prime minister of England
(7)   The man who killed Smith is as yet unknown.

These sentences *can* be interpreted as meaning the same respectively as

(8)   I know *who the current Prime Minister of England is*
(9)   It is as yet unknown *who the killer of Smith is,*

where the content of the definite description appears in a form *transparently* representing a question.

**7** Other definite phrases, appearing as the complements of certain verbs, *must* be construed as equivalent to a question clause, and as representing questions.

(10)   She asked the price of eggs ( = what the price of eggs is)
          the time of day ( = what time of day it was)
          the baby's name ( = what the baby's name was)
          her busband's whereabouts ( = where her husband was)
          his intentions ( = what his intentions were)

These definite phrases are all transformed question clauses, and it is this fact that determines their interpretation

**8** Thus it determines their *referential* characteristics. In 'She asked the price of eggs', 'the price of eggs' refers to what she asked—to wit a *question*—and it specifies which question she asked. Accordingly it is equivalent to

(11)   She asked what the price of eggs is

and thus to

(12)   She asked the question, what is the price of eggs?

And this is true if it is true that

(13)   She asked "what is the price of eggs?"

This supports the idea that the interrogative definite description refers to an entity of speech, the object of a locutionary act.[3]

**9** This means that such phrases as 'the price of eggs' are not used herein to *refer* to the thing that "fits the description", where what "fits the description" '*the f*' is just what the *f* may be said to be. Thus from

(14)   Mary asked the time of day

and

(15)   The time of day was eight-thirty

it does not follow that

(16) *   Mary asked eight-thirty.

But not only does it not follow; this last sentence is nonsense. This is explained on the view that *what* Mary asked when she asked the time of day was a *question*. The particular question she asked is indicated, if not referred to, by the phrase, "the time of day". Thus we have a kind of definite phrase which is in a sense "opaque", but not in the sense that substituting co-referential expressions fails to preserve truth-value. For the situation in (14) and (15) is not one in which 'the time of day' refers in each occurrence to one and the same thing. That is, (15) 'The time of day was eight-thirty' does not say or mean that

---

[3] Similarly, with *tell*:
      (a) He told her the price of eggs,
is, I would suggest, from
      (b) He told her the answer to the question, What is the price of eggs?,
which is confirmed by the fact that in
      (c) He told her the answer
'the answer' is the object of 'tell'. (Cf.
      (d) *He told her the question What is the price of eggs.)
Thus if
      (e) The answer to the question is 90 cents a dozen
it will follow that
      (f) He told her (said) 90 cents a dozen,
which will be true if
      (g) He told her (said) "90 cents a dozen"
again indicating that what he told her, and thus what the grammatical object of 'tell' here refers to is an entity of speech.

(16)*    The time of day was identical with eight-thirty.

**10** What *is* expressed by "The time was eight-thirty" may *instead* be regarded as an answer, specifically, to the wh. question, What time is it? I say 'instead' because sentences *asserting* identities in an important sense do not give answers to any natural wh. question. If the question is asked

(17)    Who was Tully? [4]

and the response is

(18)    Tully was the same man as Cicero

what the respondent has stated is *not* an answer to the question. (Indeed his saying (18) *tends* often to imply that he doesn't know, or is merely *hinting* at, the answer.[5]) Likewise to say that the price of eggs is identical with the price of hamburger is not to answer my question, 'What is the price of eggs?'; I didn't ask you what it is *the same as*, I asked you what it *is*.

**11** Now of course, if you should happen to know what the price of hamburger is, then I will have brought it about that you know the price of eggs, and that you *have* the answer to your question. But still, what I said *isn't*, or doesn't *state*, that answer. Likewise if you know who Cicero was (say, that he was a Roman orator and statesman), (18) will provide the information you want fully as well as a sentence which actually states an answer, like "Tully was a Roman orator and statesman who also bore the name Cicero". The information you go away

---

[4] Question (18) "Who was Tully?" contrasts with
    (a) Who was it who was *called* Tully?
(which is a subject-wanting question; it supplies the *predicate* 'was called Tully'; cf. §12 below. Its direct answers include
    (b) It was Cicero who was called Tully.
    (c) *Cicero* was called Tully
but *not*
    (d) *Cicero* was the same man as Tully.
[5] It is I think an interesting curiosity that there is no *natural* wh-question corresponding to, and which might be answered by, a genuine identity stating sentence like (18). The sentences
    (a) What man was Tully the same man as?
    (b) What is the morning star identical with?
are distinctly *unnatural*, if not ungrammatical. They might be used for such special purposes as eliciting a reminder of something (some fact or example) one already knows, or of testing someone's memory. But they are not questions one asks in order to *learn* the answer, i.e., to come to know something he had not known, and they are in that sense at least *unnatural* questions.

with is the same in either case. The notion of a sentence "stating the answer" to a question which I am here invoking is plainly distinct from the notion of a sentence the utterance of which will bring it about that one knows the answer to that question. I am concerned instead with a formal *syntactic* relation which obtains between certain indicative and certain interrogative questions. (I will depend heavily on the *formal* nature of this relationship in the late going.)

## *III*

### SUBJECT-WANTING AND PREDICATE-WANTING QUESTIONS

**12** I shall be making use of a distinction between what I shall call "subject-wanting" questions and "predicate-wanting" questions. The sentence

(19)    Who is the man who murdered Smith?

is ambiguous. It may be read as

(20)    Who murdered Smith?

that is, as what I call a "subject-wanting" question. Here the inquirer himself supplies the predicate he is concerned with ('murdered Smith') and what he *wants* is the subject to which it may be ascribed. That will be supplied by giving him an expression that will replace the interrogative pronoun—for example, someone's name—yielding a true statement. That is a subject-wanting question. Or, the question may be instead a predicate-wanting question,

(21)    Who *is* that man, who is the man who murdered Smith?

This is the question that might be asked after we've nabbed the murderer, but find him to be a stranger who carries no identification or credit cards. I call this a "predicate-wanting" question, because the inquirer knows who it was who murdered Smith (he knows it was the man the police have in custody) and wants to know something *about him*: what may be predicated of him.

**13** While there is much that is unclear about this distinction, it is clear enough that *such* a distinction exists. And it has a clear *syntactic* reality. Thus the question reported in

(22)    He asked "What is the GNP?"

is ambiguous in the same sort of way. It might be answered either

    (23)   One trillion dollars

or by

    (24)   The total value of all goods and services purchased nation-
           ally in a given year.[6]

Now I shall regard (24) as the answer to a *subject*-wanting question, for
this reason: the question appropriately answered by (24) may be paraphrased by "What is it that *is called*, or referred to as, 'the GNP'?" in
which version it is clear that a *predicate*, "is called 'such and such' ", is
supplied and that what is wanted is its subject. Let us (somewhat
artificially) regard *stating* or *giving* the amount of something (or the
price, or the meaning, or the time), as a variety of predication; then (22)
taken in the sense "He asked $x$ to state the amount of the GNP", that is,
the question answerable by (23), will be a *predicate*-wanting question.[7]
Notice that it is only when the inquirer is asking a predicate-wanting
question, in asking (ambiguously) "What is the price of eggs?" that it
will be true to say

    (21)   He asked the price of eggs

employing the interrogative definite description. (It would not be true
to say (21) if he would have been satisfied to learn that the price of eggs
is what you have to pay for eggs.)

    **14** Such facts as these indicate that syntax is sensitive to the
subject-, predicate-wanting distinction; for presumably there is a
transformational relationship between the indirect speech report (21),
which is unambiguous, and the ambiguous

---

[6] In a radio interview a certain Indian philosopher had been deploring the kind of person
who did not aspire to knowledge of the ultimate truth; the interviewer, in momentous
tones, finally asked "And, Professor ———, what *is* the ultimate truth?" Philosopher: "It
is that truth which illuminates all reality".

[7] This is not finally satisfactory, and it indicates that this initial effort to characterize the
distinct interpretations of wh-questions needs work. (Nonetheless I think the required
refinements would affect only details of the main argument of this paper.) It is not
satisfactory because in stating the price or giving the meaning, i.e., in saying what it is,
I am not *really* saying something *about* the price or meaning. And if "is 90 cents" does
not express a "real predicate" likewise its subject "*the price*" is not a "real subject". The
real subject is *eggs*. Similarly, in 'The meaning of "clandestine" is *surreptitious*', 'is
*surreptitious*' does not express a "real predicate" of *the meaning of 'clandestine'*, and
that is not a "real subject", the real subject is the *word* 'clandestine'.

(22)    He asked what the price of eggs is,

and direct report

(23)    He asked "What is the price of eggs?"

And if so then (22) and (23) must have two underlying *syntactic* forms, corresponding to the two kinds of questions. Notice similarly that

(24)    The police know the killer

is not ambiguous in the same way as is

(25)    The police know who the killer is.

**15** My analysis of attributives will turn on certain distinctive syntactic capacities of names, vis-à-vis wh-questions and attributive definite descriptions. So it is relevant to observe that the subject-wanting, predicate-wanting ambiguity of (18) does *not* characterize such a sentence as

(26)    Who was Tully?

This can express *only* a predicate-wanting question. That is, the answer to it can be stated only by a sentence which says something about or predicates something of Tully, as does

(27)    Tully was a Roman statesman and orator.

It cannot be answered, as I urged above in §10, by saying

(28)    Tully was Cicero,

a sentence which strictly speaking says nothing about, and predicates nothing of, Tully. Thus also, "Who was Tully?" cannot be a subject-wanting question *because such* questions must *supply* a predicate. But being Tully (as opposed to be named or called Tully, or being a Tully) is not what we want to regard as a property, nor therefore do we take 'was Tully' to be a predicate, in the relevant intuitive sense. (This intuition is required to appreciate the wit of the title "The Importance of Being Earnest".) Now "Who was Tully?" supplies only a name, and if a name cannot serve as a predicate, it can only be a subject that is supplied. This explains why (28) will not answer the question, for it supplies only another name, and not the required predicate. However, (27) does supply the predicate, 'being a Roman statesman and orator', and therefore qualifies as an answer to question (26).[8]

## IV

### THE SYNTACTIC STRUCTURE OF ATTRIBUTIVES

**16** Attributive definite descriptions are definite phrases which occur in sentences such as those of the form (iv) below (the minimal acoustic realization of an attributive sentence), *and also* occur in a higher wh.question clause (ii) which occurs inside a higher wh.ever-clause (i), in the fuller representation of the phrase structure of such a sentence:

(i)     Wh. ever it may be
(ii)    Wh. is THE $F$
(iii)   I say that
(iv)    THE $F$ is $g$

This is the proposition I shall try to defend in this section. I must say a word about what constitutes a defense of such a proposition. I am claiming that the syntactic structure of apparently so simple a sentence as 'The murderer of Smith deserves our thanks' is represented by the configuration (i)-(iv) above. Such proposals are founded on the principle that the meaning of a sentence is determined by the constituents of that sentence, and their syntactic relations. That principle requires that some of those constituents may be unexpressed, *postulated* to account for the sentence meaning what it does. I postulate the existence of three (i-iii) unexpressed clauses in the structure of the superficially simple sentence, in order to account for the fact that one of the meanings of the sentence 'The murderer of Smith is insane' is *whoever murdered Smith is insane.* Plainly I must hold that that *is* one of the meanings of the sentence, and that controversial claim is explicitly defended below in section *V.* But the vindication of the view that the sentence in question is ambiguous in meaning must lie largely in the persuasiveness of the syntactic account of the two interpretations.

---

[8] Perhaps one can in this way explain why questions like "Who was Tully the same man as?" or "What is the morning star identical with?" are as unnatural as they are, given the assumption that a natural question is one or the other, either subject-wanting or predicate-wanting, and that the former must supply a predicate and the latter a subject. The curious question 'Who was Tully the same man as?' supplies only a subject, and yet its answer must furnish not a predicate but a second subject.

That requires that the postulation of these higher clauses should be defended on syntactic grounds, that is, as required in order to retain the optimal set of *grammatical* rules capable of accounting for the distribution of morphemes in grammatical sentences of the language. The defense of the third clause is deferred until section *VI*. I first turn to the wh.ever clause, represented by (i) and (ii).

**17** Consider first the import of the wh.ever clause. Any wh.ever-clause (such as 'Whoever murdered Smith') declares the irrelevance, to what follows, of having an answer to some wh-question—such a question as 'Who is the man who murdered Smith?' But such questions, I have been saying (§12), are ambiguous between what I call subject-wanting and predicate-wanting interpretations. As we should expect, then, there are uses of whoever-clauses appropriate to *either* of the two ways in which the wh-question may be taken.

(29)    They don't know [the answer to the question] Who murdered Smith. But WHOEVER HE IS, the murderer of Smith must be insane.

(30)    They've arrested the murderer, but they don't know who he *is* [that is, the answer to the question Who *is* the man who they know to have murdered Smith]. But WHOEVER HE IS, (even if he's the son of the governor) the murderer of Smith will get the chair.

Now the sentence,

(31)    The man who murdered Smith is insane

is ambiguous, between a referential and an attributive use or sense. Recasting the sentence with *certain* whoever clauses merely preserves this ambiguity, as happens in

(32)    Whoever the man who murdered Smith may be, he is insane.

This is still ambiguous. It might declare the irrelevance either of a subject- *or* of a predicate-wanting question. Those whoever-clauses which have the definite phrase in their *subject* (as does (32) where it *precedes* the main verb of the clause) retain the ambiguity: that is, those of the form, Whoever *the f is*, the *f* is *g*.

**18** My claim that the sentence 'The murderer of Smith is insane' has two meanings is supported by the fact that there are *un*ambiguous sentences which express the attributive meaning of that sentence; these include

(33)   Whoever murdered Smith, the murderer of Smith is insane
(34)   Whoever it may have been who murdered Smith, the murderer of Smith is insane
(35)   Whoever it may be who is the murderer of Smith, the murderer of Smith is insane.

These unambiguous paraphrases share a *syntactic* characteristic: in each of them, the definite phrase 'the murderer of Smith' is represented as a *predicate* expression—either as in (33) occurring in verbal form as a predicate expression 'murdered Smith', or as in (34) and (35) retaining the nominal form but occurring *following* the main verb of the whoever-clause, in the predicate or verb phrase, as a *predicate-nominal*. (In the still ambiguous form (32), once again, the phrase occurs as the *subject* of the verb 'may be'.) So it is these forms, (33)-(35) that are the unambiguous and structure-revealing paraphrases. And again, we may hope to have identified in this structural representation, which displays a complex relation between two predicate expressions, the syntactic basis for the fact that attributive sentences are understood as expressing a connection between two properties—between the property of being the murderer of Smith and the property of being insane.

**19** Accordingly, my claim is that attributive definite descriptions occur in sentences which have in their underlying structure a higher wh.ever clause in the *predicate* of which the definite phrase occurs. Now *such* a wh.ever clause, notice, expresses the irrelevance to the predication being made on the *f*, of having an answer to some *subject*-wanting question. The irrelevant question is 'Who is the murderer of Smith?' in the sense 'Who murdered Smith?' The predicate ('murdered Smith') is furnished, and we want its subject—though I do not need it to tell you that the murderer is insane.

**20** The structure I postulate includes the complex form of 'Whoever it may be who murdered Smith' rather than the simpler 'Whoever murdered Smith'. This has the advantage for my purposes of displaying in the structural representation the clause 'Who murdered Smith', which expresses the question declared or understood to be irrelevant to the predication. But perhaps a better reason for postulating that clause emerges from consideration of such sentences as

(39)   Whoever $\begin{cases} \text{murdered Smith,} \\ \text{it was who murdered Smith,} \end{cases}$ it was a madman.

Now the 'it' in the lower clause is of course not the demonstrative 'it' of 'It's Superman', but rather a pronoun representing some constituent of the sentence itself. (Thus 'It was a madman' is a fragment, which makes sense only in certain linguistic contexts.) And there is a possible sentence

(41)   Whoever murdered Smith, it was a madman who planned it,

which of course cannot be expressed by (39), since we recognize that the person who planned the murder may not have been identical with the murderer. What constituent the 'it' of (39) might represent is clear from its paraphrase

(40)   Whoever murdered Smith, it was a madman *who murdered him.*

Of course, (39) cannot be paraphrased by

(41)*  Whoever murdered Smith it was a madman *whoever murdered him.*

But if 'it' can in this way represent the clause *who murdered Smith,* there seems to be reason to suppose the identical clause should appear in the tree, and is concealed in the abbreviated form *whoever murdered Smith*: thus that the explicit form is the two-clause construction *whoever it may be who murdered Smith.*[9]

**21** Notice that only *subject*-wanting questions will form wh-ever clauses with *it* or dummy subjects, as it were marking the place where the subject is wanting. Thus if asked the subject wanting question 'Who wrote *Syntactic Structures?*' one may say

(42)   I don't know who wrote *Syntactic Structures,*
       but $\begin{cases} \text{it was one smart cookie.} \\ \text{it was some enemy of Nixon's.} \end{cases}$

But if asked the unambiguously predicate-wanting question, 'Who *is* Noam Chomsky?', one cannot similarly reply

---

[9] I think this argument has some force, whether 'it' is to be regarded as a kind of anaphoric pronoun or as merely a dummy subject left in the subject place by cleft sentence formation: for even on the latter treatment, on which (40) comes from (40a) 'Whoever murdered Smith, a madman murdered Smith', the possibility of this being reduced to (39) suggests that a higher 'who murdered Smith' completes the sense.

(43)* I don't know who Noam Chomsky is,

but $\begin{cases} \text{it is one smart cookie.} \\ \text{it is some enemy of Nixon's.} \end{cases}$

**22** I shall now offer my main evidence for the view that simple attributive sentences like 'The inventor of the miniskirt deserves our thanks' have the same syntactic structure as the sentence 'Whoever it may be who invented the miniskirt, the inventor of the miniskirt deserves our thanks'. The evidence I offer is of this general nature: there are constraints upon the selection of predicate phrases for the relevant wh.ever-clauses; violations of these constraints result in clearly *ungrammatical* sentences such as

(44) * Whoever invented the miniskirt was Mary Quant.

And, there are sentences, such as

(45) The inventor of the miniskirt was Mary Quant

in which the definite description *cannot be given the attributive interpretation*, cannot be being used attributively. We may account for this fact on the hypothesis that the reason (45) will not support that interpretation, is that to interpret it thus would require taking its constituents to stand in syntactic relationships which, according to the same grammatical rule that is violated by (44), it is impossible that they should stand in. The impossibility of reading the definite description in (45) attributively, and of using it attributively, may be explained by reference to the same theoretical postulates already required to account for the ungrammaticality of (44), and thus without complicating the grammar. But the rule constraining predicate selection which allows the predicate 'deserves our thanks' but disallows 'is Mary Quant', must operate on a range of subject expressions which is defined by their *syntactic* structure or classification. If one and the same rule is to define both the grammatical predicates of wh.ever-clauses and the predicates permitting the attributive interpretation of a definite description, then definite descriptions receiving that interpretation must represent the *same* syntactic structure as is exhibited by those wh.ever-clauses. The reason (45) is unambiguous, then, will be that it cannot be taken to represent (or cannot be derived from) the structure of (44), that being illicit; the definite description in (45) must obviously be governed by selection restrictions other than those that govern wh.ever clauses (given that (45) *is* permitted) and therefore it must represent some different structure. It represents a structure distinct from that of (44), obviously, but also, it must represent a structure distinct from that of the *unambiguously attributive* definite description occurring in

(46)    I don't know who invented the miniskirt, but *the inventor of the miniskirt* deserves our thanks.

For there is evidently a rule which blocks the embedding of (45) in such a context:

(47) *    I don't know who invented the miniskirt, but *the inventor of the miniskirt* was Mary Quant.

This sentence, with the *definite* phrase, is ungrammatical—just as (44), with the *wh.ever*-clause, is ungrammatical. Accordingly, we may hypothesize that in certain contexts of the form 'I don't know wh. is the $f$, ... the $f$ ..., the definite phrase (in its second occurrence) is constrained by the *same* predicate selection rule that governs the relevant wh.ever-clauses, i.e., in *or out* of such contexts—and thus that the rule violated by (44) is one and the same rule that is violated by (47). This hypothesis is confirmed by the fact that, of course,

(48)    I don't know who invented the miniskirt, but whoever invented the miniskirt deserves our thanks

is acceptable. This suggests that the predicates that the rule *allows* for the wh.ever-clause are just those allowed in such contexts as (46) for the definite phrase. But now, if these two constructions, apparently syntactically diverse, are in fact governed by the same predicate selection rule, then we must postulate an *identity* of syntactic form *underlying* the surface differences displayed by the relevant (attributive) definite descriptions and the wh.ever clauses. Then the definite description in (45), which will not accept the attributive interpretation, must represent some different syntactic structure from that represented by what is superficially the same phrase, as it occurs in (46), where it admits *only* the attributive interpretation. All this falls in place on the hypothesis that that structure underlying the attributively interpreted definite description, and thus *one* structure underlying the ambiguous definite description of (3), is just that represented by:

wh.ever it may be that is the $f$, the $f$ is $g$.

**23** Obviously the same constraints that operate on sentences with wh.ever clause subjects, like (44), also operate where the wh.ever clause appears in a higher clause, permitting

(49)  Whoever (it may have been who) invented the miniskirt, she deserves our thanks,

(50)  Whoever (it may have been who) wrote *Syntactic Structures*, it was one smart cookie,

but not

(51)*  Whoever (it may have been who) invented the miniskirt, $\left.\begin{array}{l}\text{she}\\\text{it}\end{array}\right\}$ is Mary Quant.

(52)*  Whoever (it may have been who) wrote *Syntactic Structures*, it was Noam Chomsky.

That is, the same constraint operates on the selection of predicates for those pronouns (*she*, *it*) which find their antecedent or interpretation in the predicate of a wh-clause ('who invented', or 'is the inventor of the miniskirt') embedded to a wh.ever-clause.

**24** Consider that set of nominal expressions which *cannot* occur grammatically in predicates of wh.ever-clauses, or in predicates of subjects relevantly associated with such clauses (as discussed in (24))—where the wh-clauses concern subject-wanting questions. My account makes these predictions: that set of expressions is precisely that set which cannot occur as predicate nouns, in the predicate of an attributive definite description. And, those predicates which *are* possible predicates of attributive definite descriptions are just those that are possible predicates of the relevant wh.ever-clauses (etc.).

**25** On the present view, the predicates which are permitted should be just those which do not fully satisfy the underlying subject-wanting wh-question, those which fail to state the answer to the question, Who is it who is the *f*? The predications which are *not* permitted will be those which *do* state the full answer to that question, such as those stating *the name* of the person who is the *f*. They seem also to include certain exhaustive *demonstrative* phrases. Thus consider

(53)*  Whoever invented the miniskirt, it is $\left\{\begin{array}{l}\text{the}\\\text{that}\end{array}\right\}$ girl over there right behind the fern.

(54) *  Whoever it was who left that hat, $\begin{Bmatrix} \text{it} \\ \text{he} \end{Bmatrix}$ is $\begin{Bmatrix} \text{the} \\ \text{that} \end{Bmatrix}$ man there running down the street.

and, *predictably*, we find that the descriptions in the following sentences *cannot be attributive*:

(55)   The girl over there right behind the fern invented the miniskirt
(56)   The man there running down the street left this hat.[10]

**26** It may be argued that very similar facts characterize wh.ever-constructions formed from *other* interrogative pronouns as well.

(57) *  Whenever she arrives it will be at five o'clock CST, Mon., Oct. 23, 1972 A.D.
(58)   The time of her arrival will be at five o'clock CST Mon., Oct. 23, 1972 A.D. (NO ATTRIBUTIVE READING (?))
(59)? * Whatever the price of eggs is it is 90 cents a dozen
(60)   The price of eggs is 90 cents a dozen (NO ATTRIBUTIVE READING (?))

Here the noun phrases seem completely to satisfy the subject questions

(61)   When will she arrive?
(62)   What is the price of eggs?

Where the noun phrase does not completely answer the question, the attributive interpretation is again possible

[10] Notice there that where the underlying question is a *predicate*-wanting question, demonstrative phrases *may* occur: thus whereas
   (a) *Whoever it may be who is the killer of Smith, he is that man there running down the street
is out, a sentence involving a predicate-wanting question, like
   (b) Whoever the man who killed Smith may *be*, he is that man there running down the street
is possible. On the other hand,
   (c) *Whoever the killer of Smith is, he is Jones,
is deviant on either interpretation. Names, here unlike demonstratives, evidently satisfy the question as to who someone is, even when demonstratives do not: thus
   (d) I don't know who the killer *is*, but I know he is that man there.
but not
   (e) *I don't know who the killer is, but I know that he is John Jones.
   (f) I don't know who the killer is, but I know that his name is John Jones,
is acceptable.

(63)   The time of her arrival will be in the afternoon
(64)   Whenever she arrives it will be in the afternoon
(65)   The price of eggs is high/around 90 cents a dozen.
(66)   Whatever the price of eggs is it is high/around 90 cents a dozen.

Other sentences like

(67)   Wherever the coin will be found it will be in John's hand,

*may* be interpreted attributively, but that interpretation forces us to suppose, for example, John's hand to be very large indeed, for only on some such out of the way supposition can the phrase 'in John's hand' fail to answer completely the question

(68)   Where is the coin?

I am persuaded by a remark of Saul Kripke's regarding this, that in fact sentences like (57) and (59) are *not* ungrammatical, for one can imagine a situation in which we operate on two different dating schemes or monetary scales and employ exactly the same terms with the same senses in each scheme. This seems to open up the possibility of reading (58) and (60) attributively.

**27** But names (and demonstratives) are a different matter. It is impossible to imagine any analogous indeterminacy about the use of a name which might allow us to interpret the sentence *'Whoever invented the miniskirt, it was Mary Quant' as grammatical or 'The inventor of the miniskirt is Mary Quant' as involving an attributively used description. Let us test this. Consider the case of "Sedan Chair", which was the code name assigned to a certain disgruntled Humphrey insider by the Watergate mob. We do not know who it was who was called "Sedan Chair". Suppose now that intimate letters of Humphrey's to Tricia Nixon are found stuffed up Charles Colson's stovepipe. "Who betrayed Humphrey?" we ask, and the answer is "Sedan Chair". But that is to say that we *know* who betrayed Humphrey, and the sentence 'The man who betrayed Humphrey was Sedan Chair' does *not* receive the attributive interpretation—thus it does not mean the same as *'Whoever betrayed Humphrey it was Sedan Chair'. Neither does it mean the same as the sentence 'The traitor was the man they called "Sedan Chair" '—which *may* be taken attributively. In the same way, while you can say

(69)  I don't know who betrayed him, but it was the man they called "Sedan Chair"

(70)  Whoever it was who betrayed him, it was the man they called "Sedan Chair",

I maintain that you cannot say

(71) *  I $\begin{Bmatrix} \text{don't know} \\ \text{can't say} \end{Bmatrix}$ who betrayed him, but it was Sedan Chair

(72)  *Whoever it may be who betrayed him, it was Sedan Chair.

One may waver on this, because the name can be heard as if in quotes:

(73)  I don't know $\Big\}$ who betrayed him, (but) it was "Sedan
      Whoever it was $\Big/$ Chair".

Such quotes represent a deleted verb of saying, and to "hear" them is to recognize that the sentence thus means roughly the same as (69-70).

**28** Obviously I reject the view that names are disguised descriptions, notwithstanding the fact that they may be bent to that purpose; doing so, I think, clearly involves linguistic deviation. Behind all this is Mill's insight that proper names have no connotation, no meaning; that it is not by the properties of things that their names attach to them, and thus naming them attributes no properties to them. Syntax is not insensitive to this fact.

**29** A theory of the phenomena I have mainly emphasized must account for these *two* things: First, it must account for the ungrammaticality of certain complex sentences attaching certain predicate phrases to definite descriptions. Secondly, it must account for the impossibility of using the corresponding definite descriptions attributively, where they occur in grammatical simple sentences with the *same* predicates. One might seek to do this by postulating the syntactic rules required to account for the ungrammatical sentences, and then certain *additional* rules governing the *use* of definite phrases, which debars the attributive use in conjunction with certain predicates. But then the total theory would have to employ for these purposes *two* sets of rules, syntactic rules *and* rules of use. But these two kinds of rules *can* be viewed as doing one and the same job—that is, the one job of selecting predicates for two kinds of subject constructions which have the same meaning. For 'the murderer of Smith' *can* mean the same as 'Whoever murdered Smith'. Surely, our knowledge that *'Whoever killed Smith is Jones' is not a grammatical sentence is essentially of a piece with our knowledge that 'The killer of Smith is Jones' cannot be read attributively. These are not two separate things, and an account of descriptions which reflects this is to be preferred, *ceteris parabus*, to one which does not.[11]

## V

### Two Alternative Accounts

**30** The suggestion that the surface structure of a sentence like 'Whoever it may be who is the *f*, the *f* is *g*' represents the deep structure of sentences of the surface form 'The *f* is *g*' where that definite description is attributive, is contrary to Donnellan's view about attributives. In his article on attributives Donnellan said

> In general, whether or not a definite description is used referentially or attributively is a function of the speaker's intentions in a particular case. "The murderer of Smith" may be used either way in the sentence "The murderer of Smith is insane." It does not appear plausible to account for this, either, as an ambiguity in the sentence. The grammatical structure of the sentence seems to me to be the same whether the description is used referentially or attributively: that is, it is not syntactically ambiguous. . . . These, of course, are intuitions; I do not have an argument for these

---

[11] Similarly, the theory of English should reflect the fact that our knowledge that
   (a) *You shut the door, will she?
is an ungrammatical sentence, is essentially connected with our knowledge that
   (b) Shut the door, will she?
cannot be read imperatively (but only indignantly). It may be useful to compare the argument given in §29 with *one* argument for the almost universally accepted "understood 'you'" analysis of imperatives. The indignant interpretation of (b) is possible because the subject of the main clause may be a deleted 'she', which will agree with the subject of the tag "will she?", the requirement of such agreement being what renders (a) ungrammatical. It is the rule that secures such agreement that requires us to postulate a deleted 'you' as the subject of
   (c) Shut the door, will you?
and of
   (d) Shut the door.
And it is our understanding that an imperative involves a certain predication on the *addressee*, that allows (c), but not (b), the imperative reading, second person being the person of address. (Incidentally, (c) can also have the indignant interpretation; cf. 'Insult my wife, will you?'. An unambiguously imperative structure would be that of 'Shut the door, if you will'.) Thus to account for our interpretation of (b), we invoke a rule (of agreement) which is postulated to account for the ungrammaticality of (a)—and that rule dictates that (b) cannot have the second person subject required of any imperative.

conclusions. Nevertheless the burden of proof is surely on the other side. (p. 297)

I of course am inclined to think the sentence *is* ambiguous, and that the ambiguity is syntactic in nature. I think it is ambiguous because *one* thing the sentence might mean is this: whoever murdered Smith is insane. Here is an argument for saying that that is one meaning of the sentence, rather than just one thing a speaker might mean by it. Generally, it will not follow generally from the fact that I said "*p*" and meant thereby that *q*, that I *said* that *q*. If I say "The cat is on the mat" but mean that spring is coming, I have for all that certainly not *said* that spring is coming. It *will* follow that I said that *q* if the thing I meant on that occasion is also one of the ('nonoccasional') meanings of the sentence. Thus, if I say "Visiting relatives can be boring", meaning that it can be boring to visit relatives, then I will have *said* it can be boring to visit relatives. Now, if I say "The murderer of Smith is insane", meaning that whoever murdered him is insane, I will have *said that* whoever murdered him is insane. That is a true *oratio obliqua* report of what I *said*. That it is a true report would be explained by supposing that that is one of the meanings of the sentence.

**31** But it is not the only explanation, and the argument is not irresistibly persuasive. The situation is that we have two apparently conflicting ways in which we might seek to account for the facts about attributives, and the question whether the sentence has two meanings or one may best be referred to the larger question, which of these two competing accounts is superior: that developed in the present paper, on which the sentences are regarded as ambiguous in meaning and representing two distinct syntactic structures, or the other one —favored by Donnellan—in which one regards the sentence as *un*ambiguous in meaning, and takes the phrases merely to be *used* in two different ways. The characteristic implications of the attributive use, for example, that there is some connection between the properties expressed by the definite description and the properties being ascribed to it, will on the latter view be attributed to considerations external to the grammar itself, such as certain conventions governing discourse in general, informal inductions from the speech situation, or the like.

**32** Advocates of one analysis will claim greater simplicity for their own account and charge the other with unnecessarily complicating the total theory of language. The two uses view will be charged with multiplying rules beyond necessity and the two meanings view with multiplying meanings beyond necessity. On a general sketch of the two views, it is a Mexican standoff. One must descend to the actual detail of the two accounts to decide whether one is superior to the other.

**33** But before making a brief effort to do just that, it is as well to temper the apparent conflict between the two views, and moderate our claims. For instance, the two-meaning partisan need not take exception to Donnellan's remark that "whether or not a definite description is used referentially or attributively is a function of the speaker's intentions in a particular case." For while holding that the sentence "The murderer of Smith is insane" is ambiguous in meaning, I would also hold that what a speaker *means by* it (no less than how he is *using* the definite phrase) in a particular utterance, is precisely a function of his intentions in that case. (We might of course differ on the way we choose to characterize those intentions.) Thus while without question the *sentence* 'Mary was nice to visit' is ambiguous, what a speaker means by it is a function of his intentions "in a particular case", and thus so is what it means on that occasion. Notice that one might also say that whether a speaker is using 'Mary' as the grammatical object of 'visit' or as its subject, that being what determines what he means, likewise turns on his intentions in the given case. But that *too* is consistent with our saying that the sentence itself is ambiguous, and syntactically ambiguous.

**34** Secondly, regarding the charge of multiplying meanings unnecessarily. That the multiplication is unnecessary has of course not been conceded. But however that may be, it is worth saying that the thesis that the sentence has two meanings is not ontologically expansive, for of course we are not "committed" by this view to the existence of an extra *entity*; it is not an issue quite like the postulation of two atomic particles where an alternative view requires only one. On the view that the meaning of a sentence is (*roughly*) nothing other than what might properly be meant by it, the claim that a sentence has two meanings is (roughly) just the claim that there are two things that might properly be meant by it.

**35** On the other side, the two-use theorist is charged (as in §29) with duplicating functions in the total theory of language, specifically of requiring a syntactic rule to explain certain distributional facts and, redundantly, a "rule of use" to explain why the description in "The one who did it was Harry" cannot be used attributively. But to make this charge stick, it has to be shown, first, that what is required for the latter task is indeed a "rule"—perhaps a certain informal induction to the speaker's intentions can be described which will suffice; and secondly, that if some rule *is* required in the account, it is one that is not required also by independent considerations.

**36** It is clear that neither account has been sufficiently developed to test its claims decisively. For my part, I have not attempted to show that the sentences in question can be generated from the suggested deep structures by well-established and independently motivated transformational rules; perhaps the syntacticians' verdict will be that the analysis would require introducing new, and otherwise unwanted, rules into the grammar. On the other side, no explanation has actually been offered of how well-established and independently motivated principles of conversational implication might account for the distinctive facts about the attributive use.

**37** Let us explore briefly the prospects of the two-use theory, when it comes down to explaining one particular fact: the fact that definite descriptions cannot be used attributively in sentences like 'The inventor of the miniskirt is Mary Quant'. The two-use account will require, obviously, an appropriate characterization of what it is to use a description attributively, so that we can say just what it is that the description cannot be being used to do, in such a sentence. I suggest this:

> To use a definite description *attributively* in a sentence (the $f$ is $g$) is to use it in such a way as to convey, or implement the intention of conveying, the same thing that would be conventionally and expressly conveyed by the same sentence with the appropriate wh.ever-clause prefixed to it (wh.ever it may be that is the $f$, the $f$ is $g$.) [12]

Now to say something *explicitly* of the latter form, such as 'Whoever invented the miniskirt, the inventor of the miniskirt deserves our thanks', is expressly and by conventional linguistic means to indicate that

(C)     the speaker says even without knowing, or would say even without knowing who invented the miniskirt, that its inventor deserves our thanks.

That (C) is conveyed is beyond relevant doubt determined by the rules of English, given the express occurrence of the whoever-clause; that is (or alternatively), it is something one knows owing to his competence as a speaker of English. But the same thing, (C), *might* be being conveyed and understood also when one says that same sentence

---

[12] Admittedly, this draws heavily on my own characterization, but it does not do so in a tendentious way; e.g., the characterization does not imply that the two sentences mean the same thing.

*minus* the whoever prefix ('The inventor of the miniskirt deserves our thanks'). According to the two-use theory, this is a fact we know about the possible ways of using the description contained, not a specifically about what the sentence might mean, or its grammatical structure. Therefore, that (C) might be being conveyed is not something specifically determined by the rules of English. But what determines that if one were to say 'The inventor of the miniskirt was Mary Quant', that (C) could *not* be conveyed? (The two-use theorist will agree, presumably, that, were the sentence prefixed with the whoever-clause, it *would* be determined by the rules of English that (C) *was* being conveyed.) The fact is that one who utters that sentence—'The inventor ... is Mary Quant'—cannot be doing so with the intention that it should be understood that he would say that Mary Quant invented the miniskirt whoever it might have been who invented the miniskirt. He "cannot" have such an intention because it is an impossibly incoherent intention to have. Of course, the two-meaning theorist may well agree with *that*, but hold that that is why the sentence can't be uttered with the attributive meaning, that is, that that is why one "cannot" mean by it that whoever invented the miniskirt, she is Mary Quant (cf. §33). And, both sides may agree that it is an incoherent intention because (this being one way to put it) it is to intend it to be believed that one might know that the inventor of the miniskirt is Mary Quant no matter who it was who invented the miniskirt, *therefore* even if it was *not* Mary Quant who did it.

**38** But perhaps this, at last, locates the crux of the issue. The question concerns the nature of this inference marked by "therefore". The inference evidently involves this assumption: to know that it was Mary Quant who invented the miniskirt *is* to know who invented the miniskirt. (To know that it was a person, or the only person, *named* Mary Quant does not constitute knowing who invented the miniskirt.) But what is the nature of this proposition? In my submission it expresses specifically *linguistic* knowledge, reflecting recognition of the syntactic differences between the expressions "is Mary Quant" and "is named 'Mary Quant'" (or 'deserves our thanks'). The same proposition explains why we can say

(78)   He's named Harry Jenkins, but I $\left\{\begin{array}{l}\text{can't say}\\\text{don't know}\end{array}\right\}$ who he is

but not

(79)*   He's Harry Jenkins, but I $\left\{\begin{array}{l}\text{can't say}\\\text{don't know}\end{array}\right\}$ who he is.

Now there are not two distinct states of affairs, that of being named Harry Jenkins and that of being Harry Jenkins. Therefore, so far as their relative capacity to communicate knowledge of the state of affairs that obtains, of the way things are, the two sentences "The man is Harry Jenkins" and "The man is named Harry Jenkins" do not differ. To recognize the difference between such sentences as (78) and (79) is just to recognize that the act of stating the answer to a question cannot be analyzed just in terms of the imparting of desired knowledge about the situation that obtains. The imparting of such knowledge is neither necessary nor sufficient for stating the answer to a question. What *is* required is that one should do so by uttering a sentence of a certain syntactic form, such that that *sentence* answers the question. There is a *syntactic* relation obtaining between pairs of interrogative and indic- ative sentences, such that the latter *answers* the former. And this is what is expressed by the proposition that saying that Mary Quant invented the miniskirt constitutes answering the question, who invented the miniskirt?

**39** If so it is not a *conversational* implicature, in Grice's terminology, of saying 'The *f* is NAME' that the speaker gives it to be understood that he knows who it is who invented the miniskirt: it is a *conventional* implicature. Thus it is a conventional implicature of one's saying 'The inventor of the miniskirt is Mary Quant', that blocks the attributive use, or interpretation, of the definite description. For these reasons it seems to me that the attempt to explain such things in terms *purely* of informal inductions or general conversational maxims, will fail: and the two-use view, then, will as charged have to postulate what is genuinely a *rule* or *stipulation* that giving the name of the *f* constitutes saying who it is who is the *f*". And this rule will indeed be redundant, merely duplicating the function of whatever rules or grammatical devices render the sentence *"Whoever invented the miniskirt is Mary Quant" an ungrammatical sentence of English.

**40** The point I am laboring to make may become clearer if approached from one other angle. I claim that such sentences as

(80) *  I don't know who left that hat here, but it was Jim Martin
(81) *  Without knowing who left that hat here I can tell you that the guy who left it was Jim Martin

are ungrammatical. I think the opposition—the two-use man—has to *deny* that they are ungrammatical. He might hold that instead they are grammatical sentences essentially like Moore's paradox sentences:

(82)   I don't know that it is raining, but it is raining

(83)   I don't know that Jim Martin left it, but it was Jim Martin who left it,

that is, that they are grammatical but manifest impossibly incoherent intentions, this last being strictly a psychological or logical proposition, not a linguistic one. Now I am inclined to agree that (82) and (83) are not ungrammatical. But how do we decide this? Not on the basis of their relative audible screwiness. Rather, the decision must involve the judgment that there is no grammatical rule violated by (82) and (83). And this seems sound, because there are no grammatical *relations* obtaining between the clauses, or their constituents, such that the rules governing such relationships are being violated. (Cf. the case discussed in footnote 11.) But now my position is precisely that in (80) and (81) there *does* obtain such a syntactic relationship, specifically that between the question-clause 'who left that hat' and the clause 'it was Jim Martin'—that is, that relationship which also obtains between interrogative sentences and indicative sentences which *answer* them. The deviance of (80) and (81), I hold, is owing to a violation of rules governing that syntactic relation; thus to a violation of syntactic rules. If so, they *are* ungrammatical sentences and not merely functionally self-stultifying ones like (82) and (83).

## VI

### WH.EVER-CLAUSES

41 How exactly does the wh.ever-clause contribute to the meaning of the attributive sentence? In particular what is the relation between the dependent clause 'whoever killed Smith', and the independent clause 'The killer of Smith is insane'? It does not seem that the whoever-clause can modify any of the *constituents* of the main clause. That is, the attributive sentence is unlike

(83)   She takes that lamb wherever she goes,

in which the *wherever* clause is evidently part of the verb phrase. Construing

(84)   The killer is insane whoever he is

analogously, yields the idea that the killer has multiple personalities, all crazy; but that interpretation is not the one we want, and it is not necessarily attributive. Again, it seems clearly wrong to suppose the whoever-clause modifies the subject phrase, as if to say, 'The killer of Smith, whoever it may be who is *he*, is insane', whatever exactly that might possibly mean.

**42** Instead, the whoever-clause stands outside the main clause, somehow modifying the entire sentence, 'The killer is insane'. But again, it is not like such sentence adverbs as 'obviously' or 'certainly' or 'surprisingly': that is, it does not say something *about* the proposition or fact that the killer is insane—that it is surprising, or obviously true.

**43** My suggestion about the wh.ever-clause is that it is a kind of adverbial construction modifying some higher clause like 'I say'. The idea that all indicative sentences involve such a higher structure has of course been argued by John R. Ross, and other linguists. Peter Schreiber,[13] for instance, points out that in such sentences as

(85)    Frankly,
        To be frank,  } Marge is sort of boring

(since there is no way of being boring which is the frank way, nor is Marge boring in order to be frank) the adverb *frankly* must modify some verb of *saying*; and this suggests structures like

(86)    I say frankly that Marge is sort of boring
        To be frank I must say that Marge is sort of boring.

In the same way I suggest that the structure of whoever sentences is

(87)    I say whoever it may be who is the *f*, the *f* is *g*.

Notice that *wh.ever*-clauses can be paraphrased by *regardless* clauses: "whoever it may be who is the *f*" means the same as "regardless who it may be who is the *f*." (Apparently, 'regardless wh.' and 'wh.ever' stand in complementary distribution: there is no \*'Regardless whoever did it . . .'; this fact indicates that they are two realizations of one and the same semantic role.) Now *regardless*-clauses express conditions which *might* be thought to stand in the way of something's being the case. Thus

(88)    It doesn't matter } how cold it gets, my car starts
        Regardless
(89)    However cold it gets, my car starts

---

[13] "Style Disjuncts and the Performative Analysis," *Linguistic Inquiry*, III, 3 (1972). See also Ross, "On Declarative Sentences," in R. Jacobs and P. Rosenbaum, *Readings in English Transformational Grammar* (Waltham, Mass.: Ginn, 1970).

are fine, whereas

(90)   ? It doesn't matter ⎫ how cold it gets, my car is a Ford
       ? Regardless       ⎭
(91)   ? However cold it gets, my car is a Ford

make no *apparent* sense, for there is no apparent way that its being
cold might stand in the way of my car's being a Ford.

**44** Now how do we interpret

(92)   It doesn't matter ⎫
       Regardless        ⎬ who left this hat, he's got an enormous
       Whoever it was    ⎭ head.

There is no apparent way that its being one person rather than another
who left his hat here *might* be relevant to the size of the head of the one
who did it—any more than how cold it is might be relevant to the make
of my car. Neither is it the case that my not *knowing* who left the hat
might stand in the way of that person's *having* an enormous head.
Whether I know or don't know who it is who left it is obviously
irrelevant to the size of his head. What it is not irrelevant to, and what
it might stand in the way of, is *my* knowing and thus my *saying* that
he's got an enormous head. So that is why I suggest that the structure
must be that of 'I *say* wh.ever it may be who is the *f*, the *f* is *g*.' The
wh.ever-clause says that the answer to the question Wh. is the *f*?
doesn't matter. But what is it that it doesn't matter *to*? Not to its being
the case that the *f* is *g*, but rather to one's being able to *say* that the *f* is *g*.

**45** This view also yields the right account of the sense in which
attributive sentences express a connection between the properties, of
being the *f* and of being *g*. To repeat it: if one gives it to be understood
that one says that the *f* is *g* regardless of the answer to the question
Who is the *f*?, the question arises, How *can* one say such a thing? If we
presume rationality and good faith on the part of the speaker, this
becomes the question, How could one know, or think he knew, that the *f*
is *g*, independently of his knowing who or what it is that is the *f*? And
the answer must be that the speaker's reason for saying of the *f*, that it
is *g*, must be in part that the *f* is the *f*. We hypothesize that he says that
the man who killed Smith is insane, on the basis of the sole fact one may
be presumed to know, independently of his knowing who killed Smith,
about the man who killed Smith, namely, that he is the man who killed
Smith. And, we figure, the speaker thinks that no one could have done
what that man did (whether "what he did" was kill a human being, kill

the kindly Smith, kill him in such a way, or risk the noose) unless he were insane.

**46** Now typically perhaps, the fact that the *f* is the *f* provides reason for saying that the *f* is *g* because either being the *f* entails being *g*, or because the *f*'s being *g* *would explain* its being the *f*, or it's having some property entailed by its being the *f*. But this is not always the situation. Consider, for instance

(93)    The man in the anteroom is the killer.

Suppose that we knew that one of the suspects assembled in the anteroom was the killer, and that they have been examined and exonerated one by one until there remains only one suspect. Here we may assert (93) attributively, without supposing that his being the killer explains his being the man in the anteroom or anything entailed thereby, or that his being the killer is the only explanation for his being the man in the anteroom. That is, in this case, the connection between the properties of being the killer and being the last man left in the anteroom have no connection *except* for the fact that the possession of the property of being in the anteroom provides reason for thinking or a basis upon which one might know, and thus for *saying*, of that person that he has the other property, of being the killer. So that is the sense I give to the idea that attributive definite descriptions "express a connection between properties". In particular, notice that there need be no connection between the properties in question obtaining in the nature of things; there need be no causal connection.[14]

---

[14] Compare in this connection the character of general statements, and the distinction between accidental and lawlike propositions. The rough proportion to be explored between general and singular statements here is this: accidental are to lawlike general statements as referential are to attributive singular statements. Consider,

    (a) Everybody I meet is doing well. (Calvin Coolidge)
    (b) Everyone here has hair.
    (c) Anyone who is here must be interested in philosophy.
    (d) Any mass falling in a vacuum (whatever that mass may be, (stone or feather))
falls at a velocity that increases by equal amounts in any two equal times.

The speaker who asserts an accidental generalization does *not* give it to be understood that his reason for saying of, e.g., every person here, that he has hair, is that everyone here is assembled *here*. Whereas in (c), my reason for saying of anyone who is here, that he must be interested in philosophy *is*, in part, that he is *here*, i.e., at this philosophical meeting. Regarding a statement enunciating a natural law, like (d), it is understood that the predicate is true of any mass, because any mass, whatever it may be, has mass. There is the view that a natural law expresses a causal connection between properties. Might this be a special case of the connection between subjects and predicates which characterizes attributive definite descriptions?

## *VII*

### ATTRIBUTIVES AND REFERENCE

**47** Donnellan and before him Linsky criticize views of referring which would make it a necessary condition of referring to a thing $x$ by a descriptive phrase, that $x$ should satisfy that description. One can refer to what is not an $f$ as an $f$. And one may therein be *saying* something about the thing to which he referred. If in saying, "Her boyfriend is a fool", I am referring to the person who is in fact her husband, I am nonetheless saying something *about* her husband. But Donnellan *contrasts* this situation with that of the attributive phrase, with resulting inaccuracies in his characterization of attributives. In particular, Donnellan maintains that unless the presumption that someone murdered Smith is true, then when one says "The murderer of Smith is insane", using the phrase attributively, "no one has been said to be insane".

**48** This seems to me wrong. In the first place, *within* the definite phrase there are terms which may be being used referentially: for instance, 'Smith' in the phrase 'the murderer of Smith' may be being used referentially. The speaker may be referring to the dead man as Smith, but when his head is located we learn that the dead man is Jones. We will understand that the man who said that the murderer of Smith is insane was referring to the murderer of Jones. But then surely someone *has* been said to be insane. Further, suppose that insanity is exculpating of the charge of murder. On Donnellan's account the man who said 'The murderer of Smith is insane' using the phrase attributively could not possibly have said anything true. But what he presumably *meant* was that the *killer* of Smith is insane, and surely he was referring, if incorrectly, to the *killer* of Smith as the "murderer" of Smith. Now he has, I think, *said that* the killer of Smith is insane; he *certainly* has said *of* the killer of Smith that he is insane. So someone *has* been said to be insane. And, I think, a reference has been made.

**49** Donnellan's characterization of attributives features an alleged contrast between descriptions used to refer to some particular thing which the speaker has in mind, on the one hand, and attributives on the other. But first, while we think we know what this is driving at, the phenomena evade this particular attempt to catch them. For one *can* say that on the attributive interpretation, the speaker is referring to *whoever it was who killed Smith*, and even that he had a *particular person* in mind, to wit, *whoever it was who killed Smith*. If the speaker is not referring to any particular person that he has in mind *as being* the killer of Smith, then that just shows that, indeed, he is not referring to a person of whom it is true that the speaker has him in mind as being the killer of Smith. It doesn't show that he's not referring to anyone. In his final paragraph (p. 303), Donnellan, apparently recognizing something of this, says, "If there is anything which might be identified as reference here, it is reference in a very weak sense—namely, reference to whatever is the one and only φ, if there is any such". But it is not reference in a "weak sense", it is reference pure and simple.

**50** To take this view is in no way to deny that there are constraints on what expressions one may substitute in framing a true statement of what has been said, when one says, speaking attributively, 'The murderer of Smith was insane'. If it should turn out to be Jenkins who murdered Smith, it will nonetheless *not* be true that the speaker had said that Jenkins was insane, nor that he said of, or about, Jenkins that he was insane. After all, what he did say, according to me, was that *whoever* murdered Smith was insane, and there is no true identity proposition expressed by the ungrammatical sentence *'Whoever murdered Smith was Jenkins' which would force such conclusions. The only expressions substitutable, saving grammaticality, will be those capable of an attributive interpretation, and the only interpretation of the resulting sentences which will save truth will be the attributive interpretation.

**51** And indeed, one cannot (saving truth) substitute *every* attributively interpretable definite description (which with the description used will express a true identity proposition). Consider the cases of inaccurate attributive reference considered above in §48. I said that where the dead Jones was mistaken for Smith, the man who said "The murderer of Smith is insane" may truely be held to have said that the murderer of Jones is insane. But this is right *only* on certain suppositions about the "connection of properties." If it is the fact that the murderer *decapitated* his victim (whoever the victim might be), that is rightly understood to make the speaker say that the murderer is insane, *then* the reference to the victim as Smith, and thus to the murderer as the murderer of Smith, can be corrected as suggested. For the reference to the murderer as the murderer of *Smith* is *accidental; that is, not determined by the reasoning that supports or explains the predication.* If the reasoning does *not* involve the premise that decapitation is the act of a madman, but instead the premise just that killing saintly *Smith* in particular is the act of a madman (perhaps whereas we will agree that Jones deserved what he got), then I think that we will *not* revise the description. It will not be true that the speaker said that the murderer of Jones ( = whoever murdered Jones) is insane. Again, consider the situation wherein insanity is exculpating of murder, concerning which I alleged that we can truly revise the speaker's language and claim that he said that the *killer* of Smith is insane. Again, it depends on the connection of properties being expressed. If it is to be understood that the reason that the man is being said to be insane is precisely because he would have to have been insane to have killed with premeditation, malice, and the capacity to distinguish right from wrong, *then* we will *not* be free, I think, to say that he said that the *killer* ( = whoever killed him) was insane. Generally, it is apparent that our freedom to revise the speaker's language in framing *oratio obliqua* reports is constrained against misrepresentation of the reasoning which underlies the utterance. There is a question of *correctly* representing his thought.

**52** In his closing paragraph, having conceded that attributives might be said refer in some weak sense, but not to refer to any particular thing, Donnellan alludes to the lack of particularity of such reference, and concludes thus:

> But this lack of particularity is absent from the referential use of definite descriptions precisely because the description is here merely a device for getting one's audience to pick out or think of the thing to be spoken about, a device which may serve its purpose even if the description is incorrect. More importantly, perhaps, in the referential use as opposed to the attributive, there is a *right* thing to be picked out by the audience and its being the right thing is not simply a function of its fitting the description. (p. 303)

I have been arguing that there is a right thing to be "picked out" or thought of by the audience, where the description is used attributively, as well as where it is used "referentially"—or as I should prefer to say, "demonstratively", since I think that both uses *are* referential ones. This is the substance of the issue concerning the referential powers of the attributive use. And the fact is that, when someone says "The murderer of Smith is insane", there *is* a question whether it is *right* or *wrong* to suppose that he is therein referring to, and saying something about, whoever it was who murdered *Jones*, or *Smith*, or whoever it was who *decapitated* Jones, or whoever it was that planned the deed, of exactly who *in particular* he is referring to, and thinking of.

**53** There is nothing in my treatment of attributives, in acknowledging their referential power which provides aid and comfort to the widely discredited idea that what one is referring to, what one is saying what he is saying *about*, is a matter determined purely and simply by the meaning of the phrase one uses in referring to it or speaking about it. It is never "simply a function of its fitting the description" that a thing is that thing about which a speaker is saying something, or in that sense, the subject of a statement. Neither does my account contain horrible implications of actually existing objects of actual indeterminate identity: if I should refer to the inventor of the wheel, that is, to whoever it was who invented it, it is merely absurd to say that I am committed to the truth of the proposition that there exists some person who is whoever invented the wheel. I am, however, "committed" to the proposition that someone invented the wheel, and, I think, if that should be false, then my situation is just like that of one who says "The present king of France is bald". That is, there will be a disinclination to say that I have said something about, or referred to, anyone, or said anything either true or false—again, *unless* I was referring to someone as "the inventor of the wheel" or "the present king of France" *incorrectly*, mistakenly referring to some existing person I had in mind.[15]

## *VIII*

### CONCLUSION AND A CONJECTURE

**54** I said at the outset that my main purpose was to understand how attributive sentences both refer to and predicate something of a particular subject "*by and while therein expressing a connection between properties*". Having tried to solve it, I wish now to state more explicitly the problem I saw in this, and to enter some last conjectural remarks.

First, where I *assert* a connection of "properties" quite explicitly, as in 'The discovery of the calculus required enormous intelligence', I do not explicitly say anything *about*, nor do I *refer to*, the person who discovered the calculus. But I held that in saying 'The man who discovered the calculus must have been enormously intelligent' (un-

---

[15] Connected with this is Donnellan's account of the differing origins of the presupposition that there is someone who fits the description, in the referential and the attributive uses respectively. He said that in the attributive use, that presupposition arises from the fact that unless it is true "the purpose of the speech act will be thwarted". It seems to me clear that the truth of that presupposition is *as* essential, i.e., as *in*essential, to the success of the speech act involving the attributive as it is to the one involving the referential description. Perhaps the presupposition which must be true in order for anyone to have been said to be insane is not that someone murdered Smith, but that someone should have done something which might be referred to as (might be thought to be) the murdering of Smith. But there is an analogous presupposition which must be true in the referential case, in order for anyone to have been said to be insane: sc. that there is someone who might be referred to as (thought to be) the murderer of Smith.

derstood attributively) I am saying something about and referring to
a particular man, that is, presumably to the man who discovered the
calculus, while *"therein"* expressing a connection of properties. The
possibility of this seems sufficiently well explained, given what has
been said about the character of the reference, and secondly given the
appropriate distinction between what one *asserts* and what one
*expresses*: for the 'connection of properties' is not being asserted, but
is rather *expressed*, owing to an inference that must be drawn if the
speaker is to be thought to have had any sufficient basis for asserting
what he did assert.

**55** Secondly, and more obscurely, I said that the reference is made
'*by* expressing' such a connection. Consider this important premise of
Russell's:

> ... it seems scarcely possible to believe that we can make a judg-
> ment or entertain a supposition without knowing what it is that
> we are judging or supposing about.[16]

But we *can* say "I do not know who left that hat, but the man who left
it must have had a big head", which may appear to be doing just that.
Of course, Russell's view was that 'the man who left it' does *not* stand
for a constituent of the proposition judged to be true. (To the extent
that we may take Donnellan's referentially used definite descriptions
to be among those that designate what Russell might have called a
constituent of the judgment being expressed, and accept his view that
in using definite descriptions attributively we are not saying anything about some particular thing to which we are referring, Donnellan
may be considered a supporter of Russell's position, where it is restricted to attributives.) But Russell's premise actually bears up quite
well, without driving us to these doctrines. For "knowing what it is
that we are judging about" does not require what Russell thought it
did. It does not require that one should know the thing by *acquaintance* that one is judging about or saying something about: one is not
required to know Nixon in order to say something about Nixon.
Neither does it require that one should know what the thing *is*, or who
the person *is*, that he is saying something about (that is, the answer to
what I called the predicate-wanting question). It is enough to know,

[16] "Knowledge by Acquaintance and Knowledge by Description" (1910), reprinted in
*Mysticism and Logic* (New York: Doubleday, 1957), p. 212. Russell describes the quoted
statement as "the chief reason" for accepting as true "The fundamental epistemological principle in the analysis of propositions containing descriptions...: Every
proposition which we can understand must be composed wholly of constituents with
which we are acquainted."

for example, that it is the man who left his hat to whom one is referring and about whom one is saying something. That is, one must know the answer to the (subject-wanting) question, 'To whom are you referring?'

**56** But what does it take to know the answer to that question? Whatever it takes, one thing is clear: the correct answer to the question is not necessarily given just by repeating the phrase that one has used to refer to whoever it may be that he is referring to. For again, it may not *be* the murderer of Smith to whom one is referring when he says "The murderer of Smith is insane". There may be a sense in which one *must* know what he's referring to, perhaps associated with the sense in which he must know what his intentions are. However it would still not be true that his intentions are whatever fits the description he gives of them, nor that he is referring to or thinking of whatever satisfies the description he gives of the thing he's referring to or thinking about.

**57** It may seem that if the meaning of the phrase does not determine the subject of the statement, then there is nothing which *can* do so, in circumstances wherein it is understood that the statement is made as if without knowing who murdered Smith. But the fact is that even so, the reference may be determinate, as it must be—if we are genuinely to have said that anything is so. The determinateness of the reference, its "particularity", is evident from the possibility of giving correct and incorrect answers to the question, What is it that is being referred to? And this determinateness is the contribution, one may say, of that which determines the correctness of such answers. But the meaning of the phrase cannot be consulted as a *criterion* of the correctness of such answers, in such a way that the referent is simply whatever it may be that willy nilly fits the description used in making the reference. It seems that instead the fact that one uses a particular phrase enters into the determination of what his statement is about as nothing more nor less than a piece of *evidence* relevant to the inductive identification of that thing. Finally identifying that subject, I am inclined to think, is a matter of discovering a certain correct hypothesis which would *explain* the utterance of the sentence, and thus, in that sense, arriving at an *understanding* of the utterance.[17] That is a conjecture, of course, but there is nothing in the study of attributives to discourage one from pursuing that conjecture. On the contrary.

**58** To attain an understanding of a speaker's having uttered a

[17] The larger context of this idea is developed in my "Show and Tell," forthcoming in the proceedings of the 1972 Annual Fall Colloquium, of the University of Western Ontario, "Forms of Representation."

sentence of the form, 'Wh.ever it may be that is the $f$, the $f$ is $g$', consistently with the assumption that he is saying that something is so, is to understand how he could say—i.e., how he thinks he could know—that that thing was so, without knowing who or what it is that is the $f$. That is *not* simply the question, how might he think he knew that whatever actually fits the description has the property attributed by the predicative expression he uses. For if the indications are that he could not think he knew *that*, or think that we would think he knew that, then we ask, What is it that he might think he knows, or think that we would believe that he knows, that would explain his saying 'The $f$ is $g$', consistently with the plausible attribution to him of such misapprehensions, erroneous presuppositions, linguistic errors, and so on, as are indicated by the evidence? This is the kind of question we face, whether dealing with the demonstrative or with the attributive use of referring expressions.

**59** In the demonstrative case—someone says "The redhead over there by the diving board knocks me out"—we ask, Who, in this scene, might he think fits the description 'redhead over there by the diving board', given what he's saying about that person, and given his relative competence with respect to each question, (a) the fittingness of the description, and (b) the truth of the predication? Given his sexual proclivities, and the fact that he can see well enough apart from his color blindness, we rule out the only redhead, a boy, and figure that the person he is referring to is a certain brunette girl, who is a knockout, and not the blonde, who is not. We work back and forth from subject to predicate.

**60** Exactly the same kind of considerations determine the reference of the attributive definite description: Who might the speaker be saying what he is saying *about*, given what he is evidently saying about it? And, given what he is evidently saying it about, what is he saying? But here we have the additional factor that he is saying it, *whoever* it may be who fits the description. This means that his basis for saying what he says cannot derive from any knowledge or beliefs that would require his knowing or thinking that he knows what fits the description.[18] It must then derive from his knowing or thinking he

---

[18] Consequently, the competence of his perceptual judgment cannot have the same relevance, and the particularity or determinateness of the reference cannot be traced to that one thing fitting the description which enters causally into the perceptual acquisition of the evidence or knowledge upon the basis of which the statement is made. Thus, in order to think one knows, on the basis of one's *perception* of him, that the person referred to the killer of Smith is insane—e.g., because he *looks* like a madman—one must have *seen* him, of course, but more than that one must think that he knows who it is that killed Smith, or is being referred to as the killer of Smith: sc. that man that he saw.

knows that from the fact that a thing fits the description it may be inferred that it has the property predicated of it; and thus from his knowing or thinking that, in that sense, the predicated property is "connected" with the property in terms of which the thing about which one is speaking is described. But now the question becomes: Given what he is saying about the thing he is saying something of, what might he know or believe, that would explain his uttering that sentence, 'The murderer of Smith is insane, whoever it may be'? That is, what might he know of *such* a nature *without* knowing who murdered Smith? Might it be that any *murderer* is insane? any *killer*? anyone who would kill *Smith*? or anyone who would *decapitate* a man? Suppose that the murderer and the decapitator were different people. The right answer will identify the particular person he is talking about—whether whoever murdered him, or whoever decapitated him. And the right answer may turn in part on what it is that the speaker is saying about whoever it may be that he is speaking of. Suppose that he is saying that that person was foolish to the point of madness, given what they will do to the murderer. Then it will apparently be the *murderer* that he is referring to. But suppose that he means that whoever decapitated Smith must be actually psychotic: then it will be whoever it was (whether it was the murderer or not) who cut Smith's head off, that the speaker is speaking of, and he that has been said to be insane. (It will be he and *not* the murderer, notwithstanding the fact that the speaker may assume that the decapitator is the murderer.)

**61** It is in this connection that I say that it is '*by*' expressing a certain connection of properties that, without knowing who it is that fits the description I use, that I may yet do something such that from what I do, it may be known of that person that he has the property I ascribe to him: that is, that it is '*by*' expressing a certain connection of properties that I may *say that* something is so, say about some *particular* thing, that it is thus and so.[19]

---

[19] I have profited from discussing these issues with Tom Patton, Fred Dretske, Lloyd Eggan, Berent Enc, Joe Chassler, and Peter Schreiber, and also, so I hope, from critical remarks of Gil Harman and Saul Kripke.

# Pragmatic Presuppositions[1]

## ROBERT C. STALNAKER

*Cornell University*

There is a familiar intuitive distinction between what is *asserted* and what is *presupposed* in the making of a statement. If I say that the Queen of England is bald, I presuppose that England has a unique queen, and assert that she is bald. If I say that Sam regrets that he voted for Nixon, I presuppose that Sam voted for Nixon, and assert that he feels bad about it. If I say that Ted Kennedy is the only person who could have defeated Nixon in 1972, I presuppose that Ted Kennedy could have defeated Nixon in 1972, and assert that no one else could have done so. Philosophers have discussed this distinction mainly in the context of problems of reference. Linguists have discussed it in many other contexts as well. They have argued that the phenomenon of presupposition is a pervasive feature of the use of natural language, one that must play a role in the semantic analysis of many words and phrases.

The principal criterion that has been used to identify presuppositions can be stated in the following way: *Q* is presupposed by an assertion that *P* just in case under normal conditions one can reasonably infer that a speaker believes that *Q* from either his assertion or his denial that *P*. One who denies the example statements listed above—who says that the Queen of England is *not* bald, that Sam does *not* regret that he voted for Nixon, or that Ted Kennedy is *not* the only

[1] This paper was read at the University of Texas conference on performatives, conversational implicature, and presupposition in March, 1973, as well as at New York University. I, and I hope the paper, benefited from stimulating comments by linguists and philosophers at both places.

person who could have defeated Nixon in 1972, normally makes the
same presuppositions as the person who makes the affirmative statements. Linguists have used this criterion to identify many examples
of the phenomenon. The criterion, and many of the examples, are
relatively clear and uncontroversial; it is clear that there is a phenomenon to be explained. But it is much less clear what kind of
explanation of it should be given. Granted that either the statement
that the Queen of England is bald, or the speaker who makes it,
presupposes that England has a unique queen. But what is it about the
statement, or the speaker, which constitutes this fact? There are two
very different kinds of answers to this question.

The first answer is that presupposition is a semantic relation
holding between sentences or propositions. This kind of account
draws the distinction between presupposition and assertion in terms
of the content or truth-conditions of the sentence uttered or the
proposition expressed. Here is an example of such a definition: a
proposition that $P$ presupposes that $Q$ if and only if $Q$ must be true in
order that $P$ have a truth-value at all. The presuppositions of a proposition, according to this definition, are necessitated by the truth,
and by the falsity, of the proposition. When any presupposition is
false, the assertion lacks a truth-value.

The second answer is that presupposition should be given a
pragmatic analysis. The distinction between presupposition and assertion should be drawn, not in terms of the content of the propositions expressed, but in terms of the situations in which the statement
is made—the attitudes and intentions of the speaker and his audience.
Presuppositions, on this account, are something like the background
beliefs of the speaker—propositions whose truth he takes for granted,
or seems to take for granted, in making his statement.

The pragmatic account is closer to the ordinary notion of presupposition, but it has frequently been assumed that the semantic
account is the one that is relevant to giving a rigorous theoretical
explanation of the linguistic phenomena. I want to argue that this
assumption is wrong. I will suggest that it is important for correctly
understanding the phenomena identified by linguists to give the second kind of analysis rather than the first. In terms of the pragmatic
account, one can give intuitively natural explanations of some facts
that seem puzzling when presupposition is viewed as a semantic relation. The pragmatic account makes it possible to explain some particular facts about presuppositions in terms of general maxims of
rational communication rather than in terms of complicated and *ad*
*hoc* hypotheses about the semantics of particular words and particular

kinds of constructions. To argue this, I will sketch an account of the kind I want to defend, and then discuss some of the facts identified by linguists in terms of it.

Let me begin by rehearsing some truisms about communication. Communication, whether linguistic or not, normally takes place against a background of beliefs or assumptions which are shared by the speaker and his audience, and which are recognized by them to be so shared. When I discuss politics with my barber, we each take the elementary facts of the current political situation for granted, and we each assume that the other does. We assume that Richard Nixon is the President, that he recently defeated George McGovern by a large margin, that the United States has recently been involved in a war in Vietnam, which is a small country in Southeast Asia, and so forth. That we can reasonably take these facts for granted obviously makes our communication more efficient. The more common ground we can take for granted, the more efficient our communication will be. And unless we could reasonably treat *some* facts in this way, we probably could not communicate at all.

Which facts or opinions we can reasonably take for granted in this way, as much as what further information either of us wants to convey, will guide the direction of our conversation—will determine what is said. I will not say things that are already taken for granted, since that would be redundant. Nor will I assert things incompatible with the common background, since that would be self-defeating. My aim in making assertions is to distinguish among the possible situations which are compatible with all the beliefs or assumptions that I assume that we share. Or it could be put the other way around: the common background is defined by the possible situations which I intend to distinguish among with my assertions, and other speech acts. Propositions true in all of them are propositions whose truth is taken for granted.

Although it is normally inappropriate because unnecessary for me to assert something that each of us assumes the other already believes, my assertions will of course always have consequences which are part of the common background. For example, in a context where we both know that my neighbor is an adult male, I say "My neighbor is a bachelor," which, let us suppose, entails that he is adult and male. I might just as well have said "my neighbor is unmarried." The same information would have been conveyed (although the nuances might not have been exactly the same). That is, the *increment of information*, or of content, conveyed by the first statement is the same as that conveyed by the second. If the asserted proposition were accepted, and added to the common background, the resulting situation would be the same as if the second assertion were accepted and added to the background.

This notion of common background belief is the first approximation to the notion of pragmatic presupposition that I want to use. A proposition $P$ is a pragmatic presupposition of a speaker in a given context just in case the speaker assumes or believes that $P$, assumes or believes that his addressee assumes or believes that $P$, and assumes or believes that his addressee recognizes that he is making these assumptions, or has these beliefs.

I do not propose this as a definition or analysis, first since it is far from clear what it is to believe or assume something, in the relevant way and second since even assuming these notions to be clear, the definition would need further qualification. My aim is not to give an analysis but rather to point to a familiar feature of linguistic contexts which, I shall argue, is the feature in terms of which a certain range of linguistic phenomena should be explained. The notion has, I think, enough intuitive content to enable us to identify a lot of particular cases, and the general outlines of the definition are clear enough to justify some generalizations about presuppositions which help to explain the facts. Before defending this claim by discussing some of the facts, I will make two remarks about the general notion.

First, note that it is persons rather than sentences, propositions or speech acts that have or make presuppositions. This goes against the prevailing technical use of the term, according to which presuppositions, whether semantic or pragmatic, are normally taken to relate two linguistic things. One might define such a relation in terms of the pragmatic notion in something like one of the following ways: (a) One might say that a sentence $x$ presupposes that $Q$ just in case the use of $x$ to make a statement is appropriate (or normal, or conversationally acceptable) only in contexts where $Q$ is presupposed by the speaker; or (b) one might say that the statement that $P$ (made in a given context) presupposes that $Q$ just in case one can reasonably infer that the speaker is presupposing that $Q$ from the fact that the statement was made; or (c) one might say that the statement that $P$ (made in a given context) presupposes that $Q$ just in case it is necessary to assume that the speaker is presupposing that $Q$ in order to understand or interpret correctly the statement. As stated, these suggested definitions are vague, and each is different from the other. But I do not think it would be fruitful to refine them, or to choose one over the others. It is true that the linguistic facts to be explained by a theory of presupposition are for the most part relations between linguistic items, or between a linguistic expression and a proposition.

They are, as I interpret them, facts about the constraints, of one kind or another, imposed by what is said on what is appropriately presupposed by the speaker, according to various different standards of appropriateness. But I think all the facts can be stated and explained directly in terms of the underlying notion of speaker presupposition, and without introducing an intermediate notion of presupposition as a relation holding between sentences (or statements) and propositions.

This last point is a strategic recommendation, and not a substantive claim. As I said, one *could* define such a notion in various ways; I just doubt the theoretical utility of doing so. My purely strategic motive for emphasizing this point is that I want to avoid what I think would be a fruitless debate over which of various explications of the notion of pragmatic sentence presupposition best accords with the use of the term "presupposition" by linguists. I do not want to deny that, in an adequate theory of conversation, one will need a notion or notions of conversational acceptability, and that once one has such a notion one has all the material for a definition of pragmatic sentence presupposition. A rough definition of "conversational acceptability" might be something like this: a speech act is conversationally acceptable in the relevant sense just in case it can reasonably be expected to accomplish its purpose in the normal way in which the normal purposes of such speech acts are accomplished. But such a notion would get its content from an account of the mechanisms by which the normal purposes of speech acts are accomplished, and the notion of speaker presupposition is intended to be one theoretical concept useful for giving such an account. It is in this way that it is a more basic concept than the concept of conversational acceptability.

Second, let me suggest one way that the definition given above needs to be qualified. In normal, straightforward serious conversational contexts where the overriding purpose of the conversation is to exchange information, or conduct a rational argument, what is presupposed by the speaker, in the sense intended, is relatively unproblematic. The presuppositions coincide with the shared beliefs, or the presumed common knowledge. The difficulties in applying the notion come with contexts in which other interests besides communication are being served by the conversation. If one is talking for some other purpose than to exchange information, or if one must be polite, discreet, diplomatic, kind, or entertaining as well as informative, then one may have reason to act as if the common background were different than one in fact knows it to be. For example, when I talk to my barber, neither of us expects to learn anything; we are talking just to be civil, and to pass the time. If we haven't much to say, we may act as if the background of common knowledge is smaller than it really is. "Cold today, isn't it?" "Sure is, windy too." "Well, spring will be here before long." Although there is little actual communication going on here, it is clear that what is going on is to be understood in terms of genuine communication. We are pretending to communicate, and our pretense can be explained in terms of the same categories as a serious exchange of information.

In other cases, a speaker may act as if certain propositions are part of the common background when he knows that they are not. He may want to communicate a proposition indirectly, and do this by presupposing it in such a way that the auditor will be able to infer that it is presupposed. In such a case, a speaker tells his auditor something in part by pretending that his auditor already knows it. The pretense need not be an attempt at deception. It might be tacitly recognized by everyone concerned that this is what is going on, and recognized that everyone else recognizes it. In some cases, it is just that it would be indiscreet, or insulting, or tedious, or unnecessarily blunt, or rhetorically less effective to openly assert a proposition that one wants to communicate.[2]

Where a conversation involves this kind of pretense, the speaker's presuppositions, in the sense of the term I shall use, will not fit the definition sketched above. That is why the definition is only an approximation. I shall say that one actually does make the presuppositions that one seems to make even when one is only pretending to have the beliefs that one normally has when one makes presuppositions. Presupposing is thus not a mental attitude like believing, but is rather a linguistic disposition—a disposition to behave in one's use of language as if one had certain beliefs, or were making certain assumptions.[3]

---

[2] This is a special case of what Grice has called *exploitation*, since the speaker exploits the rules governing normal conversation in order to communicate something which is not explicitly said. See H. P. Grice, "Logic and Conversation," unpublished.

[3] It was suggested by Jerry Sadock (personal communication) that the definition should be modified in another way to account for examples of the following kind: I am asked by someone who I have just met, "Are you going to lunch?" I reply, "No, I've got to pick up my sister." Here I seem to *presuppose* that I have a sister even though I do not assume that the speaker knows this. Yet the statement is clearly acceptable, and it does not seem right to explain this in terms of pretense, or exploitation. To meet this problem, Sadock suggests replacing the clause in the definition, "speaker assumes or believes that the addressee assumes or believes that *P*" with the clause, "speaker assumes or believes that the addressee *has no reason to doubt* that *P*."

The reason I resist this suggestion, even though I recognize the force of the example, is that some basic generalizations about speaker presuppositions would fail if it were adopted. For example, one important generalization, alluded to above, is that it is unnecessary, in fact inappropriate, to assert what is presupposed. But consider a

The presumed background information—the set of presuppositions which in part define a linguistic context—naturally imposes
constraints on what can reasonably or appropriately be said in that
context. Where the constraints relate to a particular kind of grammatical construction, or to a particular expression or category of
expressions, one has a linguistic fact to be explained. This is the case
with the sample sentences with which I began. One of the facts could
be stated like this: it is inappropriate to say "The Queen of England is
bald" (or to say "the Queen of England is not bald") except in a
context in which it is part of the presumed background information
that England has a queen. Compare this with a description that interprets the phenomena in terms of a semantic concept of presupposition: the proposition expressed by "the Queen of England is bald"
has a truth-value only if England has a unique queen. The first description, in contrast to the second, makes no claim at all about the
content of the statement—about the truth-conditions of what is said.
The description in terms of the pragmatic notion does not rule out a
semantic *explanation* for the fact that a certain presupposition is
required when a certain statement is made, but neither does it demand such an explanation. That is, one *might* explain why it is appropriate for a speaker to say "the Queen of England is bald" only if
he presupposes that England has a queen in terms of the following
two assumptions: first, that the statement lacks a truth-value unless

---

routine lecture or briefing by an acknowledged expert. It may be that everything he
says is something that the audience has no reason to doubt, but this does not make it
inappropriate for him to speak. The problem is that the modification would work only
for cases where the addressee could infer what was being presupposed from the overt
speech act. But this is not the only case where speaker presuppositions are important.

Two alternative responses to the example are possible: (a) one can explain it in
terms of exploitation; (b) one can deny that there is a presupposition made at all in this
kind of example.

To respond in the first way is, I admit, to stretch the notion of exploitation, first
because the example lacks the flavor of innuendo or diplomatic indirection which
characterizes the clearest cases of communication by pretense, and second because in
the best cases of exploitation, it is the main point of the speech act to communicate
what is only implied, whereas in this example, the indirectly communicated material is
at best only a minor piece of required background information. Nevertheless, the
explanation of how communication takes place in this example may be thought to be
similar in form to explanations of how it takes place in the more familiar cases: the
addressee infers that the speaker accepts that $Q$ from the fact that he says that $P$
because normally one says that $P$ only when it is common background knowledge that
$Q$.

To take the second option is to deny the generalization that the speaker *always*
presupposes the existence of a unique referent (in the relevant domain of discourse)
fitting any definite description (like "my sister") which he uses. To make this plausible,
one would have to give an explanation of why one is *usually* expected to presuppose
the existence of a unique referent when one uses a definite description—an explanation which also explains the exceptions to the rule.

England has a queen, and second, that one normally presupposes that one's statements have a truth-value. But one also might explain the fact in a different way. The *facts* about presuppositions, I am suggesting, can be separated from a particular kind of semantic explanation of those facts. This separation of the account of presupposition from the account of the content of what is said will allow for more diversity among presupposition phenomena than would be possible if they all had to be forced into the semantic mold. Let me suggest, more specifically, four of the advantages of making this move.

First, if presupposition is defined independently of truth-conditions, then it is possible for the constraints on presuppositions to vary from context to context, or with changes in stress or shifts in word order, without those changes requiring variation in the semantic interpretation of what is said. This should make possible a simpler semantic theory; at the very least, it should allow for more flexibility in the construction of semantic theories. For example, D. T. Langendoen points out in a paper on presupposition and assertion that normally, if one said "my cousin isn't a boy anymore" he would be asserting that his cousin had grown up, presupposing that he is male. But one might, in a less common context, use the same sentence to assert that one's cousin had changed sexes, presupposing that she is young.[1] If a semantic account of presupposition is given of this case, then one must say that the sentence is therefore ambiguous. On the pragmatic account, one just points to two different kinds of situations in which a univocal sentence could be used.

Second, if presupposition is defined independently of truth-conditions, then one can separate the question of entailment relations from the question of presupposition. On the semantic account, presupposition and entailment are parallel and incompatible semantic relations. $A$ presupposes that $B$ if and only if $B$ is necessitated by *both* $A$ and its denial. $A$ entails $B$ if and only if $B$ is necessitated by $A$ but *not* by its denial. Thus the claim that the sentence, "Sam realizes that $P$" *entails* that $P$ conflicts with the claim that that sentence presupposes, in the semantic sense, that $P$. But using the pragmatic account, one may say that sometimes when a presupposition is required by the making of a statement, what is presupposed is also entailed, and sometimes it is not. One can say that "Sam realizes that $P$" entails that $P$—the claim is false unless $P$ is true. "Sam does not realize that

[1] D. Terence Langendoen, "Presupposition and Assertion in the Semantic Analysis of Nouns and Verbs in English," in *Semantics: An Interdisciplinary Reader in Philosophy, Linguistics and Psychology*, ed. by Danny D. Steinberg and Leon A. Jakobovits (Cambridge, England: Cambridge University Press, 1971).

$P$," however, does not entail that $P$. That proposition may be true even when $P$ is false. All this is compatible with the claim that one is required to presuppose that $P$ whenever one asserts or denies that Sam realizes it.

Third, the constraints imposed by a statement on what is presupposed seem to be a matter of degree, and this is hard to explain on the semantic account. Sometimes no sense at all can be made of a statement unless one assumes that the speaker is making a certain presupposition. In other cases, it is mildly suggested by a speech act that the speaker is taking a certain assumption for granted, but the suggestion is easily defeated by countervailing evidence. If a speaker says to me, "Sam was surprised that Nixon lost the election," then I have no choice but to assume that he takes it for granted that Nixon lost. But if he says, "If Eagleton hadn't been dropped from the Democratic ticket, Nixon would have won the election" (without an "even" before the "if" or a "still" after the "Nixon"), there is a suggestion that the speaker presupposes that Nixon in fact did not win, but if the statement is made in the right context, or with the right intonation, the suggestion is overruled. This difference in degree, and variation with context is to be expected on the pragmatic account, since it is a matter of the strength of an inductive inference from the fact that a statement was made to the existence of a background assumption or belief.

Fourth, and perhaps most important, the pragmatic analysis of presupposition, because it relates the phenomena to the general communication situation, may make it possible to explain some of the facts in terms of general assumptions about rational strategy in situations where people exchange information or conduct argument. One way to explain the fact that a particular assertion requires or suggests a certain presupposition is to hypothesize that it is simply a fact about some word or construction used in making the assertion. In such a case, the fact about the presupposition requirement must be written into the dictionary, or into the semantics. But since we have an account of the *function* of presuppositions in conversations, we may sometimes be able to explain facts about them without such hypotheses. The propositions that $P$ and that $Q$ may be related to each other, and to common beliefs and intentions, in such a way that it is hard to think of a reason that anyone would raise the question whether $P$, or care about its answer, unless he already believed that $Q$. More generally, it might be that one can make sense of a conversation as a sequence of rational actions only on the assumption that the speaker and his audience share certain presuppositions. If this kind of explanation can be given for the fact that a certain statement tends to require a certain presupposition, then there will be no need to complicate the semantics or the lexicon.

For example, consider the word "know." It is clear that "$x$ knows that $P$" entails that $P$. It is also clear that in most cases when anyone asserts or denies that $x$ knows that $P$, he presupposes that $P$. Can this latter fact be explained without building it into the semantics of the word? I think it can. Suppose a speaker were to assert that $x$ knows that $P$ in a context where the truth of $P$ is in doubt or dispute. He would be saying in one breath something that could be challenged in two different ways. He would be leaving unclear whether his main point was to make a claim about the truth of $P$, or to make a claim about the epistemic situation of $x$ (the knower), and thus leaving unclear what direction he intended or expected the conversation to take. Thus, given what "$x$ knows that $P$" means, and given that people normally want to communicate in an orderly way, and normally have some purpose in mind, it would be unreasonable to assert that $x$ knows that $P$ in such a context. One could communicate more efficiently by saying something else. For similar reasons, it would normally be inappropriate to say that $x$ does not know that $P$ in a context where the truth of $P$ was in question. If the speaker's reason for believing his assertion were that he thought that $P$ was false, or that he thought that $x$ didn't believe that $P$, or didn't have reason to believe that $P$, then his statement would be gratuitously weak. And it would be unusual for a speaker to be in a position to know that one of these situations obtained, without knowing which.

This is a tentative and incomplete sketch of an explanation. Much more would have to be said to make it convincing. My point is to make it plausible that, in some cases at least, such explanations might be given, and to argue that where they can be given, there is no reason to build specific rules about presuppositions into the semantics.

I want now to illustrate these advantages of the pragmatic account by looking at some linguistic facts in terms of it. The two sets of facts I will consider are taken from two recent papers by Lauri Karttunen.[5]

First, on a distinction between two kinds of factive verbs. It is well known that among verbs which take a nominalized sentence complement (for example *believe, know, intend, see*) one can distinguish a subclass known as factive verbs (*know, regret, discover, see*, as contrasted with *believe, intend, assert, claim*). A number of syntactic

---

[5] Lauri Karttunen, "Some Observations on Factivity" and "Presuppositions of Compound Sentences," *Linguistic Inquiry*, IV (1973).

and semantic criteria are used to draw the distinction, but the distinguishing mark that is relevant here is the following: if $V$ is a factive verb, then $x$ $V$'s *that P* presupposes (and, I would say, entails as well) that $P$. If I assert or deny that Jones regrets, realizes, or discovers that Nixon won the election, then I presuppose that Nixon did in fact win. Karttunen has drawn a further distinction among two kinds of factive verbs which, he argues, requires a distinction between two kinds of presupposition relations. One kind of factive verb (labeled the *full factives*) includes *regret, forget* and *resent*. The basis for the distinction is as follows: with full factives, it is not only an assertion or denial of the proposition $x$ $V$'s *that P* that requires the presupposition that $P$, but also the *supposition* that $x$ $V$'s *that P* in the antecedent of a conditional, or the claim that the proposition *might* be true. With semi-factives, it is only the assertion or denial that require the presupposition. For example, consider the two statements

*Sam may regret that he voted for Nixon.*

*If Sam regrets that he voted for Nixon, then he is a fool.*

Because these two statements clearly require the presupposition that Sam voted for Nixon, *regret* is seen to be a full factive.

The following is Karttunen's example to illustrate the contrast between full factives and semi-factives. Compare

$$\textit{If I} \left\{ \begin{array}{l} \textit{regret} \\ \textit{realize} \\ \textit{discover} \end{array} \right\} \textit{later that I have not told the truth,}$$
*I will confess it to everyone.*

In the first statement, the speaker clearly presupposes that he has not told the truth. In the other two cases, he clearly does not presuppose this. Thus *realize* and *discover* are seen to be semi-factives.

To explain the difference, Karttunen postulates a distinction between a strong and a weak kind of semantic presupposition. If $P$ is necessitated by *Possibly Q*, and by *Possibly not-Q*, then $Q$ strongly presupposes that $P$. Weak semantic presuppositions are defined in the usual way.

In discussing this example, I want to dispute both the data, and the theoretical account of them. I agree that there is a sharp contrast in the particular example given, but the matter is less clear if one looks at other examples. Consider:

*If Harry discovers that his wife is playing around, he will be upset.*

*If Harry had discovered that his wife was playing around, he*
  *would have been upset.*
*If Harry had realized that his wife was playing around, he would*
  *have been upset.*
*Harry may realize that his wife has been playing around.*
*Harry may never discover that his wife has been playing around.*

There is, I think, in all these cases a presumption that the speaker presupposes that Harry's wife is, or has been, playing around. The presumption is stronger in some of the examples than in others, but it seems to me that in some of them it is as strong as with *regret*. Further, if we assume that with the so-called semi-factives like *discover* and *realize*, there is *always* a presumption that the speaker presupposes the truth of the proposition expressed in the complement, we can still explain why the presumption is defeated in Karttunen's particular example. The explanation goes like this: if a speaker explicitly supposes something, he thereby indicates that he is not *pre*supposing it, or taking it for granted. So when the speaker says "if I realize later that *P*," he indicates that he is not presupposing that he will realize later that *P*. But if it is an open question for a speaker whether or not he will at some future time have come to realize that *P*, he can't be assuming that he already knows that *P*. And if he is not assuming that he himself knows that *P*, he can't be assuming that *P*. Hence *P* cannot be presupposed. A roughly parallel explanation will work for *discover*, but not for *regret*.

One can explain another of Karttunen's examples in a similar way. Consider the three questions:

$$Did\ you \begin{cases} regret \\ realize \\ discover \end{cases} that\ you\ had\ not\ told\ the\ truth?$$

Here *realize* seems to go with *regret* and not with *discover*. The first two questions seem to require that the speaker presuppose that the auditor did not tell the truth, while the third does not. Again, we can explain the difference, even while assuming that there is a presumption that the presupposition is made in all three cases. The reason that the presumption is defeated in the third case is that the speaker could not make that presupposition without assuming an affirmative answer to the question he is asking. But in general, by asking a question, one indicates that one is not presupposing a particular answer to it. This explanation depends on the particular semantic properties of *discover*, and will not work for *realize* or *regret*.[6] It also depends on the fact that the subject of the verb is the second-person pronoun. Hence if the explanation is right, one would expect the presupposition to reappear in the analogous third-person question, "Did Sam discover that he hadn't told the truth?" It seems that it does.

Since on the pragmatic account, the constraints on presuppositions can vary without the truth-conditions changing, we can allow presupposition differences between first- or second-person statements and questions and the corresponding third-person statements and questions without postulating separate semantic accounts of propositions expressed from different points of view. So, while we have noted differences in the presuppositions required or suggested by the following two statements,

> If Harry discovers that his wife has been playing around, he will be upset.
> If I discover that my wife has been playing around, I will be upset (said by Harry).

This difference does not prevent us from saying that the two statements both have the same semantic content—that the same proposition is expressed in both cases. It would not be possible to say this on a semantic account of presupposition.

If the explanations I have sketched are on the right track, then we can account for at least some of the differences between factive and semi-factive verbs without distinguishing between two different kinds of presupposition relations. We can also account for some differences among semi-factives, and differences between first- and third-person statements without complicating the semantics. The explanation depends on just two things: first, some simple and very general facts about the relation between pragmatic presuppositions

---

[6] The relevant difference between *realize* and *discover* is this: because *realize* is a stative verb, a past tense statement of the form *x didn't realize that P* must be about some particular time in the past (determined by the context), and not about *all* times in the past. This means that *x didn't realize that P* may be true, even though *x now* knows that *P*. Therefore, a speaker may assume that his addressee knows or assumes that *P* without prejudging the question whether or not he realized (at the relevant past time) that *P*. In contrast, because *discover* is an inchoative verb, *x didn't discover that P* may be about *all* times in the past. For this reason, normally, *x didn't discover that P* implies that x has not *yet* discovered that *P*, and so does not now know that *P*. Therefore, if a speaker presupposes that *P*, he assumes that *x has* discovered that *P*, and so assumes a particular answer to the question he is asking.

and assertions, questions, and suppositions; second, on the ordinary semantic properties of the particular verbs involved.[7]

The second set of facts that I will discuss concerns the presuppositions of compound sentences: How do the presuppositions required by a conditional or conjunctive statement relate to the presuppositions that would be required by the component parts, stated alone? In general, what is the relation between the presuppositions required by an assertion that $A$ and the assertion that $B$ on the one hand, and by an assertion that $A$ *and* $B$ or that *if* $A$, *then* $B$ on the other? Karttunen defends the following answer to the question: let $S$ be a sentence of the form $A$ *and* $B$ or *If* $A$, *then* $B$. $S$ presupposes that $C$ if and only if either $A$ presupposes that $C$, *or* $B$ presupposes that $C$ and $A$ does not semantically entail that $C$. In other words, the presuppositions of a conjunction are the presuppositions required by either of the conjuncts, *minus any required by the second conjunct which are entailed by the first.* The presuppositions of a conditional are the presuppositions of either antecedent or consequent minus those required by the consequent and entailed by the antecedent. So if I say "Harry is married, and Harry's wife is a great cook," I assert, and do not presuppose, that Harry is married. But the second conjunct, stated alone (*Harry's wife is a great cook*), would require the presupposition that Harry is married. The sentence with conjuncts in reverse order would be unacceptable in any normal context (*Harry's wife is a great cook, and Harry is married*).

Now if we regard Karttunen's generalization as a generalization about *semantic* presuppositions, then we will interpret it as a hypothesis about the way the truth-value (or lack of it) of a conjunction or conditional relates to the truth-values of the parts. The hypothesis has the consequence that the conjunction *and* is not truth-functional, since the truth-value of a conjunctive statement will in some cases depend on entailment relation between the conjuncts. It has the consequence that *and* is not symmetric. $A$ *and* $B$ may be false

---

[7] Two disclaimers: First, I do not want to leave the impression that I think I have explained very much here. I have not made any attempt to explain the source of the presumption that the complements of both factive and semi-factive verbs are presupposed. I have tried to explain only how the presumption is canceled in certain cases. Also, the presumption is clearly harder to defeat in some cases than in others: harder with *realize* than with *discover*, and harder with full factives than with semi-factives. I have said nothing that would explain this. My hope, however, is that such explanations can be given using the general strategy which I am recommending. Second, I do not want to deny that there are systematic differences between factives and semi-factives. One difference is that full factives all require not only the presupposition that the proposition expressed in the complement is true, but also the presupposition that the subject of the verb knows or knew that it is. None of the semi-factives require or suggest this second presupposition; in fact, they rule it out.

while *B and A* lacks a truth-value. Finally, it has the consequence that the simple conjunction *and* is governed by mysteriously complicated rules.

On the other hand, if we regard Karttunen's generalization as a generalization about *pragmatic* presuppositions, then we can reconcile it with the standard truth-functional account of *and*, and we can explain the generalization without postulating any *ad hoc* semantic or pragmatic rules. The explanation goes like this: first, once a proposition has been asserted in a conversation, then (unless or until it is challenged) the speaker can reasonably take it for granted for the rest of the conversation. In particular, when a speaker says something of the form *A and B*, he may take it for granted that *A* (or at least that his audience recognizes that *he* accepts that *A*) after he has said it. The proposition that *A* will be added to the background of common assumptions before the speaker asserts that *B*. Now suppose that *B* expresses a proposition that would, for some reason, be inappropriate to assert except in a context where *A*, or something entailed by *A*, is presupposed. Even if *A* is *not* presupposed initially, one may still assert *A and B* since by the time one gets to saying that *B*, the context has shifted, and it is by then presupposed that *A*.[8]

As with the explanation sketched in the earlier discussion, this explanation rests on just two things: first, a simple pragmatic assumption about the way presuppositions shift in the course of a conversation—an assumption that says, roughly, that a speaker may build on what has already been said; second, an uncontroversial assumption about the semantic properties of the word *and*—in particular, that when one asserts a conjunction, he asserts both conjuncts. If we interpret presupposition to mean *pragmatic* presupposition, then we can deduce Karttunen's generalization from these two almost trivial assumptions.

The analogous generalization about conditional statements is explainable on equally simple assumptions. Here we need first the assumption that what is explicitly *supposed* becomes (temporarily) a part of the background of common assumptions in subsequent conversation, and second that an *if* clause is an explicit supposition. Again, Karttunen's generalization can be derived from these obvious assumptions.

I have been arguing in this paper for the fruitfulness of separating semantic from pragmatic features of linguistic expressions and situations, and of explaining a certain range of phenomena in terms

---

[8] In a paper given at the Texas conference on performatives, conversational implicatives, and presuppositions, Karttunen put forward an explanation of his generalization which is very similar to this. Our accounts were developed independently.

of pragmatic rather than semantic principles. This goes against the trend of the work of generative semanticists such as George Lakoff and John Ross, who have emphasized the difficulty of separating syntactic, semantic, and pragmatic problems, and who have sometimes suggested that such distinctions as between syntactic and semantic deviance or semantic and pragmatic regularities are of more use for avoiding problems than for solving them. Partly to respond to this concern, I will conclude with some general remarks about the distinction between semantics and pragmatics, and about what I am *not* recommending when I suggest that the distinction be taken seriously.

First remark: semantics, as contrasted with pragmatics, can mean either the study of *meaning* or the study of *content*. The contrast between semantic and pragmatic claims can be either of two things, depending on which notion of semantics one has in mind. First, it can be a contrast between claims about the particular conventional meaning of some word or phrase on the one hand, and claims about the general structure or strategy of conversation on the other. Grice's distinction between conventional implicatures and conversational implicatures is an instance of this contrast. Second, it can be a contrast between claims about the truth-conditions or *content* of what is said—the proposition expressed—on the one hand, and claims about the *context* in which a statement is made—the attitudes and interests of speaker and audience—on the other. It is the second contrast that I am using when I argue for a pragmatic rather than a semantic account of presuppositions. That is, my claim is that constraints on presuppositions are constraints on the contexts in which statements can be made, and not constraints on the truth-conditions of propositions expressed in making the statements. I also made use of the other contrast in arguing for this claim. I conjectured that one can explain many presupposition constraints in terms of general conversational rules without building anything about presuppositions into the meanings of particular words or constructions. But I make no general claim here. In some cases, one may just have to write presupposition constraints into the dictionary entry for a particular word. This would make certain presupposition requirements a matter of *meaning*, but it would not thereby make them a matter of *content*. There may be facts about the meaning of a word which play no role at all in determining the truth-conditions of propositions expressed using the word.

Second remark: in recommending a separation of content and context I am not suggesting that there is no interaction between them. Far from it. The semantic rules which determine the content of a sentence may do so only relative to the context in which it is uttered. This is obviously the case with sentences using personal pronouns, demonstratives, quantifiers, definite descriptions, or proper names. I suspect it happens in less obvious cases as well. But this interaction does not prevent us from studying the features which define a linguistic context (such as a set of pragmatic presuppositions) in abstraction from the propositions expressed in such contexts, or from studying the relationships among propositions in abstraction from the contexts in which they might be expressed.

A final remark: in some cases, distinctions such as that between semantic and pragmatic features may be used as a way to set problems aside. Some linguists have accused other linguists of using the distinction between syntax and semantics in this way. Deviant sentences which seem to conflict with syntactic generalizations are not treated as counterexamples, but instead are thrown into a "semantic wastebasket" to be explained away by some future semantic theory. In the same way, some may be suspicious that I am setting up a pragmatic wastebasket, and recommending that all the interesting problems be thrown away.

I do not think that this is always a bad procedure, but it is not what I am suggesting here. I am recommending instead the development and application of a pragmatic theory in which detailed explanations of phenomena relating to linguistic contexts can be given. It is true that traditionally the more well-developed and the more rigorous linguistic theories have focused on questions of grammar and content, while the discussions which emphasized the role of conversational context have been more informal and less theoretical. But there is no necessity in this. Potentially at least, a theory of pragmatics, and the notion of pragmatic presupposition can be as precise as any of the concepts in syntax and semantics. Although the explanations I have sketched in this paper are informal and incomplete, I think they suggest a strategy for giving explanations of linguistic phenomena relating to contexts which are both rigorous and intuitively natural.[9]

---

[9] I have been accused, partly on the basis of this concluding paragraph, of being overly optimistic about the possibility of a formal theory of pragmatics which is both rigorous and sufficiently detailed to provide substantive explanations of linguistic phenomena. This accusation may be just, but my main point here is independent of this. However easy or difficult it proves to be to develop an adequate theory of conversation, one cannot simplify the task by building conversational rules into a semantic theory of the content of what is said.

# The Refutation of Conventionalism

## HILARY PUTNAM

### Harvard University

I shall discuss conventionalism in Quine's writings on the topic of radical translation, and in the writings of Reichenbach and Grünbaum on the nature of geometry.

Let me say at the outset that Quine and Reichenbach are the two philosophers who have had the greatest influence on my own philosophical work. If Quine's ideas have not had the full influence they deserve, it may be in part because of the intensely paradoxical nature of the doctrines put forward—or seemingly put forward—in *Word and Object*. The doctrines of *Word and Object*—in particular the indeterminacy of radical translation—look wrong to many philosophers. Since these doctrines are thought by Quine himself to follow from the doctrines put forward in "Two Dogmas of Empiricism," they cast doubt on "Two Dogmas" itself. My contention here will be that the impossibility of uniquely correct radical translation does not follow from the critique of the analytic-synthetic distinction. I believe that Quine is right in his critique of the analytic-synthetic distinction, but wrong in his argument for the impossibility of unique radical translation. By showing that one does not have to accept Quine's arguments for the impossibility of unique radical translation, I hope, therefore, to clarify just what it is in Quine's work that is true and important.

Similarly, I think that Reichenbach understood the importance of non-Euclidean geometry for epistemology as it has not been understood by philosophers in general to the present day. I think that he understood the issues surrounding the verifiability theory of meaning

215

in his book *Experience and Prediction* far more deeply than they have been generally understood, and I think his writings on the philosophical foundations of induction clarify the nature of the problems in an unparalleled way, even if Reichenbach's particular solutions cannot be accepted. In Reichenbach's case too, it is a peculiar kind of conventionalism that seems to flow from his work that has led philosophers to downgrade him or even to dismiss him as just a "positivist." Again, I think this conventionalism need not, in fact, follow from Reichenbach's work, and does not follow from the best of his work, and that separating the wheat from the chaff in Reichenbach's work may enable his work too to achieve the philosophical influence that it so richly deserves.

One last preliminary remark: in one respect the situation is more complicated with respect to the views of both of these men than the preceding remarks would indicate. With respect to Quine, the situation is so confused that one perhaps should distinguish between *two* Quines—$Quine_1$ and $Quine_2$. $Quine_1$ is the Quine who everybody thinks wrote *Word and Object*. That is to say, the Quine whose supposed proof of the impossibility of radical translation, of the impossibility of there being a unique correct translation between radically different and unrelated languages is discussed in journal article after journal article and is the topic of at least 50 percent of graduate student conversation nowadays. $Quine_2$ is the far more subtle and guarded Quine who defended his formulations in *Word and Object* recently at the Conference on Philosophy of Language at Storrs, Connecticut. In the light of what Quine said at Storrs, I am inclined to think that *Word and Object* may have been widely misinterpreted. At any rate, Quine seems to think that *Word and Object* has been widely misinterpreted, although he was charitable enough to take some of the blame himself for his own formulations. In what follows, then, I shall be criticizing the views of $Quine_1$, even if $Quine_1$ is a cultural figment, not to be identified with the Willard Van Orman Quine who teaches philosophy at Harvard. It is the views of $Quine_1$ that are generally attributed to Willard Van Orman Quine, and it is worthwhile showing what is wrong with those views. If I can have the help of $Quine_2$—of Willard Van Orman Quine himself—in refuting the views of $Quine_1$, then so much the better.

There is a similar problem with respect to the work of Reichenbach. The arguments for the conventionality of geometry that are widely attributed to Reichenbach do not, in fact, appear in the writings of Reichenbach. They appear rather in the writings of Adolf Grünbaum. The conclusions that Reichenbach himself draws from his analysis of the status of geometry in the last pages of *Philosophy of*

*Space and Time* are not only different from Grünbaum's, they are quite incompatible with Grünbaum's. Thus, here too we have to distinguish between two Reichenbachs: Reichenbach$_1$, alias Adolf Grünbaum, and Reichenbach$_2$, alias Hans Reichenbach. In what follows, it will be the views of Reichenbach$_1$, that is, Adolf Grünbaum, that I shall be concerned to refute. At the end of this essay I will say something about the views of both Quine$_2$ and Reichenbach$_2$.

## THE STRATEGY OF THIS PAPER

The strategy of this paper is to try and show that a single argument underlies the work of both Grünbaum and Quine$_1$. That this is even something that could be true is not evident on the surface. At first blush, Grünbaum's writings on the Philosophy of Space and Time, like those of Hans Reichenbach, appear to be full of extremely substantive and topic-specific considerations. The arguments seem to depend on facts about space. Similarly, Quine's writings on radical translation are imbedded in the context of linguistic theory, or at least in the context of philosophical discussion of linguistic theory. There is a great deal of talk about linguistic questions, such as the nature of grammaticality, the nature of language, psychology of language learning, and so on. All of these considerations appear to be topic-specific to linguistics and philosophy of language. But topic-specificity can be an illusion. One of the accomplishments of the axiomatic method in mathematics has been to bring out a sense in which the same proof may occur in what look like totally different areas of mathematics. Once we see the structure of a mathematical argument, we may often see that the conclusion depended on very little that was specific to one mathematical domain as opposed to another. I am going to argue here that there is a general *conventionalist ploy* which appears in many different areas of philosophy, and that the conclusions of Quine and Grünbaum do not in fact depend on any specific facts about space or about geometry, but are simply instances of this same conventionalist ploy. I shall also argue that the ploy is fallacious and that the conclusions to which it leads should be viewed as suspect in every area of philosophy.

## REICHENBACH AND GRÜNBAUM ON SPACE AND TIME

Reichenbach used to begin his lectures on the Philosophy of Space and Time in a way which already brought an air of paradox to the subject. He would take two objects of markedly different size, say an ash tray and a table, situated in different parts of the room, and ask the students, "How do you know that one is bigger than the other?"

The students would propose various ways of establishing this, and Reichenbach would criticize each of these proposed tests. For example, a student might suggest that one could simply *measure* the ash tray and *measure* the table and thus verify that the ash tray is smaller than the table. Then, Reichenbach would ask the student, "How do we know that the measuring rod stays the same length when transported?" Or, someone might say that we can simply *see* that the table is larger than the ash tray, but then Reichenbach would point out that sight is reliable only if light travels in straight lines. Perhaps light travels in curved paths in such a way that the table, although the same size as the ash tray, or even smaller than the ash tray, does not look smaller than the ash tray. Or, someone might propose, again, to bring the ash tray over to the table. When we set the ash tray down on the table, we see that the ash tray is clearly smaller than the table. This assumes the stipulation that if one object coincides with a proper part of another, then the first object is smaller than the second.

Granting this as a definition, or partial definition, of 'smaller than' in the case of objects which are together, that is, actually touching in an appropriate way, then we have only established that the ash tray is smaller than the table when the ash tray is actually touching the table. How do we know that the ash tray is smaller than the table when the ash tray and the table are separated?

The question reduces to the question, "How do we know that the ash tray doesn't change size when transported?" which is just the question we had about the measuring rod. It might be objected that when I move the measuring rod or the ash tray around the room—say, I carry them around the room in my hand—I do not feel the ash tray or the measuring rod get larger or smaller. But perhaps my hand gets larger or smaller, and that is why I don't feel a difference!

One might try to rule out this whole line of questioning on some *a priori* philosophical ground or other; for example, "the series of questions has to come to an end." But it is necessary to be careful here. The series of questions Reichenbach is asking is formally just the same as the series of questions that Einstein asked about "How do we ever know that two events at a distance happen simultaneously?" It cannot be in principle illegitimate to ask such questions or even to push them back and back as Einstein and Reichenbach did. And the Einstein example shows that this kind of epistemological questioning can have great value, at least in exposing hidden presuppositions of everyday discourse, and perhaps, as Einstein and Reichenbach thought, in exposing definitional elements in what we mistakenly take to be purely factual statements as well. Reichenbach's conclusion, from his own line of questioning, was that the statement that the measuring rod stays the same length when transported cannot be *proved* without vicious circularity. And he proposed that this statement or some such statement must be regarded as a *definitional element* in geometrical theory. We naïvely think that it is a matter of fact that watches run at the same rate when transported and that measuring rods stay the same length when transported. Neither statement can be maintained to be true without qualification in a relativistic world, as Einstein showed; and in a Newtonian world, or in a world in which all objects are transported at the same rate relative to some fixed inertial system, the two sets of statements can be maintained to be true only in the sense of being adopted as a definition, according to Reichenbach and according to Einstein, at least on Reichenbach's reading of Einstein.

At this point, let me leave the views of Reichenbach$_2$—that is, Reichenbach, and move to the views of Reichenbach$_1$—that is, Grünbaum. The conclusion that Grünbaum draws from the situation just described is the following:

There are certain axioms that any concept of distance, that is to say any *metric*, has to satisfy. For example, *for any point* x *in the space, the distance from* x *to* x *is zero; for any points* x *and* y *in the space, the distance from* x *to* y *equals the distance from* y *to* x; *for any three points in the space* x, y, z, *the distance from* x *to* y *plus the distance from* y *to* z *is greater than or equal to the distance from* x *to* z; *distance is always a nonnegative number; the distance from* x *to* y *is zero if and only if* x *is identical with* y. But any continuous space that can be metricized at all, that is, over which it is possible to define a concept of distance satisfying these and similar axioms, can be metricized in infinitely many different ways.

Now, let $S$ be a space which is homeomorphic to Euclidean space, and let $M_1$ and $M_2$ be metrics such that $S$ is Euclidean relative to $M_1$ and $S$ is Lobachevskian relative to $M_2$. Grünbaum's conclusion, based largely although not exclusively on Reichenbach's discussion, is that there is no fact of the matter as to whether $S$ is Euclidean or Lobachevskian or neither. The choice of a metric is a matter of convention. The space $S$ cannot "intrinsically" have metric $M_1$ rather than $M_2$, or $M_2$ rather than $M_1$. If we adopt a convention according to which $M_1$ is the metric for the space $S$, then the statement "$S$ is Lobachevskian" will be true.

Let me emphasize that Grunbaum is *not* saying that any two metrics will lead to equally simple physical laws, or that any two metrics are such that it would be *feasible* to use either one in everyday determinations of distance. It is possible that the world be such that if we use the metric $M_1$, then the laws of nature would assume, let us say, a Newtonian form. If we then went over to a metric $M_2$, according to which the space is Lobachevskian, the laws of nature would become incredibly complicated. It is even likely that everyday questions about distance—for example, "What is the distance from my house to my car?"—could not be feasibly answered if we went over to the metric $M_2$. Nevertheless, Grunbaum insists, this does not show that the metric $M_2$ is somehow not the true metric of the space $S$, or that in some sense the metric $M_1$ *is* the true metric of the space $S$.

Secondly, it should be emphasized that Grunbaum is not just talking about space in the sense of ordinary three-dimensional space. Although most of his examples are drawn from this case, he means his remarks to apply just as well to the question of the metricization of space-time. In a relativistic world, there is indeed a sense in which the choice of the metric for just three-dimensional space is relative. But the choice of a metric for space-time—that is, the choice of a $g_{ik}$ tensor—is not ordinarily regarded as a matter of convention. But Grünbaum has emphasized that on his view this is a matter of convention just as the choice of a metric for space in a Newtonian world is, on his view, a matter of convention.

Since the gravitational field is identified with the $g_{ik}$ tensor by Einstein, it follows that there is, on Grünbaum's view, no fact of the matter as to which is the correct equation for the gravitational field. The choice of a nonstandard $g_{ik}$ tensor would lead to an immensely complicated form for the law of gravitation. Very likely, space-time distances could not practically be computed using such a tensor, that is, it would be totally unfeasible to use it in practice. Nevertheless, on Grünbaum's view, there would be no sense in which our space-time objectively did not have such a nonstandard $g_{ik}$ tensor, and there is no sense in which our space-time objectively does have the standard $g_{ik}$ tensor.[1]

[1] My criticism of Grünbaum's views are presented at length in reference [2]. Grünbaum's replies to these criticisms in [1], Chapter III. I have not previously replied to Grünbaum's rejoinder, because I felt that, although it clears up some misunderstandings (e.g., the status, on Grünbaum's view, of the law $F = ma$), it does not answer the main criticisms made in [2]. But, for the purposes of the present paper, let me consider Grünbaum's treatment of the question of the conventionality of the space-time metric in the GTR (General Theory of Relativity), as he replies to me in [1]. This is a clear consequence of Grünbaum's view: *any* continuous space can be metricized in more than one way, and for *any* continuous space, the choice of a metric is a matter of convention (according to Grünbaum). Since the 4-space of general relativity is a continuous space, the conventionality of *its* metric is an immediate consequence of his thesis. Moreover, this consequence is explicitly drawn by Grünbaum himself: "what does impress me, in concert with Riemann and Clifford, is that *after* the term 'congruent' is already preempted to mean extensional equality, there is nothing in the nature of the continuous physical manifolds which would requires us to *ascribe con-*

## Radical Translation

Chapter 2 of Quine's *Word and Object* contains what may well be the most fascinating and the most discussed philosophical argument since Kant's Transcendental Deduction of the Categories. On one page, Quine—evidently Quine₁—writes: "There can be no doubt that rival systems of analytical hypotheses can fit the totality of dispositions to speech behavior as well, and still specify mutually incompatible translations of countless sentences insusceptible of independent control." But a bit of explanation is in order.

Quine is talking here about the following context. A linguist is trying to translate an alien language into his home language. The two languages are supposed not to be cognate. Also the two linguistic communities are supposed to have a minimum of shared culture. In particular, there is no standard translation from the alien language into the home language. The alien language is often thought of by Quine as a primitive language, a "jungle" language, which is being translated for the first time. A translation manual is called by Quine an analytical hypothesis. Constructing a translation manual in such a context is undertaking the enterprise Quine calls *radical translation*.

*gruence*, i.e., *spatial* or *spatiotemporal equality*, to certain disjoint intervals as opposed to others." ([1], p. 226.) I argued in [2] that this consequence is unacceptable, for reasons similar to those given in the present paper.

Grünbaum's reply was to reiterate that the choice of a metric is a matter of convention ("descriptive simplicity"), while accusing me of saddling him with the view that it is not *simpler* to use the standard $g_{ik}$ tensor: "Nothing in this [Grünbaum's conception] precludes the use of the criterion of *descriptive simplicity* and *convenience* to employ a particular kind of metrization, and thereby to select a unique class of classes of congruent intervals to the exclusion of others in certain theoretical contexts." ([2], p. 219, italics mine.) Yet on p. 209 Grünbaum had written: "It is now plain that nothing about my claim that the insight contained in Riemann's doctrine has substantial relevance to the GTR requires that there be alternative *space-time* congruences *in addition to* the undeniably present alternative time congruences and alternative space congruences. And, as will become clear in the sequel, Riemann's conception accommodates the GTR's unique space-time congruences as well as the alternative congruences of time and space." In fact, what "becomes clear in the sequel" is that "Riemann's insight" *does* require that there be "alternative space-time congruences", but that one choice of a metric may be "descriptively simpler." Thus, on p. 217 Grünbaum states explicitly: "If the term 'transport' is suitably generalized so as to pertain as well to the extrinsic metric standards applied to intervals of time and of space-time respectively, then this claim of conventionality holds not only for time but also *mutatis mutandi* for the *space-time continuum* of *punctual events*!" (Emphasis in the original.)

Grunbaum also charges that I do not know the fact that in the GTR (and even the Special Theory of Relativity) one frequently uses coordinate time rather than proper time. The basis for this charge is the following paragraph in [2]:

"... we are *not* free in general relativity to employ any metric tensor other than $g_{ik}$. It is possible to choose the reference system arbitrarily and still arrive at the same

Quine's procedure will be only very sketchily reviewed here. What Quine does is to assume that we can somehow identify *assent* and *dissent* in an alien language. Modulo this assumption, he argues that we can at least riskily identify *truth functions* in an alien language. We can distinguish *occasion sentences*, sentences such as "This is a chair" to which some stimulations prompt assent, and other stimulations prompt dissent, and distinguish them from *standing sentences*—sentences such as "Australia is in the Southern Hemisphere". Standing sentences have the property that speakers, once they have been prompted to assent to them or dissent from them, continue to assent to them or dissent from them without further immediate stimulation from the environment.

Quine's central theoretical notion in this chapter is the notion of *stimulus meaning*. The stimulus meaning of a sentence is identified by Quine with the set of stimulations of a native speaker's nerve endings which would *prompt assent* to the sentence in question. Two

---

covariant laws of nature in general relativity *only* because we are *not* allowed to "choose" a space-time metric. Grünbaum obscures this situation by asserting that in general relativity we sometimes *do* employ non-standard "definitions of congruence"; he further asserts that our freedom to do this is a consequence of the alleged "insight" that we discussed above. This seems puzzling in view of the fact that all observers employ the same $g_{ik}$ tensor in general relativity, until one realizes how Grünbaum employs his terms. What he is pointing out is the fact that the customary rule of correspondence (employing a clock at rest in the reference system to determine local time) is not valid under exceptional circumstances (on a rotating disk). But correspondence rules always break down under some exceptional circumstances. Thus no special insight is needed to allow for the fact that the $g_{ik}$ tensor of the theory is to be preserved over the readings of a clock situated on a rotating disk! In sum: our alleged "freedom" to *choose a different $g_{ik}$ tensor* (a different space-time metric) *at the cost of complicating the laws of nature is in fact never employed in the general theory of relativity.* All observers are required to "choose" the *same* space-time metric [p. 242].

There was a careless slip here: I should have written "no special insight is needed to account for the fact that the customary coordinate time (based on the center of the rotating disk) is preserved over the readings of a clock situated on the rotating disk". Otherwise the paragraph is correct. In the Special Theory of Relativity, time normally refers to "t component of space-time distance, where t is the contextually definite time axis." (This analysis is given explicitly, for spatial rather than temporal distance, in my [3].) Far from denying that "time is used in the sense of "coordinate time" (or "distance" in the sense of "coordinate distance") this *emphasizes* this fact. That alternative *time* metrics are used follows from this theory of the reference of "time". But this fact that time (as opposed to space-time) is *relational* in this way; does not follow from the mere *continuity* of time. In the STR it is a theorem that the readings of an ideal clock at rest in the rest system agree with *coordinate* time (not "proper time", unless Grünbaum means the clock's *own* proper time, which is a tautology). This is what I called a "correspondence rule" (assuming that coordinates are chosen so that the velocity of light is constant in the rest system). In the GTR this still holds whenever special relativistic approximations are good enough. But, in the case of the clock on the rotating disk, it is not convenient to choose coordinates so that this theorem holds. So what?

stimulations would prompt assent to each of the two sentences. A sentence is *stimulus analytic* for a speaker if he assents to it under all possible conditions of stimulation, *stimulus contradictory* if he dissents from it under all possible conditions of stimulation.

Our previous definition of the occasion sentence may be restated in terms of the notion of stimulus meaning. Thus: a sentence is an occasion sentence if a speaker assents to it or dissents from it just in case a stimulation in its stimulus meaning (respectively, the stimulus meaning of its negation) is presented within a certain time interval, the modulus of stimulation. Quine ingeniously proposes to define the *observation sentences* as those sentences which are (1) occasion sentences and (2) possess *intersubjective stimulus meaning*. In other words, *a sentence is an observation sentence just in case it is an occasion sentence, and it has the same stimulus meaning for every speaker of the linguistic community.*

We may now say just what an *analytical hypothesis* is in a more technical way. An analytical hypothesis is a general recursive function whose domain is the set of all sentences of the alien language and whose range is a subset, possibly a proper subset, of the set of all sentences of the home language, and which has the following properties: 1) If $a$ is an observation sentence of the alien language, then $f(a)$ is an observation sentence of the home language, and $f(a)$ has the same stimulus meaning for speakers of the home language as $a$ does for speakers of the alien language. 2) $f$ commutes with truth functions, that is to say, $f(a \lor b)$ equals $f(a) \lor f(b)$, etc. 3) if $a$ is a stimulus

---

In summary: Grünbaum (1) accuses me of believing that "time" always means "proper time", and (2) replies to the charge I *didn't* make, that it isn't *simpler* to use the standard $g_{ik}$ tensor (space-time metric). The whole point is that Grünbaum's use of the term "descriptive simplicity" *begs* precisely the philosophical question at issue: I am attacking *precisely* this use of the distinction between "descriptive simplicity" (no "fact of the matter") and "inductive simplicity" (where there is a "fact of the matter"). [Grünbaum misses just this point when he writes "here Putnam has a quite mistaken idea of what Schlick, Reichenbach, and I mean by saying that two descriptions differ only in 'descriptive simplicity' as contrasted with differing in factual content (or in inductive simplicity): when saying that the difference between the descriptions associated with various alternative metrizations of the Newtonian time continuum is one of mere descriptive simplicity, we are surely *not* saying that there are no facts to be described, for the very concept of descriptive simplicity presupposes that there *are* facts to be described more or less simply." Passing over the suggestion, that "Putnam" thought descriptive simplicity meant "no facts to be described"—poor soul!—we reply that the "very concept" of descriptive simplicity presupposes that there is *no fact of the matter* as to *which* of the alternative descriptions is true—assuming at least one is—and that this is the claim under attack.] Grünbaum says only one thing that replies to my criticism—that there is no basis, apart from the conventionalist ploy discussed in this paper, for describing certain choices as mere matters of "descriptive simplicity". He says that a continuous space has no "intrinsic" or "built in" metric. But this is no help.

analytic (respectively, stimulus contradictory) sentence of the alien language, then $f(a)$ is a stimulus analytic (respectively, stimulus contradictory) sentence of the home language. If the linguist is bilingual, then condition 1) can be strengthened to condition 1'): if $a$ is an occasion sentence of the alien language, then $f(a)$ is an occasion sentence of the home language, and the stimulus meaning of $a$ for the linguist is the same as the stimulus meaning of $f(a)$ for the linguist. These are, in my paraphrase, Quine's conditions 1)-4), 1')-4) of Chapter 2.

The thrust of Chapter 2 is as follows: first Quine says in the sentence quoted above that it is possible to have "rival" analytical hypotheses which "fit the totality of speech behavior to perfection" and which "still specify mutually incompatible translations of countless sentences insusceptible of independent control." Now let $f_1$ and $f_2$ be two such rival analytical hypotheses. Then Quine's view is that there is no "fact of the matter" as to whether the translations provided by $f_1$ are the correct translations from the alien language into the home language, or whether the translations provided by $f_2$ are the correct translations from the alien language into the home language. There is no such thing as correct translation in any absolute sense. The notion of correct translation has to be relativized to an analytical hypothesis. The translations provided by $f_1$ are the correct translation relative to $f_1$, tautologically. And similarly the translations provided by $f_2$ are the correct translations relative to $f_2$, tautologically. Although Quine does not put it that way, he might have summed this up, or at any rate Quine$_1$ might well have summed this up by saying that *the choice of an analytical hypothesis is a matter of convention.*

## THE CONVENTIONALIST PLOY

What is the common structure to the argument of Grunbaum and the argument of Quine$_1$? Each argument falls into the following normal form: a set of conditions is given which (partly) specifies the extension of a notion. In the case of geometry, these conditions are the axioms which must be satisfied by a metric. In the case of radical translation, these conditions are Quine's conditions 1)-4) or 1')-4) plus the condition that the function $f$, that is the translation manual, be general recursive. Secondly, a claim is made that the conditions given *exhaust* the content of the notion being analyzed. Grunbaum emphasizes again and again [2] that any notion of distance that satisfies the

---

[2] E.g., Grünbaum writes, [1], pp. 248-249: "Putnam is insensitive to the fact that whereas the meaning of 'congruent' has been changed with respect to the *extension* of the term [when we go over to a different metric—H.P.], its meaning has not changed at

axioms for a metric is equally entitled to be termed *distance*, and equally entitled in a particular case to be termed the distance from an object $x$ or point $x$ to an object or point $y$.

In *Word and Object*, it is *not* claimed that conditions 1)-4) "cover all available evidence". For as Quine remarks, the linguist can go bilingual and thus avail himself of 1')-4) instead of 1)-4) as constraints on an analytical hypothesis. But 1')-4) are supposed (by Quine₁, anyway) to exhaust all the possible evidence for an analytical hypothesis. This seems to be implicit in the statement on page 71, "Even our bilingual, when he brings off translations not allowed for under 1')-3), must do so essentially by the method of analytical hypotheses, however unconscious." It looks implicit again on page 72 when Quine₁ writes, "and yet countless native sentences, admitting no independent check, not falling under 1')-3), may be expected to receive radically unlike and incompatible English renderings under the two systems." (Note the identification of "admitting no independent check" and "not falling under 1')-3)." And the claim that 1')-4) [or 1')-3), since 4) has been dropped as superfluous] are all the "independent checks" there are, seems to be made implicitly once more on page 74 when Quine, in the process of listing causes of "failure to appreciate the point," writes: "A fifth cause is that linguists adhere to implicit supplementary canons that help to limit their choice of analytical hypotheses. For example, if a question were to arise of equating a short locution to 'rabbit' and a long one to 'rabbit part' or vice versa, they would favor the former course, arguing that the more conspicuously segregated wholes are likelier to bear the simple terms. Such an implicit canon is all very well, *unless mistaken for a substantive law of speech behavior*" (our italics).

Once a set of constraints has been postulated as determining the content of the notion in question—the notion of *distance* or of *metric*, in the case of geometry; the notion of *analytical hypothesis*, or more colloquially *translation*, in the case of linguistics—a proof is given that the constraints in question do not determine the extension of the

---

all with respect to designating a spatial equality relation! ... According to [the classical] account, the intension of a term determines its extension uniquely. But the fact that "being spatially congruent" means sustaining the relation of spatial equality does not suffice at all to determine its extension uniquely in the class of spatial intervals. In the face of the classical account, this nonuniqueness prompted me to refrain from saying that the relation of spatial equality is the "intension" of "spatially congruent"; by the same token, I refrained from saying that the latter term has the same intension in the context of a nonstandard metric as when used with a standard metric. But since the use of "spatially congruent" in conjunction with *any one* of the metrics $ds^2 = g_{ik}\,dx^i dx^k$ does mean sustaining the spatial equality relation, I shall refer to this fact by saying that "congruent" has the same "nonclassical intension" in any of these uses."

notion in question. There can be two or more different metrics which assign different distances to the same intervals, and which satisfy the axioms for a metric; there can be rival analytical hypotheses which specify incompatible translations and which conform to 1')-3) or 1')-4).

As a final step, the claim is advanced that whenever there are incompatible objects that satisfy the constraints given, then there is no fact of the matter as to which of the objects is the correct one. There is no fact of the matter as to which of the two metrics is the correct one provided they both agree with the topology of the space in question; there is no fact of the matter as to which of the two analytical hypotheses is the correct one as long as they both conform to 1')-3) or 1')-4).

*The structure of the argument shows what is wrong with the argument,* I think. *Conventionalism is at bottom a form of essentialism.* It is not usually identified as essentialism because it is a favorite of reductionist philosophers, and we think of reductionist philosophers as anti-essentialists, and anti-reductionist philosophers as essentialists. Nevertheless, it *is* a form of essentialism, even if it is not one with which Plato or Aristotle would have been happy.

What the conventionalist does is to claim that certain constraints *exhaust the meaning* of the notion he is analyzing. He claims to intuit not just that the constraints in question—the axioms for a metric or Quine's conditions 1')-3) or 1')-4)—are *part* of the meaning of the notion of a metric or of the notion of an analytical hypothesis, but that *any further condition* that one might suggest *would definitely not be part of the meaning* of the notion in question, and also *would not be a "substantive law"* about the notion in question (since a "substantive law" would presuppose that the extension of the notion in question had somehow been fixed, and the conventionalist intuits that there is nothing to fix it beyond the conditions that he lists). Once we recognize that this is the structure of the conventionalist argument, we can also detect it in many other areas of philosophy.

Consider *emotivism* in ethics, by way of example. The emotivist claims that ethical sentences typically have some emotive force. He intuits that a certain standard emotive force is part of the meaning of ethical sentences. It is part of the meaning of "That was a good thing you did" when uttered in a moral context that the speaker feels approval, or that the speaker is performing an act of "Commending" or something of that kind. Notice, however, that even if this is right, typical emotivist conclusions—for example, that ethical sentences lack truth value—do not follow from this. Emotivism derives its punch from a further claim—the claim that the emotive force of ethical sentences *exhausts their content*. The emotivist claims to intuit not only that ethical sentences have a certain emotive meaning, but that any descriptive component that might be proposed is *not* part of their meaning.

This is hardly an empirical claim. It may well be that actions satisfying certain descriptions—for example, *torturing small children just for the fun of it*—are universally despised and condemned. *Even so*, the emotivist insists that it would be a *mistake* to regard it as part of the meaning of an ethical sentence to the effect that a certain action is good or permissible or not wrong, that it does not satisfy one or those descriptions. It would be a mistake because not satisfying those descriptions is *simply not part of the content* of the ethical sentences in question, even if the factual claim that *the act commended does not satisfy any one of those descriptions* is universally understood to be conversationally implicated by the ethical sentence. No descriptive component is or could be part of the meaning of an ethical sentence. Also, an ethical sentence could not, just as a matter of fact, have a descriptive truth condition. For to say that it has certain truth conditions, as a fact and not as a matter of its meaning, would presuppose that its extension has somehow been fixed, and there is nothing to fix the extension of an ethical term other than its meaning, and its emotive meaning exhausts its meaning.

We see now why conventionalism is not usually recognized as essentialism. It is not usually recognized as essentialism because it is *negative* essentialism. Essentialism is usually criticized because the essentialist *intuits too much*. He claims to see that *too many* properties are part of a concept. The negative essentialist, the conventionalist, intuits not that a great many strong properties are part of a concept, but that only a few *could be* part of a concept. But he still makes an essentialist claim.

## The Refutation of Conventionalism

Once we understand the structure of the conventionalist argument, we also perceive the difficulty in which the conventionalist lands himself. In one respect, it is a triviality that language is conventional. It is a triviality that we might have meant something other than we do by the noises that we use. The noise 'pot' could have meant what is in fact meant by the word 'dog', and the word 'dog' could have meant what is in fact meant by the word 'fish'.

Let us call this kind of conventionality TSC (Trivial Semantic Conventionality). Grunbaum emphasizes that he does not intend the thesis of the conventionality of the choice of a metric to be an instance of TSC. The thesis that there is no fact of the matter as to whether *distance* is *distance as defined by the metric* $M_1$ *or distance as defined by the metric* $M_2$, is not to be interpreted as meaning that the word 'distance' might have been assigned to a different magnitude, as, for example, 'pressure' might have been assigned to *temperature*, and 'temperature' might have been assigned to *pressure*. The thesis is rather that, even *given* what we mean by 'distance', there is no fact of the matter as to which is the true distance. And certainly Quine$_1$ does not think he is telling us that 'translation' might have meant, for example, *postage stamp*. The question is just this: *Can* the conventionalist successfully defend the thesis that the choice of a metric or the choice of a translation manual is a matter of convention, and *not* have his thesis be either false or truistic, that is, be either false or an instance of TSC? In my opinion he cannot. The conventionalist fails precisely because of an insight of Quine's. That is the insight that *meaning*, in the sense of reference, is a function of theory,[3] and that

---

[3] This insight must not be confused with Feyerabend's position, that a term cannot have the same reference in substantially different theories ("incommensurability"). Thus, let $T_1$ and $T_2$ be two theories containing the word "eau". $T_1$ and $T_2$ may be *very* different theories; yet the best translation of "eau" into *our* language may well be "water" in both cases. If we accept the statement that water is $H_2O$, then we will say that

  "eau" in $T_1$ refers to $H_2O$

and also that

  "eau" in $T_2$ refers to $H_2O$

even if this contradicts $T_1$ or $T_2$. Theory *helps* to determine translation; but translation does not have to make *all* of a theory come out *true*. Thus change of theory does not always imply change of extension. (I agree with Quine that to ask when a change in theory is a change in *intension* is a bad question.)

Moreover, in translating a term, we may take into account not just the theory of the speaker, but the theory of other speakers to whom the speaker is causally linked. Thus, this kind of "theory dependence" of reference is not incompatible with the sort of causal theory of reference for magnitude terms suggested in [4].

Coming to the geometry case: suppose Oscar accepts just the atomic statements about "distance" that we accept about $f(x, y, z, t, x', y', z', t')$, where $x, y, z, t$ and $x', y', z'$, $t'$ are the coordinates of the points, and $f$ satisfies the axioms for a metric. Suppose also, that Oscar accepts $f = ma$, that he postulates strange forces acting on measuring rods in order to preserve the statement that "distance = $f(x, y, z, t, x', y', z', t')$", etc. Finally, suppose that Oscar is "bilingual" relative to us, and he *tells* us that when he says "distance" he means distance, that his theory is *right* and ours is *wrong*, etc. In this case we will decide that Charity begins at home, and choose homophonic translation. We will say that Oscar's word "distance" refers to distance in *our* sense, and that Oscar's theory is just false.

If asked, "How do you know it's false?" (given that Oscar's theory doesn't imply any false predictions), we will point to the fact that Oscar's theory assumes *improbably* complicated mechanisms. In short, speaking from the perspective of *our* theory, we the enterprise of trying to list the statements containing a term which are true by virtue of its meaning, let alone to give a list of statements which *exhausts* its meaning, is a futile one. If Quine is right in this, and I think he is, then there is no reason, given the problem that Reichenbach so brilliantly sets before us, why we have to opt for a conventionalist solution. Reichenbach convincingly shows that reference is not, so to speak, an act of God. We cannot suppose that the term 'distance' intrinsically refers to one physical magnitude rather than another. But its reference need not be fixed by a convention. It can be fixed by *coherence*.

Let us try to formulate total science in such a way as to maximize internal and external coherence. By *internal coherence* I mean such matters as simplicity, and agreement with intuition. By *external coherence*, I mean agreement with experimental checks. Grunbaum certainly has not *proved* that there are two such formulations of total science leading to two different metrics for physical space-time. And $Quine_1$ certainly has not *proved* that there are two distinct analytical hypotheses both in agreement with a maximally simple and intuitive psychology, linguistic theory, and so on.

Thus, consider the following case: Suppose metric $M_1$ is one which leads to a Newtonian physics for the entire world. Suppose that metric $M_2$ leads to a physics according to which all objects are contracting toward the center of a certain sphere at a uniform rate. This contraction is undetectable because, according to the physics based on the

---

will say that Oscar is wrong and our theory is *truer*, not just *descriptively simpler*—i.e., there is a "fact of the matter", and simplicity is here one indicator of *truth*.

On the other hand, if Oscar himself regards the difference between us as "semantic", if he doesn't postulate any strange forces—if he just talks as we would if our present language were changed in the one respect that "distance" *meant* "$f(x,y,z,t,x-',y',z',t')$"—then we will obey the principle of Charity, and translate Oscar's word "distance" as "$f(x,y,z,t,x',y',z',t')$". In this case, we will say that the difference between Oscar's theory and ours is one of descriptive simplicity. (It is also an instance of Trivial Semantic Conventionality.)

Quine's position (i.e., $Quine_2$'s position) is that there is no sharp line between case 1 and case 2. Relative to one analytical hypothesis, ("*distance*" *means* "$f(x,y,z,t,x-',y',z',t')$") the choice between Oscar's theory and our theory in the second case is a matter of descriptive simplicity; relative to another analytical hypothesis ("*distance*" *means* "*distance*") the choice is one between falsity and truth. But there *may not be* any grounds for choosing between these analytical hypotheses—no "fact of the matter as to whether or not there is a fact of the matter". $Quine_1$'s position, on the other hand, is that there are *always* these two possibilities, and hence there is *never* a fact of the matter as to whether a choice is one of descriptive simplicity or falsity versus truth (or falsity versus *different* falsity). Grünbaum's position is that the choice is *always* one of descriptive simplicity. My position is that sometimes one analytical hypothesis is correct, and the choice is one of descriptive simplicity; sometimes the other is correct, and the choice is one of truth versus falsity (or of factual content versus different factual content, to put it more precisely); and sometimes the choice is arbitrary.

metric $M_2$, measuring rods themselves are contracting at the same rate. The universal contraction affects all measuring rods in the same way. A measuring rod made of Jell-O is deformed by the *universal force* that we postulate to account for the contraction to exactly the same extent as a measuring rod made of steel, not withstanding its much lower resistance to deformation. The laws of the physics based on the metric $M_2$ are infinitely more complicated than the laws of the physics based upon the metric $M_1$. The fundamental principles of the physics based on the metric $M_2$—the existence of universal forces, and the universal contraction toward the center of the sphere—are totally counterintuitive; and distances according to the metric $M_2$ cannot be computed in practice and are totally unusable in practice.

According to Grunbaum, there is no fact of the matter as to which is the true geometry plus physics—the conjunction of the metric $M_1$ with the physics based upon the metric $M_1$, or the conjunction of the metric $M_2$ with the physics based upon $M_2$. If, however, coherence can determine *reference*, then why should we not say that in a world one of whose admissible descriptions is the metric $M_1$ and the physics based upon the metric $M_1$, the distance according to the metric $M_1$ is what we *mean* by distance, that is, that it is to *this* magnitude that we are referring when we use the word 'distance'? [4]

If we take this line, then we will say that forces, according to the physics corresponding to the metric $M_1$, are what we mean by 'force'—that is, that it is to these that we are referring when we use the word 'force'. We will also say that there are no universal forces causing our measuring rods to contract in an undetectable way and that it is simply not the case that all the objects in the world are contracting toward the center of a sphere.

---

[4] Suppose, for example, we modify the example in n. 3 by 1 letting Oscar's theory be methodologically preferable to ours, rather than methodologically inferior. Then, instead of translating "distance" by "$f(x,y,z,t,x',y',z',t')$", we would do better to use homophonic translation, and, in addition, to *adopt Oscar's theory*. (In this case we will say that (1) the magnitude Oscar calls "distance" is the one we did and do call "distance"; and (2) Oscar has *discovered* the fundamental physical law that distance = $f(x,y,z,t,x',y',z',t')$, and our theory was in some respects mistaken. On this account, the *reference* of "distance" has not changed; only our *beliefs* about it have changed.

Grunbaum's position in [1], p. 367 is that even if it were the case that the reference of "distance" is fixed by what we described in [2] as constraints on the form of physical theory as a whole (and not by a stipulation that the length of the measuring rod be constant after the correction for the action of differential forces)—even if, in our present terminology, the reference is fixed by external and internal coherence—the choice of those constraints (standards of coherence) as the determinant of the con-gruences in the space is itself conventional. The choice of a metric would *still* be *conventional* even if there is no one specifiable sentence that expresses the *convention*. Conventionality follows, according to Grünbaum, from the fact that the metric is not "built in" to the space.

The point that we could use the metric $M_2$ and the physics corresponding to the metric $M_2$ will then be an instance of TSC. It is not that there are universal forces, or even that there is no fact of the matter as to whether or not there are universal forces. It is simply that by 'force' we could have meant something else—something of no conceivable interest, in fact—and that by 'distance' we could have meant something else, and that there is a certain correlation between the, let us call it 'shmorce', and the, let us call it, 'shmistance', between the end points of a body. That there is a correlation between the *shmorce* acting on a body and the *shmistance* between its end points is not a very interesting fact. It is only by relabeling 'shmorce' *force* and relabeling 'shmistance' *distance* that we can make it *appear* to be an interesting fact. When we use the word 'distance', we are customarily referring to distance, that is, to a certain physical magnitude, even if it is not fixed by any *convention* which physical magnitude it is that we are referring to.

This case may be contrasted to the relativistic case. In the relativistic case, there are a number of different definitions of distance which lead to equally simple laws of nature. Thus, in the relativistic case there really is a relativity of the *spatial* metric, and the choice of any one of the admissible spatial metrics may be described, somewhat unhappily in our opinion, as a matter of "convention." But, as far as we know, the choice of any nonstandard *space-time* metric would lead to infinite complications in the form of the laws of nature, and to an unusable concept of space-time distance. Thus, as far as we know, the metric of space-time is not relative to anything. There is no interesting sense in which we can speak of a conventional "choice" of a metric for space-time in a general or special relativistic universe.

## RADICAL TRANSLATION

I wish now to discuss Quine's position as it would be developed in detail by Quine$_1$ in strict analogy to Grunbaum's development of Reichenbach's position. I should emphasize that the position I shall develop for Quine$_1$ in this section is not a position which the actual Quine—Quine$_2$—in fact accepts. Nevertheless, I think it will have value to develop and criticize it.

Although Quine is especially interested in radical translation, the considerations in *Word and Object* are meant to apply also to translation between familiar languages, and even to English-English translation. It is just that the nature of the problem and of the solution is supposed to be clearer in the case of radical translation. I shall, therefore, in this section develop two translation manuals for the English-English case. The first is just homophonic translations, that is, the identity function. The second translation is more complicated. Let us pick two standing sentences which are neither stimulus analytic nor stimulus contradictory, say, "The distance from the earth tó the sun is 93 million miles", and "There are no rivers on Mars". We define the function $f$ as follows:

1. $f($"The distance from the earth to the sun is 93 million miles"$)$ = "There are no rivers on Mars".
2. $f($"There are no rivers on Mars"$)$ = "The distance from the earth to the sun is 93 million miles".
3. If $S$ is any nontruth functional sentence (i.e., any sentence which has no *immediate* truth functional constituents except itself), then $f(S) = S$.
4. $f$ commutes with truth functions.

It is clear from this definition that $f$ is a general recursive function. Moreover, $f$ is the identity on every occasion sentence. Also, $f$ preserves stimulus analyticity, and $f$ commutes with truth functions. Thus, $f$ satisfies Quine's conditions 1')-4). According to Quine$_1$, there is, therefore, no fact of the matter as to whether the correct translation of the sentence "The distance from the earth to the sun is 93 million miles" is the one given by the identity function, that is, "The distance from the earth to the sun is 93 million miles", or the correct translation is the one given by $f$, that is, "There are no rivers on Mars".

Imagine now that a speaker reasons out loud as follows: "The distance from the earth to the sun is 93 million miles; light travels 186,000 miles a second; that is the reason it takes 8 minutes for light from the sun to reach the earth."

If we accept the analytical hypothesis, $f$, then we have to interpret this speaker as reasoning as follows: "There are no rivers on Mars; the speed of light is 186,000 miles per second; that is the reason it takes 8 minutes for light from the sun to reach the earth." If we take the speaker, call him Oscar, to be speaking sincerely, then we have to attribute to him a very strange psychology. Since he does not say anything which we can translate as *explaining a reason for thinking* that there is a connection between the nonexistence of rivers on Mars, and the fact that it takes 8 minutes for light from the sun to reach the earth, we have to suppose that Oscar *just believes* that there is a connection between the nonexistence of rivers on Mars and the one-way trip time for light traveling from the sun to the earth, and that no explanation can be given of how Oscar *comes to believe this*, and no *route* can be provided *to this belief* which would make it plausible to us that a human being in our own culture could have such a belief. Quine₁, of course, maintains that just as there is no fact of the matter as to whether Oscar means *the distance from the sun to the earth is 93 million miles*, or means *there are no rivers on Mars*, so there is likewise no fact of the matter as to whether standard psychological theory or the highly nonstandard psychological theory which attributes such a strange and unexplained inferential connection to Oscar is correct. The underdetermination of translation by conditions 1')-4) becomes an *underdetermination of psychology, sociology, anthropology, and so on, by all conceivable empirical data.*

It is instructive to try to meet Quine₁'s arguments in various ways and to see why the counterarguments fail, or at least why they fail to convince Quine₁. Thus, suppose we argue as follows. It is a striking fact that any two human cultures can intercommunicate. In Quine's terminology, what this fact comes to is that it has proved possible, even in the case of the most different languages and cultures, to construct an analytical hypothesis which is actually usable, and on the basis of which actual communication can and does take place. This is, of course, an empirical fact. It is logically possible that we should someday find a "jungle" language such that any analytical hypothesis at all that met Quine's 1')-4) would be so hideously complex as to be unlearnable, or would involve attributing to the "jungle" speakers inferential connections as weird as those that *f* requires us to attribute to Oscar, or both. One plausible explanation of the universal intercommunicability of all human cultures is that there are at least *some* facts about human psychology which are universal, that is, independent of culture. It is not that people in another culture cannot have crazy beliefs—there are plenty of people in our own culture who have what any one of us would count as crazy beliefs. It is rather that in all or at least a great number of cases, when one person has what another would count as a crazy belief, it turns out to be possible to specify a *route* to that belief, a way in which the person got to that belief, which renders it at least partly intelligible to the other, that a human being might come to such a belief. If this assumption is true as a substantive statistical law, then the fact that accepting the analytical hypothesis *f* requires us to assume that Oscar violates this law, whereas accepting the homophonic analytical hypothesis does not, would count as *evidence* in favor of homophonic translation.

Quine₁ would not be convinced by this argument because he would say that there is simply no fact of the matter as to whether the analytical hypotheses that we customarily accept are correct and the

proposed psychological generalization is correct, or whether noncus-
tomary analytical hypotheses are correct and the proposed psychological generalization is false.

Another argument we might try is the following. Suppose that
future psychology and neurophysiology disclose that there are brain
processes and brain units of both physiological and functional significance, such that, if we accept one system of analytical hypotheses
relating the various languages, then there turn out to be deep
similarities between the linguistic processing that goes on in the case
of speakers of different languages at the brain level; whereas if we
adopt nonstandard analytical hypotheses, then we cannot even correlate the various linguistic processes of *producing sentences, understanding sentences, parsing sentences, making inferences in explicit
linguistic form,* with anything that goes on in terms of these or any
other natural brain processes and units. Would this not be evidence
for the correctness of the standard system of analytical hypotheses
relating the various languages? Once again, Quine₁ would answer,
"No, there is simply no fact of the matter as to whether the supposed
psychological laws are correct or not, be they stated in mentalese or
Turing machine-ese."

It will be seen that the position of our hypothetical Quine₁ is
exactly parallel to Grunbaum's and that the same objection applies to
it. If the adoption of one system of analytical hypotheses rather than
another permits a great simplification of such sciences as neurophysiology, psychology, anthropology, and so on, then why should we not
say that what we mean by 'translation' is *translation according to the
manuals that have this property*? Why should we not maintain that to
say of Oscar that when he says "The sun is 93 million miles from the
earth", he means "There are no rivers on Mars", is simply to change
the meaning of 'means' in an uninteresting way? This objection is
even stronger against Quine₁ than against Grunbaum. For, it should
be remembered, it is generally believed that Quine₁ is the Quine who
wrote "Two Dogmas of Empiricism." Since "Two Dogmas of
Empiricism" explicitly rejects the analytic-synthetic distinction, and
Quine has from "Truth by Convention" on expressed skepticism about
the notion of a convention, then he should feel highly uncomfortable
at being caught in what is after all an essentialist maneuver. His
position, after all, does not differ much, if at all, from saying that
1')-4) are *meaning postulates* for the notion of "translation", and that
they are all the meaning postulates that there are for the notion of
"translation". One would think that the Quine who wrote "Two Dogmas of Empiricism" would feel much more comfortable with what we
have called a coherence account of reference than with the idea that

reference is fixed (or left undetermined) by a finite set of meaning postulates.

## REICHENBACH ON GEOMETRY

It may shed some light on these problems to review Reichenbach's own solution to the problem that he posed in *Philosophy of Space and Time*. Reichenbach saw that the term 'distance' corresponds to a magnitude. He also saw that it is the task of philosophy to say something about the nature of this correspondence. If a word corresponds to one thing rather than another, then it must be something human beings do or specify that controls this. It is the task of philosophy, in Reichenbach's view, to say just what it is that we do or specify that controls the reference of such terms as 'distance'.

There is a superficial similarity to the thought of the later Wittgenstein here. Wittgenstein, too, saw that meaning is a function of human practice. Indeed, he saw this far more completely than any philosopher before him. But the similarity is only superficial. For Wittgenstein, when he came to see the extent to which meaning is a function of human practice, somehow also came to the conclusion—the erroneous conclusion, in my opinion—that talk about human practice obviated talk of correspondence or reference altogether. Reichenbach's perspective is the more correct one. There is a correspondence between words and things or words and magnitudes, and it is a function of human practice. A central task of philosophy is to spell out the nature of this function.

It is interesting that Reichenbach presents his solution to the problem in the form of a series of successive approximations. The first approximation—the, so to speak, first-order approximation to a solution—is to say that we specify a metric implicitly by specifying that a rigid measuring rod is to stay the same length when transported. That is to say, the length of the measuring rod is to *count as* the same even when the measuring rod is in different places. But to *literally* make a *particular* measuring rod the standard of congruence would involve insuperable difficulties. Reichenbach illustrates these difficulties charmingly by means of the following example: Suppose we were to create a standard of time congruence by specifying that the interval between the king's successive heartbeats is to *count as* the same. Then the laws of nature would assume a very strange form. For example, it would become a law of nature that whenever the king runs upstairs, then all natural processes slow down! It is therefore necessary to allow for what Reichenbach calls the *interposition of theories*. We specify, not that the measuring rod remains the same length when transported, but that the *theoretically corrected length of the meas-uring rod* is to remain the same.

At first blush, this involves us in a dangerous circularity. Correcting the length of the measuring rod for the action upon it of various forces requires a theory. The theory required is one that has the notion of 'distance', or some similar notion, as a primitive. But 'distance' is to acquire a 'meaning', that is, a specified reference, by way of the very coordinating definition that we are in the process of setting up. Thus it seems as if the constraint—that the length of the measuring rod, after correction for the action upon it of all the various forces postulated by a correct physical theory, should remain the same on transportation—is so weak as to leave *distance* still wholly indeterminate.

Reichenbach solves this problem by saying that what we have to do is impose *further* constraints upon the *form* of physical theory. The constraint that he chooses is the constraint that universal forces vanish, that is, that there be no forces with the properties that (1) the total deformation they produce upon any body is the same, independently of the internal resistance to deformation of the body; (2) the forces are permanently associated with regions of space; (3) the forces have no sources and no shields—they cannot be turned off or modified by moving their sources away or by putting shields around the objects affected.

In a later work, Reichenbach explains the same line of thinking in the following way. Choose any metric compatible with the topology of space-time. Then a true physics based upon that metric is a system of physical laws which correctly predicts the *trajectories* of all the particles when the trajectories are described in terms of that metric. If $M$ is a metric, and $P$ is a system of physics such that in some possible world $P$ is the true system of physics based upon the metric $M$, then we call $M + P$ an admissible "geometry plus physics". Now, let $M + P$ be any admissible geometry plus physics, and let $M'$ be any metric which can be obtained from $M$ by a homeomorphic mapping. Let $P'$ be a system of physics based upon $M'$ with the property that the two systems $M + P$ and $M' + P'$ lead to exactly the same predictions—not just the same predictions with respect to *observation sentences*, but the same predictions with respect to *possible trajectories*. That is to say that if we take the trajectories predicted by $M + P$ and "translate" them into the language of the metric $M'$, then those trajectories are exactly the trajectories predicted by $M' + P'$. In this case, Reichenbach speaks of the two systems of geometry plus physics, the systems $M + P$ and $M' + P'$, as *equivalent descriptions*. The set of all $M' + P'$ equivalent to a given $M + P$ is called the *equivalence class* of $M + P$. If an equivalence class has a member which satisfies the constraint described above, the constraint that universal forces vanish, then that member is called the *normal* member of the equivalence class. Reichenbach's position was that there is *one and only one true equivalence class* of geometries plus physicses—that is, there is one and only one equivalence class such that the pairs $M + P$ in that equivalence class give correct predictions with respect to the possible trajectories of bodies in our world. If someone proposes an $M + P$ which belongs to any other equivalence class, then he is presenting a false theory. Which equivalence class is the equivalence class of true geometries plus physicses is not in any sense a matter of convention. On the other hand, the choice of a geometry plus physics *from the true equivalent class* is a matter of convention; the usual convention is to *choose the normal member*.

It will be seen that the notion of a *definition* undergoes successive widening in Reichenbach's successive approximations to the definition of the metric. Even the first stipulation, the stipulation that the transported rod stays the same length, is not a definition in the technical logical sense of an explicit definition. It does not provide a nonmetrical *substitute* for metrical notions; it does not provide a way of eliminating metrical notions where they occur in science. What it does is to fix the reference of metrical notions by specifying a standard of congruence. It was for this reason that Reichenbach referred to this type of definition as a *coordinating definition*. But with the introduction of the element of "interposition of theories," and especially when it comes to pass that the work of fixing the reference of geometrical notions is mainly done by a stipulation on the *form* of geometry plus physics *as a whole*—the stipulation that universal forces vanish—the term 'definition' becomes wholly inappropriate.

Perhaps not wholly. For there is a tradition, even in mathematical logic, whereby a condition which has a unique solution is sometimes referred to as an 'implicit definition'. If Reichenbach were right, if the condition that physical theory include the statement that universal forces vanish uniquely determined the metric, then this stipulation might be termed an *implicit definition* of the metric. Reichenbach's position might then be stated simply thus: the metric is implicitly defined by the condition that universal forces vanish, together with the condition that $f = ma$, which requires that all deformations in bodies be ascribed to forces.

Unfortunately, Reichenbach is wrong. As a matter of mathematical fact, the condition that universal forces vanish does not single out a unique geometry plus physics.[5] In fact, any metric that agrees with the topology of a space at all is compatible with some "true" system of geometry plus physics according to which universal forces vanish. But this fact need not be fatal for Reichenbach's enterprise. I do not think that Reichenbach would have been terribly disturbed by the fact that the constraint that universal forces vanish is not a sufficient constraint. If we have to add the further constraints that the geometry plus physics as a whole have additional formal properties—say, that they preserve various intuitive requirements, where these requirements can be preserved without cost, and that they be maximally simple in some sense of simple which is connected with feasibility and utility in scientific practice—then why should we not add these constraints in the very same spirit that led Reichenbach to speak of the "interposition of theories"? (Note, by the way, that Reichenbach was writing of the "interposition of theories" in the very same year that Bridgman published *The Logic of Modern Physics*, a book notable for totally ignoring the interposition of theories.) If we adopt this suggestion, then we can no longer speak of the metric as having even an *implicit* definition; for our constraint on scientific theory no longer has the form of a *sentence*. But why should we retain the doctrine that reference is fixed by stipulating *sentences*?

Reichenbach should not have been bothered by the remark that the conventionality of the choice of the metric for physical space is merely an instance of TSC. In the final pages of *Philosophy of Space and Time*, he himself points out that his analysis of the metricization of space-time is meant to apply, *mutatis mutandi*, to such cases as temperature, pressure, and so on—that is, to all physical magnitudes. Grünbaum, on the other hand, insists that his doctrine is a doctrine of the *intrinsic metrical amorphousness* of space-time, that it applies to distance but it does not apply to pressure. Pressure, according to Grünbaum, has an *intrinsic* metric, whereas space-time does not.

The reason that Reichenbach should not have been bothered by our charge of TSC is simply this: he would have said that of course the choice of a metric is the choice of a 'meaning', that is, a reference, for the word 'distance'. But, he would have said, the whole philosophical problem is to say *how* we go about choosing a reference for the term 'distance'. TSC simply says that any term that refers at all could have referred to something different. That is true. The philosopher's job is to explain *how* terms can refer to something at all. Reichenbach was a philosopher pioneering in the very difficult and unexplored terrain of the theory of reference of scientific terms.

[5] See Appendix.

In one important respect Reichenbach was mistaken, however. Seduced by Einstein's own fallacious analysis of his own special theory of relativity—an analysis that Einstein later seems to retract—Reichenbach *identified* the problem of specifying the mechanism of reference for magnitude terms with the problem of separating definitional and empirical elements in scientific theory. For Reichenbach, the analytic-synthetic distinction was essential. The whole job of the philosopher reduced to the job of deciding which sentences in scientific theory are *really* analytic, appearances to the contrary, and which ones are really synthetic. But he was led to this conception of the philosopher's job precisely because he identified the problem of separating analytic and synthetic, or definitional and empirical, elements in science, with the problem of explaining the mechanism of reference of scientific terms. Reichenbach, writing twenty years before the discussions at Harvard that eventuated in Quine's "Two Dogmas of Empiricism," could not have foreseen that it would be possible to provide an answer—what we have called a "coherence account"—to the question of reference of scientific terms which not only did not presuppose the analytic-synthetic distinction, but which was in spirit fundamentally hostile to that distinction. I suggest that we retain Reichenbach's concern with explicating reference while giving up the analytic-synthetic distinction. I suggest that we agree with Reichenbach that the "choice" of a metric is an instance of TSC, while not losing interest in the question of just how it is that the reference of the term 'distance' is fixed.

## CAUSAL THEORY OF REFERENCE

In a couple of recent papers I have suggested that we extend Kripke's causal theory of reference from proper names to natural kind words and physical magnitude terms in science.[6] I will not review the details here. But suffice it to say that I do not claim that a physical magnitude term can be introduced only by a causal description. But I do claim that a customary way of introducing physical magnitude terms is via a causal description, that is, a description of the form 'By *x* I mean the magnitude that is responsible for such and such effects.' For example, Benjamin Franklin might well have given a causal description of electricity by telling us that electricity obeyed an equation of continuity, that it collected in clouds, and that when it reached a certain concentration, some of it flowed from the cloud to

---

[6] See [4] for a causal theory of reference in connection with magnitude terms, and [5] for a discussion of natural kind words and the general problem of meaning and reference.

the earth, and that this sudden flow of a large quantity of electricity took the form of what we recognize as lightning. The reader may wonder why I have not hitherto appealed to causal theory of reference in order to answer the conventionalist. Since the distance between space-time points is no longer something which enters into physical laws neither as an effect nor a cause, since space is no longer a mere arena in which physical processes take place, but an agent and an actor in the physical drama, and an actor which is itself affected by the physical drama, why should we not specify the reference of the term 'distance', or of the technical term the '$g_{ik}$ tensor', by specifying certain *causal* properties of distance or of the $g_{ik}$ tensor?

The reason why this answer would not meet the conventionalist criticism, at least by itself, is that the conventionalist is fully prepared to be a conventionalist about causes and effects *too*. If we choose a nonstandard geometry plus physics, then we will choose a nonstandard account both of the phenomena and of their causes. It is necessary, thus, at some point to argue that the reference of *cause* and *effect* is not up for grabs to the extent that the conventionalist thinks. There is no such effect as the universal contraction of all objects toward the center of a certain sphere, and there are no such causes as universal forces. The coherence account, far from being incompatible with the causal account of reference, is a necessary part of the story.

## ENTER QUINE₂

The position of Quine₁ may be explained in the following way. Let 5) be some plausible constraint that one might think of adding to Quine's constraints 1)-4) or 1')-4) in order to obtain unique or more unique translation. Such a constraint might be the constraint Quine himself suggests, that we ask that expressions which are short in English, or whatever the home language may be, correspond to short expressions in the alien language; or it might be the constraint we suggested above, that the translation manual be compatible with certain psychological or neuropsychological hypotheses; or it might be a more subtle constraint on the structure of the translation manual itself. (Geoffrey Hellman, in a recent Harvard dissertation, has explored a number of such constraints. Some of Hellman's constraints may well rule out such examples as the notorious *gavagai*.) The position of Quine₁ with respect to such a constraint 5) would be that it in no way reduces the indeterminacy of translation. For even if 5) had the property that there was in every case a *unique* translation satisfying constraints 1)-5), still there is no fact of the matter as to whether 5) is a correct constraint, and hence no fact of the matter as to whether a translation satisfying 1)-5) is correct versus a translation satisfying 1)-4) and violating 5). Translations violating 1)-4) are objectively wrong; they go against the *evidence*. But 1)-4), or rather 1')-4), are all the objective constraints there are. This is the position that we criticized above as involving the same conventionalist ploy as Grünbaum's position on the conventionalism of the metric of physical space-time, in a relativistic world, or of the metric of space in a Newtonian world.

At the Storrs Conference on the Philosophy of Language, however, Quine admitted that *Word and Object* was widely interpreted in this way, but explicitly repudiated this interpretation as unrepresentative of his intentions and his actual philosophical views. His view as he expressed it is not that there is no fact of the matter as to whether an added constraint 5) would be objectively correct or not, but that there is "no fact of the matter as to whether or not there is a fact of the matter".

This is not just an *aperçu* on Quine's part. In fact, Quine is here taking a position which is far more consonant with the position of his other writings than is the position of Quine$_1$. Quine is a realist. That is, he believes that the sentences of physical science have a truth value, and that that truth value depends upon the external world, not just upon human language or human sensation or human convention, and so on. But, like any sensible realist, Quine believes that human convention plays *some* part in the determination of the truth values of sentences of physical theory. Where he differs from, say, Reichenbach, is in holding that it is futile to try to distinguish the contributions of human convention and objective fact, sentence by sentence. Human convention and objective fact both contribute; but there are no sentences which are true just by virtue of objective fact, and no sentences which are true just by virtue of human convention.

The position of Quine$_1$ goes against this because it maintains that 1')-4) are, as it were, meaning conventions. They stipulate the meaning of 'translation'. A fifth constraint could not be a substantive law since it is underdetermined by 1')-4); therefore, it could at best amount to an arbitrary stipulation to redefine the notion of 'translation'. The position of the real Quine, Quine$_2$, is that it is a bad question to ask whether the adoption of a fifth constraint would express the discovery of a substantive law or the adoption of a new meaning for 'translation'. "Is that a statement of fact or a meaning-stipulation?" is as bad a question in linguistic theory as it is in physical theory, in Quine's view. Quine's real view thus allows that we may have further constraints over and above 1')-4). It allows that such constraints may be well motivated, motivated by just the considerations of agreement with intuition ("conservativism"), agreement with experimental evidence, fertility, coherence with the rest of science, and so on, that are operative in the growth and development of physical theory. At the Storrs Conference, Quine went on to say that it was his belief that even the discovery/stipulation of such further constraints on radical translation as might prove well motivated would still not determine a unique translation. There would still be, he expects, some indeterminacy of translation.

Note, then, that on Quine's view the indeterminacy of translation is a hypothesis, not something of which Quine claims to have a logical or mathematical proof.

## The Importance of the Indeterminacy of Translation

Quine believes that there is not a shred of scientific evidence for the existence of "propositions" as irreducible, nonbehaviorally linked, nonphysical entities, and I certainly agree with him on this. What there are, in Quine's view, are isomorphisms between languages. When we say that a sentence in a language $L_1$ has the same meaning as a sentence in a language $L_2$, no reference to irreducible propositions is needed to explain what we mean. What we mean is simply that there is an isomorphism—more precisely, a behavior-preserving mapping—of one language onto the other that sends one of the two sentences onto the other.

If this is a reasonable account of sameness of meaning, and *prima facie* it certainly seems to be, then at first blush it would seem that propositions could be restored, at least as logical constructions out of linguistic behavior. Let us simply say that two sentences express the same proposition just in case one is a translation of the other. The trouble with this proposal is that it assumes that for any two languages, if there is an isomorphism between them at all, then there is a unique isomorphism between them. This is precisely the thesis that is challenged by the hypothesis of the indeterminacy of translation. Quine's examples show that it is quite conceivable that there are two or more isomorphisms between two different languages, and that a sentence which is mapped onto a sentence $S_1$ by one of those isomorphisms may be mapped onto a different, even an incompatible, sentence $S_2$ under the other of those isomorphisms. If there are many isomorphisms between any two languages, then the notion of *sameness of meaning* has to be relativized to the isomorphism that we pick.

Even if talk of "propositions" is not meant metaphysically, it is still a very bad idea at this stage in our knowledge. For it begs just the question which is raised by the hypothesis of the indeterminacy of translation: the question whether or not isomorphism between different languages is unique, or almost unique. It should be noted that the importance of the hypothesis of the indeterminacy of translation in this respect does not depend upon the hypothesis being *true*. Recognizing that *we do not know* what constraints upon translation would determine a unique translation, if there are any reasonable constraints that would do this, and recognizing, further, that it may be that no reasonable constraints upon translation would determine *unique* translations, is enough. It is enough that the hypothesis of the indeterminacy of translation *might* be true; it is not necessary that it should be true.

## UNDERDETERMINATION OF THEORIES

Quine's reasons for believing that there will turn out to be some indeterminacy of translation, even if additional constraints upon translation prove to be justified, are basically two. He argues for the indeterminacy of translation first from the general underdetermination of scientific theories by true observation sentences, and second from ontological relativity. We shall consider the argument from ontological relativity in the next section. Let us take a look now at the underdetermination of scientific theories.

The topic of the underdetermination of scientific theories is such a large topic that we cannot undertake to really discuss it here. What we can do is very briefly consider its relevance to the topics of this paper. Our standpoint is, briefly, that it is quite unclear to what extent scientific theories are underdetermined by what, and what to make of the fact that they are underdetermined if they are.

Thus, a physicist would be likely to regard two theories as equivalent descriptions if no physically possible experiment could ever decide between them. Some scientific realists would question the justifiability of even this weak requirement, the requirement of the physical possibility of a crucial experiment. But it is important to note that when Quine says that scientific theory is underdetermined by the totality of all possible observations, he does not mean what the physicist means. He does not mean that there are two theories such that no physically possible experiment *could* decide between them, and such that both are equally acceptable on the basis of such canons as simplicity, and so on. When Quine speaks of the totality of all *possible observations*, he means the totality of all *true observation sentences*, that is, of the totality of all *ordered pairs consisting of observation sentence and a point in space-time at which that observation sentence could have been truly uttered*, whether or not someone was present at that point in space-time to truly utter it. He does not count counter-factual observation sentences, for example, "This match would have lit if it had been struck"; and *a fortiori*, he does not count sentences about what the outcomes of various experiments which were not performed *would have been* if those experiments had been performed.

To make the point clear: two theories are observationally inequiv-alent, by Quine's criterion, if one implies an observation sentence and the other implies the negation of that observation sentence. For ex-ample, if one implies "There is a red apple at the point in space-time with coordinates *xyzt*", and the other implies that "There is no red apple at the point in space-time with coordinates *xyzt*". Two observationally complete theories, that is, two theories which settle the truth value of all observation sentences, which agree in their assignment of truth values to all observation sentences, are observa-tionally equivalent, by Quine's criterion. In particular, they are still observationally equivalent even if one of them implies that *if* a cer-tain amount of energy *had been* employed in making a certain mea-surement, say, the measurement of the position of a certain particle, it would have been found in a region $r$, and the other implies that *if* that amount of energy had been employed and the measurement had been made, then the particle *would have been* found *outside* the region $r$. Of course if the measurement was made, then the statement of the result of the measurement is an observation sentence, and if the two theories disagree in the truth value they assign to that observation sentence, they are observationally inequivalent. But if we suppose that no human being ever employs the amount of energy required in making an experiment simply as a matter of sociological fact, and that therefore the experiment is never performed, then the two theories are *not* inequivalent. It seems to me that here Quine's cri-terion differs from that which is accepted by physicists. The fact that people never get around to performing certain experiments, or that people never have available enough energy to perform certain exper-iments, and the like, does not mean that two such theories become equivalent. As long as the theories imply different predictions about what *would* have happened *if* the experiments *had* been performed, then they are inequivalent, as most physicists understand the matter.

What this shows is that even if there should be observationally equivalent theories in Quine's sense, which in addition to being equiv-alent were equally simple and so on, that is, which would come out as equally good on all of the usual methodological canons, still it would not follow that there was no fact of the matter as to which of the two theories was right. The step from the underdetermination of scientific theories by the totality of true observation sentences, if it is a fact, to there being no fact of the matter as to which theory is right, is not an obvious step at all.

Sometimes Quine seems to assume that the Verifiability Theory is correct provided that the unit of meaning is taken to be scientific theory as a whole, and not the individual sentence. I am not myself persuaded that this is right; but even if we accept this, it does not follow that there is no fact of the matter as to which of two observationally equivalent theories, by Quine's criterion, is correct. For many Verificationists have counted counterfactual verification as part of empirical meaning. That is, it is customary even for Verificationists to count two theories as differing in empirical meaning in the case discussed above. Nelson Goodman has urged that the counterfactual conditionals are meaningless unless we can somehow succeed in construing counterfactual talk as highly derived talk about actual events. In Goodman's view, talk about what the outcomes would have been of experiments using higher energies than will ever be available to human beings is meaningless unless it can be translated into talk about things that actually do happen. Perhaps it would follow that there is no fact of the matter as to which of two observationally equivalent descriptions is the true theory, if we assume *both* the holistic version of verificationism *and* Nelson Goodman's stand with respect to counterfactual conditionals. For our present purposes it is enough to remark that there is no clear route from "(observationally) equivalent descriptions" to "no fact of the matter" unless we are willing to assume such difficult and problematical philosophical doctrines as the holistic version of verificationism and the rejection of counterfactual conditionals, or at least, the rejection of realism with respect to counterfactual conditionals.

Quine's position is that one can only say whether two theories are compatible or incompatible once we have fixed a background theory *and* a translation of each theory into the language of one's background theory. If they come out incompatible on that translation, then (relative to that translation) they *are* incompatible. Since we speak from the point of view of our background theory, we say there *is* a fact of the matter as to which is true—even if the two theories be observationally equivalent in the sense just discussed. Thus, Quine does not believe that there is any step, in general, from the fact that the choice between theories is underdetermined, in his sense, to there being "no fact of the matter."

In the special case of indeterminacy of translation, however, these difficulties can be sidestepped. For if we agree that meanings, insofar as they are legitimate scientific entities at all, must be functions of isomorphisms between languages and linguistic behaviors,

then evidence that there is no unique isomorphism satisfying whatever are the appropriate constraints is *ipso facto* evidence that there
are no unique meanings. If many isomorphisms satisfy the optimal
constraints, whatever they may be, then asking which of the isomorphisms translates sentences *preserving meaning*, that is, which of the
isomorphisms is *the correct translation*, is, in effect, asking which of
the isomorphisms satisfies the Great Constraint in the Sky. The
answer is that there is no Great Constraint in the Sky, and hence there
is no fact of the matter as to which of the optimal isomorphisms
satisfies it. In general, I am inclined to think that this is a reasonable
line to take.

In the case of the indeterminacy of translation, what Quine is
reminding us of is this: not any sentential function is an implicit
definition. For a sentential function to be an implicit definition it is
necessary that it should have a unique solution. That is, there must be
one thing satisfying it, and only one thing satisfying it. When we
specify an object by saying that that object is the object satisfying
certain constraints, then in the absence of any proof that there is only
one object satisfying those constraints, we are not justified in assuming uniqueness. The general underdetermination of scientific
theories by observational facts is clear only when the constraints upon
scientific theory are very weak. If the only constraints are those of
deductive consistency, then the point is trivial. Once some kind of
strong coherence is added as an additional constraint, then the extent
of underdetermination becomes quite problematical. (It is also quite
problematical why we should require, pending argument, consistency
with all true observation sentences, and not, say, consistency with all
true sentences about the actual and possible trajectories of particles.)
This appeal to the underdetermination of scientific theories by observational facts can strengthen the case for the indeterminacy of
translation only by reminding us of the logical point just made. The
constraints that it may be justifiable to place upon analytical hypotheses are not just facts about correct translation manuals; they define
what it is to be a correct translation manual. Pending proof, we cannot
assume that such a set of constraints has a unique solution.

## ONTOLOGICAL RELATIVITY

The other argument that Quine offers for the indeterminacy of
translation is the fact of ontological relativity. According to the doctrine of ontological relativity, there exist thoroughly intertranslatable theories which do not even agree on ontology, that is, on what
objects there are.

Let $T$ and $T'$ be two such theories. Then if the speakers of the "jungle" language utter sentences which may be correctly translated (according to some translation manual) by the sentences of $T$, then by composing that translation manual with the translation of $T$ into $T'$, we could equally well translate the jungle speakers as holding the theory $T'$. If $T$ and $T'$ are formally incompatible, then this gives us an example of the indeterminacy of translation. The indeterminacy of translation follows from the relativity of ontology.

There is no doubt that this ingenious argument strongly moves Quine. I should like to raise some doubts about the argument here, however. In the first place, what are the considerations that lead Quine to the doctrine of the relativity of ontology? One consideration is a formal trick. Suppose, for example, we assign numbers to all the objects in the world in some effective way. For example, we might pick some particular particle, say Oscar, and assign it the number 1. The object nearest to Oscar, if there is an object nearest to Oscar, is then assigned the number 2. If more than one object has the distance $r$ from Oscar, where $r$ is the closest any other object gets to Oscar, then among the particles with the distance $r$ from Oscar we pick the one with the smallest $\theta$ (thinking of Oscar as the center of a system of polar coordinates), and assign that object the number 2. If there are two or more particles which both have the distance $r$ from Oscar and the angle $\theta$, then we pick the one with the least $\rho$ and assign it the number 2. Continuing in this fashion, we can assign an integer to every particle in the entire universe, assuming that there are only a countable number of particles in the universe. The method has been explained only for particles existing at one time; however, it can easily be extended to a four-dimensional universe.

Now, suppose we have defined a "proxy function" in this way, that is a function mapping particles onto integers. Any physical thing, that is, any thing consisting of a finite number of particles, can then be identified with a finite set of integers. If we Gödel number finite sets of integers, which is easy to do, then we can represent both particles and finite collections of particles by means of integers. Then any theory which quantifies over physical things (over particles and finite collections of particles) can be replaced by a theory which quantifies over integers. It suffices to replace any predicate of physical things, for example, 'is red', by the corresponding predicate of integers. The notion of 'corresponding predicate' can be explained by means of an example: if the given predicate is "is red", then the corresponding predicate is "is the number which is assigned to an object which is red". Thus, the sentence "Oscar is red" goes over into the sentence "The number 1 is the number of an object which is red". If $T$ is a theory which quantifies over physical objects, and $T'$ is the corresponding theory which quantifies over integers, then there is no doubt that $T$ and $T'$ are thoroughly intertranslatable, if $T'$ has been constructed in the way just outlined. There is also no doubt that $T$ and $T'$ have a different ontology, if we accept Quine's criterion of ontological commitment. But Quine's criterion does not seem plausible to me in this case. It seems to me that a theory may presuppose objects as much through the predicates it employs as through the objects it quantifies over; and that, intuitively, $T'$ in the above example has an ontology of material objects just as much as $T$ does. Once again, a consideration offered in support of the indeterminacy of translation proves to be itself a difficult and problematical philosophical doctrine.

Quine also appeals to examples from the history of science, notably the notorious wave-particle duality. Let us take a somewhat better example than the wave-particle case; the case of a Newtonian world and the following two presentations of Newtonian theory: action at a distance theory, quantifying only over particles, and field theory, quantifying over particles and fields. These two theories do intuitively have different ontologies. Intuitively, the former says that the world consists of particles; the latter says that the world consists of particles *and fields*. And there is also no doubt that these two theories are thoroughly intertranslatable as long as we assume Newtonian physics. Thus, as long as we adopt only Quine's original constraints on radical translation, only the constraints 1')-4), then the step from the translatability of these two theories to a possible indeterminacy of translation seems sound. But the fact is that while these two theories are thoroughly intertranslatable, they are also notationally and mathematically quite different. A physicist doing his calculations in the style of field theory writes down different expressions from a physicist doing his calculations in the style of action at a distance theory. Thus, if we add to the constraints 1')-4) the further constraint that Quine himself mentions, the constraint that we choose analytical hypotheses that preserve length of expression, that is, that send short expressions in the target language onto short expressions in the home language, then it seems as if we *could* say that the calculations done by the "jungle" physicist should be translated by the calculations of the action at a distance theorist, or by the calculations of the field theorist, whichever the case might be. The fact is that the step from examples of ontological relativity, even if they be bona fide, to indeterminacy of translations is a valid step only for Quine[1].

## Summary

We have examined some of the considerations that lead Quine to the hypothesis of the indeterminacy of translation. Two of these considerations—the underdetermination of scientific theory by observational fact, and the existence of ontological relativity—seem to us quite problematical. We cannot see any sure step from these considerations to the indeterminacy of translation, but neither can we see any proof of the *determinacy* of translation. Quine is right: how much indeterminacy of translation there is, if there is indeterminacy of translation, is surely an empirical question. Like all empirical questions, it involves elements of discovery and elements of stipulation; and to ask whether any particular sentence that we may adopt as linguistic theory and translation theory develop is a meaning stipulation or a substantive law will be futile. But our purpose here has not been to discover if there is indeterminacy of translation, but rather to refute the argument of Quine₁ and the allied argument of Grunbaum. Once that argument is recognized to be an instance of the general conventionalist ploy, and that ploy is recognized as having no validity, then the way is clear for the consideration of the substantive questions raised by Reichenbach and Quine: How is the reference of scientific terms fixed? And to what extent is reference determinate?

## Appendix

In [2], I sketched a proof of the following theorem:

Theorem. Let $P$ be a system of physics (based on a suitable system of coordinates) and $E$ be a system of geometry. Then the world described by $E$ plus $P$ can be redescribed in terms of an arbitrarily chosen metric $g_{ik}$ (compatible with the given topology) *without postulating "universal forces"*, i.e., forces permanently associated with a spatial region and producing the same deformations (over and above the deformations produced by the usual forces) independently of the composition of the body acted upon. In fact, according to the new description $g_{ik}$ *plus* $P'$ (which predicts the same trajectories as $E$ *plus* $P$):

(1) All deformations are ascribed to three sources: the electromagnetic forces, the gravitational forces, and gravitational-electromagnetic interactions.

(2) All three types of forces are dependent upon the composition of the body acted upon.

(3) If there are small deformations constantly taking place in

solid bodies according to *E plus P* (as there are, owing to the atomic constitution of matter), then no matter what geometry may be selected, the new $g_{ik}$ can be so chosen that the deformations according to $g_{ik}$ plus P′ will be of the same order of magnitude. Moreover, it will be impossible to transform them away by going back to *E plus P*.

(4) If it is possible to construct bodies held together by only gravitational forces or only electromagnetic forces, then (in the absence of the other type of field) the interactional forces of the third type (postulated by *P*′) will vanish.

(5) If there are already "third type forces" according to *E plus P*, then the situation will be thoroughly symmetrical, in the sense that (i) going from the old metric to $g_{ik}$ involves postulating additional deformations (relative to the description given in *E plus P*) which are the same for all bodies, and (ii) going from $g_{ik}$ back to *E plus P* involves postulating additional deformations which are also the same for all bodies, *relative to the description given in* $g_{ik}$ *plus P′*; and the same number and kind of fundamental forces are postulated by both *P* and *P*′.

I now give a much simpler proof. (The proof will be longer, because I will be more detailed.) Afterward, I will discuss Grünbaum's criticism of the original proof.

Proof: Let *E plus P* be based on a metric $g'_{ik}$. Let $g_{ik}$ be an arbitrarily chosen metric compatible with the given topology. We replace the original notion of distance (given by $g'_{ik}$), wherever it occurs in physical laws by the appropriate function of the coordinates. The second law of motion is now destroyed, since it now reads

$$F = m\ddot{x}$$

and $\ddot{x}$, the acceleration is no longer "acceleration", owing to the arbitrary character of the old metric as viewed from the new $g_{ik}$ tensor. (We assume the new $g_{ik}$ is compatible with the original topology.) But the law $F = ma$ can be reintroduced as a definition of "force". (Here $a$ must be defined in terms of the new $g_{ik}$ tensor.) The difficulty is that so far we have only defined *total resultant force*. To obtain a resolution into component forces, we proceed as follows: Let $A$ and $B$ be two arbitrary *logically possible* differential forces (whether physically actual or not). For example, $A$ might be electromagnetic force, on the assumption that Maxwell's Laws are "locally" true (in the metric $g_{ik}$), whether they are in reality or not, and $B$ might be gravitational force, on the assumption that Newton's law (or some relativistic law, if one prefers) is locally true (in the metric $g_{ik}$), whether it is in reality or not. Without loss of generality, we assume $A + B \neq F$. Determine $C$ from the equation $A + B + C = F$. If $C$ is differential, we are through: we just set $E = A, G = B, I = C$, and the theorem follows. If $C$ is universal, we express the differential force $B$ as the sum of two differential forces $B_1$ and $B_2$ ($B = B_1 + B_2$); this can always be done. Moreover, if $B$ is Newton's law of gravity or some relativistic law, $B_1$ can be chosen to be approximately $B$; hence, approximately Newton's law or the relativistic law. Then $A + B + C = F$, and $B = B_1 + B_2$; so $A + B_1 + (B_2 + C) = F$. Since $B_2$ is differential and $C$ is universal, $(B_2 + C)$ is differential. So we just set $E = A, G = B_1, I = (B_2 + C)$, q.e.d.

Our original proof was unnecessarily complicated because we determined $E$ and $G$ in the metric $g'_{ik}$ and transformed to find them in the metric $g_{ik}$, instead of just working with the metric $g_{ik}$ and the total resultant force $F$. Our description of the procedure was as follows:

"Now set the gravitational field equal to zero, determine the total "phorce" that would now be acting on $B$, and determine from this the total force that would be acting on $B$. Call this $E$ (electromagnetic force). Similarly, set the electromagnetic field equal to zero, and obtain the total force that would be acting on $B$. Call this $G$ (gravitational force). Finally define I (interactional force) from the equation $F = E + G + I$."

In [1], Ch. III, Grünbaum gives both a "counterexample" to the theorem and a criticism of the proof. But the "counterexample" is a counterexample to what Grünbaum takes me to have meant by some statements in the proof; not an example to show the *theorem* is *false*. (If I wished to imitate Grünbaum's style in [1], I would now accuse Grünbaum of "shocking ignorance" and of not knowing the meaning of "counterexample".) So all we have is a criticism of my proof (of which the relevant part is "b'" pp. 363–364.) The criticism of my proof is based on the assumption that when I wrote "set the gravitational field equal to zero" I must have intended *either* the original physics $P$ to be used (in which case a host of objections arise, depending on the character of $P$) or the new physics $P'$ to be used, in which case one has to already know $P'$ to construct it. What I had in mind was neither of these alternatives. When I wrote "determine the total "phorce" that would now be acting on $B$", I meant determine the total "phorce" that would be acting *using any convenient system of physics* (whether it agrees with $P$ or not). (For example, one can just assume that if the gravitational field is zero, then the "phorce" that would be acting on $B$ would obey Maxwell-type laws, in the metric $g'_{ik}$, if one wishes. Similarly, one can assume that if the electromagnetic field is zero, then the "phorce" that would be acting on $B$ would obey Newton's law of gravity, if one wishes.) Then $E$, $G$, and $I$ are well defined.

Grünbaum's other criticism (p. 364) is that I do not prove that $E$,

*G*, and *I* will be differential (although it should have been clear that it is only by sheer chance that any one of them will be universal). This criticism is correct, and I have supplied details above.

Note that part (3) of the theorem holds because even if a space is, say, Euclidean relative to $g'_{ik}$ and we wish it to be Lobachevskian relative to $g_{ik}$, this is compatible with the distance between two events being almost the same in the two metrics at usual distances. (I.e., the two metrics can almost agree at nonastronomical distances.) In particular, the disagreements can be made small relative to molecular vibrations or even relative to the Compton wave length of an electron. And, since the total force *F* is always differential (since different objects have different internal forces and vibrations), total deformation cannot be transformed away.

To verify part (4), we have to put additional constraints on the forces *A* and *B* (or $B_1$), which is no problem, since these are arbitrary differential forces. Namely, let *A* and *B* never both vanish, and let neither *A* nor *B* vanish in the case of the great majority of physical objects (this is in agreement with both classical and contemporary physics). Then, instead of setting *E* = *A*, *G* = *B*, *I* = *C*, define *E*,*G*,*I* at each space-time point *p* as follows:

If $A \neq 0, B \neq 0$ at *p*, set $E = A, G = B, I = C$ at *p*.
If $A = 0$ at *p*, set $E = 0, G = B + C, I = 0$ at *p*.
If $B = 0$ at *p*, set $E = A + C, G = 0, I = 0$ at *p*.

(If it is necessary to split B into $B_1, B_2$, put instead:

If $A \neq 0, B_1 \neq 0$ at *p*, set $E = A, G = B_1, I = B_2 + C$ at *p*.
If $A = 0$ at *p*, set $E = 0, G = B_1 + B_2 + C, I = 0$ at *p*.
If $B_1 = 0$ at *p*, set $E = A + B_2 + C, G = 0, I = 0$ at *p*.)

Then *E*, *G*, and *I* are still differential, because for most bodies *E* = *A*, *G* = *B*, *I* = *C*, and these are differential forces; and *I* vanishes whenever *E* or *G* does. Part (4) of the theorem was really unnecessary, since *E* and *G* never vanish *globally*, and there is no reason why the local *I* forces should depend only on local *E* and *G* forces.

Part (5) summarizes the import of the whole theorem.

### DISCUSSION

In the above theorem we have not discussed the notion of a "rod". The reason is that, although Grunbaum and Reichenbach take "the rod corrected for differential forces" as the standard of congruence, such an object—an object that *would* stay rigid if all differential forces vanished—cannot, in general, exist in a geometry of variable curvature. If there is a "bump" in the space, then a rod which is large relative to the "bump" *must* change shape as it moves through the bump even if all differential forces (except the "tidal" force due to the curvature itself) vanish. And it makes no sense to "correct" for *tidal* forces. These are represented by vectors in tangent space, and unless we construe the tangent space as a real embedding space, we cannot say what the object would do if these were set equal to zero. (If we *do* construe the tangent space as an embedding space, then (1) the object won't even stay in the original space if the tidal forces are set equal to zero; and (2) what it will do will depend on *how* the embedding is done; not just on the intrinsic geometry of the original space itself.) For these reasons, it is customary to understand a "rod" as a *small* object in dealing with curved space—small relative to a local Euclidean (or Lorentzian, in the space-time case) frame, in the sense that, given the accuracy of the measurements in question, "tidal" effects can be ignored. (cf. *Gravitation*, by Misner, Thorne, and Wheeler pp. 393–399.)

We have followed Reichenbach in *separating* space and time, and discussed only the problem of remetricizing *space*. Earman has remarked to us that it is a defect of Reichenbach's book that he discusses space and time separately, and only discusses *space-time* at the end. Following a suggestion of Earman's (but not holding him responsible for the present discussion) we now generalize the above theorem to the case of space-time. In this case the equation $F = ma$ becomes:

$$(1)\left( m\ \frac{d^2x^i}{d\tau^2} + g'\ \Gamma^i_{jk}\frac{dx^j}{d\tau}\frac{dx^k}{d\tau} \right) = F \text{ (total force)}$$

(assuming that if the metric is g', then the connection is the unique symmetric one g' $\Gamma$ compatible with g').

In order to preserve the form of this law and predict the same particle orbits the advocate of g has to add on a rather complicated additional force *relative to the description given by g'*:

$$(2)\ F_A = F(1-\phi^2) + m\frac{dx}{d\tau'}\frac{d\phi}{d\tau'}\frac{1}{\phi} +$$

$$m\ \left( g'\Gamma^i_{jk} - g\Gamma^i_{jk}\ \frac{dx^j}{d\tau'\iota}\frac{dx^k}{d\tau'} \right)$$

(We assume g and g' are conformally equivalent: otherwise, as Earman points out the change in metric will result in causal propagation outside the null cone.) The total force is now $F' = F + F_A$, and the equation of motion is:

$$(3) \left( m \; \frac{d^2x^i + g\Gamma^i_{jk} \dfrac{dx^j \, dx^k}{d\tau' \, \delta d\tau'}}{d\tau'^2} \right) = F' \; (\text{total force})$$

The new total force $F'$ is always differential, and it can be split into parts E, G, I such that all three parts are differential and E satisfies Maxwell's Laws (locally),* G satisfies your favorite gravitational equation (locally)* and I depends on *both* masses and charges (an "interactional" force), but is not universal.

The equation (3) implies that a system consisting of two free particles whose world lines are *parallel* geodesics in a local Lorentz frame (parallelism is only defined *locally*) will be "rigid", since (3) implies that in the absence of forces, particles follow geodesics of the metric g and not g'. Of course, what types of "rods" will actually be *possible* will depend on the physics and the metric g- as Wheeler, *et al* remark:

> One need not—and indeed must not!—postulate that proper length is measured by a certain type of rod (e.g. platinum meter-stick), or that proper time is measured by a certain type of clock (e.g., hydrogen-maser clock). Rather one must ask the laws of physics themselves what types of rods and clocks will do the job. Put differently, one *defines an "ideal" rod or clock* to be one which measures proper length as given by $ds = (g_{\alpha\beta} \, dx^\alpha \, dx^\beta)^{1/2}$ or proper time as given by $d^\tau = (-g_{\alpha\beta} \, dx_\alpha \, dx^\beta)^{1/2}$ (*op cit*, p. 393).

* Apart from singularities, of course.

### BIBLIOGRAPHY

[1] Grünbaum, A. *Geometry and Chronometry in Philosophical Perspective*. Minnesota: 1968.

[2] Putnam, H. "An Examination of Grünbaum's Philosophy of Space and Time," in B. Baumrin, ed., *Philosophy of Science, The Delaware Seminar*, II, 1962-63. :Interscience Publishers, 1963.

[3] ———. "Memo on 'Conventionalism'," Minnesota Center for the Philosophy of Science (circulated privately), April 22, 1959, to appear in a forthcoming collection of my articles.

[4] ———. "Explanation and Reference," *Conceptual Change*. Glenn Pearce, ed. D. Reidel Publishing Co., 1973.

[5] ———. "The Meaning of 'Meaning'," to appear in *Minnesota Studies in the Philosophy of Science*, vol. 7 or 8, Keith Gunderson, ed. (forthcoming). A part of this has appeared in the *Journal of Philosophy* as my symposium paper at the Christmas 1973 meeting of the American Philosophical Association under the title "Meaning and Reference."

[6] Quine, W. V. O. "Two Dogmas of Empiricism," in his *From a Logical Point of View*. Cambridge, Mass.: Harvard University Press, 1953, 1961. Also reprinted in the excellent anthology edited by Jay F. Rosenberg and Charles Travis, *Readings in the Philosophy of Language*. Englewood Cliffs, N.J.: Prentice-Hall, 1961.

[7] ———. *Word and Object*. Cambridge, Mass.: MIT Press, 1960.

[8] J. Misner, K. Thorne, J. Wheeler, *Gravitation*, Freeman-Holt, 1974.

# *Truth*

## PETER UNGER

### *New York University*

Truth is one of the great, grand subjects for philosophical thought. In this respect, truth is akin to goodness and knowledge and freedom. Men seek, and also seek to understand, goodness, knowledge, freedom, and truth. I tend to be somewhat skeptical about all of these great, grand things. I suspect that there is never anything in the world to fulfill the grand ideas and, in particular, that there is nothing to answer to the idea of truth. In trying to examine what truth might be, I will try not to let this penchant for skepticism overcome my powers of judgment. In other words, I will try to be open-minded about truth, letting the accumulation of apparent evidence direct me where it may.

At the outset, one thing seems pretty clear: Whatever else may be said about truth, truth is bound to be the purported referent of our own word 'truth' in at least one important sense of this quite common common noun. On my reckoning, as with other great, grand things, the evidence for testing any account of truth is likely to be largely linguistic. More specifically, it will concern facts about our own language, English, in which this purportedly referring word occurs.

It should also be pretty clear that the word to look at first and last, indeed, most closely, is the word 'truth'. Facts about this word are the ones we most want to explain. For a variety of more or less obscure reasons, which I will try neither to discern nor excuse, this word has been avoided by contemporary philosophers of truth, even when they have an eye toward our own actual language. This has hardly been an unconscious omission, as the following quote from Austin illustrates:

'What is truth?' said jesting Pilate, and would not stay for an answer. Pilate was in advance of his time. For 'truth' itself is an abstract noun, a camel, that is, of logical construction, which cannot get past the eye even of a grammarian. We approach it cap and categories in hand: we ask ourselves whether Truth is a substance (the Truth, the Body of Knowledge), or a quality (something like the color red, inhering in truths), or a relation ('correspondence').[1] [There is here a footnote which reads: [1] It is sufficiently obvious that 'truth' is a substantive, 'true' an adjective and 'of' in 'true of' a preposition.] But philosophers should take something more nearly their own size to strain at. What needs discussing rather is the use, or certain uses, of the word 'true'. *In vino*, possibly, *'veritas'*, but in a somber symposium *'verum'*.[1]

My own belief, on the contrary, is that many contemporary philosophers have missed out on a correct account of truth largely because, like Austin, they have neglected to look carefully at 'truth'. If we look first at 'truth', we might hope later to give a better account of the relevant meaning or use of the adjective 'true'. We might also hope to explain what distinguishes a relevant use of 'true', as in 'Her statement to him was true', from uses less directly relevant to the topic of truth, as in 'Her love for him was true'. We proceed, then, to look at 'truth'.

## I

### THREE SENSES OF 'TRUTH'

There are, I think, exactly three main uses or, better, *senses* of the word 'truth'. Each of them connects rather directly with the philosophical topic of truth. They are manifest in the following three sentences:

1. The first thing he uttered was a *truth*, but the *truth* was not as informative as the lies he later produced.
2. The *truth* of what he said cannot be denied, and *truth* should always be valued.

---

[1] This is the first paragraph of J. L. Austin's "Truth," originally published in the *Proceedings of the Aristotelian Society*. Supp. Vol. XXIV (1950). In fairness, I should also refer to his "Unfair to Facts" in his *Philosophical Papers*, ed. by J. O. Urmson and G. J. Warnock (Oxford: The Clarendon Press, 1961).

3. At first, I didn't think he was telling me the *truth*, but then I remembered the *truth* about it all and realized that he was.

In the first sentence, 'truth' is, in both occurrences, a sortal or count noun. A necessary condition for a thing to be a truth is that it be true, in the relevant sense of 'true'. To dispense with talk of "the relevant sense", we may say that a thing is a truth *only if* we may speak of the truth *of* it. It seems to me that not all things which are thus true are truths: The sentence 'Though what he said was *not* true, there are many true things *in* what he said' will not mean ??'Though what he said was *not* true, there are many truths *in* what he said' (especially, perhaps, if what he said is, simply, that all men are created equal). But, whatever further refinements are needed to get a definition for 'truth' in this first sense, I will try to show that one will understand the first sense of 'truth' in terms of the second.[2]

In the second sentence, 'truth' is, in both occurrences, used to talk about, or to try to denote, a certain *property*, namely, the property of truth. This is a property which all truths have (whether or not only those things have it). In the first occurrence, we talk of a property *of something*, namely, of what he said. In the second occurrence, we talk of the same property but more abstractly, detached, so to speak, from any things which might have it. There is of course nothing at all unusual in this, nor anything peculiar to talk of truth. Talk of properties manifests this distinction quite generally: 'The innocence of the peasants was charming, but, then, innocence can be a curse'. In any case, this is evidently the sense of 'truth' which most directly relates to the philosophical topic of truth; indeed, we just now used the word in that way to mention that great, grand thing. If we can define 'truth' in this sense, we will have provided, at least in the main, a definition of truth itself. (We will then need only "to cast things in the material mode".)

In the third sentence, we find, in both occurrences, what I take to be the key or central sense of the word. What 'truth' means here will become progressively apparent throughout the remainder of this essay. But, it is well to note now that this sense may give us a way, both simple and quite natural, of defining the other two main senses. For, if what someone said was true, so that one might refer to the truth of it, then it was in (complete) agreement with the truth. Thus, truth may be defined as agreement with the truth, or as the property of being in agreement with the truth. And, then, this is the key property

---

[2] I go at this quite wholeheartedly in section X, "The Predication of Truth and The Relevant Uses of 'True'."

which all truths share. No other way of starting, or proceeding, allows for so simple or so natural a way of relating the main senses of 'truth'. This alone is some pretty strong evidence for the idea that this third sense is the central, indeed, the primitive one. It is also some evidence for our account of truth which is, in short, that truth is agreement with the truth. But, then, what is that?

Now before I proceed to answer this difficult question, I should like to express some extremely sweeping but deeply held beliefs of mine. In my belief, there is a theory of the world, and so of us and our relations to things, which is embodied in our language. However, this actually came to pass, *one instructive way to view* the present situation is as follows: The embodied theory is terribly old, having been created by some ancient forgotten geniuses, most responsible for our language. They are thus responsible by being more directly responsible for creating an ancient language, or ancient languages, of which our own is a distant descendant, along with other modern tongues. Now, these geniuses shaped their language, or languages, in such a way that they might express their theory, and might continue to develop their theory, by thinking in language. Thus, a mutual development of the theory and language went on for many years. In time, some other geniuses came to realize, one in this respect, another in that, that at least part of the theory in his language was incorrect and, indeed, badly deficient. But, it is much easier to give up a theory than the language which embodies it, and for which it is the most suitable expression. Having no other available rich language, much less the time or power to inculcate it in others, such later geniuses would continue with the language, but not take its import seriously. As time goes on, the newer theories prevail, and other people don't take that original import seriously, being too much concerned with various practical matters. Later still, the original import is almost forgotten, and, then, perhaps entirely so, people being now too much concerned with the more practical aspects and uses of language. But, the theory is there, embodied in our later languages nevertheless. And, in very many, if not all of our *own* statements, we are giving expression to parts of that theory, unwittingly and, of course, unintentionally. If a contemporary philosopher is linguistically sensitive, and if he has a strong desire to find this theory, he can reconstruct it, or large parts of it, by looking at his own language—but with as much caution as boldness.

It is with this way of viewing our language in mind, that I look into my language, English, to find a theory of truth. The theory I find (or reconstruct) will be part of a much larger theory. Connections with other parts of the whole will be important for us, but a quest for them should not expend too much of our energies. For, it is work enough, especially for one paper, to discern and express such an embodied theory of truth.

## II

### THE TRUTH ABOUT THINGS

In the central sense of 'truth', we may speak of the *whole* truth about something as well as of various things each of which is *part* of the whole truth about the thing. This is entirely smooth and colloquial. Though it may not be so colloquial, we may, if only for expository convenience, speak of each of the latter things as *a* part of the former and, so, speak of *them* as *parts* of it. It is easy to translate back to get the facts of colloquial speech which I will use this convenience to record.

In the central sense of 'truth', we may speak of the truth *about* one thing as well as the truth about *another*. Generally, this will be the same as the whole truth about the first, and then, again, about the second. The only possible exception here, apart from elliptical usage, occurs where the thing in question is a "yes-no matter", or something to be specified, when we can specify it at all, by an expression of the form 'the matter of whether or not $p$' or, more shortly, of the form 'whether $p$'. (The letter '$p$' is, as is standard, to be replaced by a *propositional clause*, in the standard sense of the expression.) Thus, the truth about China is, really, the whole truth about China, and the truth about China's size, the whole truth about China's size. Perhaps, the truth about *whether China is larger than India* is *not* the *whole* truth about that; perhaps *nothing* is such a thing. This goes with the apparent fact that there is nothing which is part of the truth about whether China is larger than India. This last thing, which has no parts, at least none which are each the truth about something, itself is simply either of two things: In case China is larger, it is that China is larger; in case it is not, it is that it is not. There being no suitable parts, there at least *seems* to be nothing which is the *whole* truth about whether $p$, just the truth about it.

In contrast, the truth about whether China is larger than India *is* part of the truth about China's size. And, *each* of these two things is part of the truth about China. What is this last part of? The truth about China is, among other things, part of the truth about *the world*, even in the grand, as against the planetary, sense of this last word. That is, it is part of the truth about *the universe*, or about *everything*. Thus, each of these things is the *whole* truth about something, *and*, except for the last, each is *part* of the whole truth about something else. Finally, in every case, when 'truth' is used in its central sense, it is used to talk about the whole truth about the world or else about something which is part of that.

The whole truth about the world is itself but part of the (whole) world, just as is a book about the whole world, or a toad, or a toothpick. And, further, we should also note that *the whole truth about* the whole truth about the world is itself but *part* of the whole truth about the world. As such, it too is, then, but part of the world. And so, too, for the whole truth about . . . the whole truth about the world, and for any of the infinite number of things that are each part of it.

The whole truth about the world is different from the whole truth about any entity in it. This may be shown even in the face of the following: It may *well* be that in order to *know* the whole truth about, say, me, you must know also the whole truth about the whole world. But even if for one to be known the other must also be, and vice versa, the two things known will be different things. For, we have as a sentence descriptive of the truth about the world:

> Part of the whole truth about the world is the truth about whether China is larger than India.

But we do not have any such descriptive sentence about the truth *about me*, not one that *makes any sense*, anyway:

> Part of the whole truth about me is the truth about whether China is larger than India.

There is something, then, which is part of the one but not of the other. And, so, the two are not the same. What we do have as a perfectly sensible sentence which is descriptive of the whole truth about *me* is this:

> Part of the whole truth about me is that I exist in a world (or as part of a world) in which there is also something which is the truth about whether China is larger than India.

And, while we *don't* have as any sentence *which makes sense:*

> Part of the whole truth about me is that China is larger than India.

we do have *this* sentence to talk some sense with:

Part of the whole truth about me is that I exist in (or as part of) a world in which (the truth about whether China is larger than India is that) China is larger than India.

Indeed, it is *this* sort of sentence which brings to our attention the idea that *so much* must be known in order for anyone to know the whole truth about me. But, then, it leaves intact our distinction between the whole truth about the world, on the one hand, and the whole truth about me, which is but part of that first thing.

All of this *presents* a metaphysical theory. At the same time it records, or manifests, many quite obviously related facts about perfectly grammatical and even rather natural discourse in our language. Thus, we may be encouraged to surmise that this theory is embodied in our language and that any theory of truth must connect with this embodied theory. Of course, this suggestion needs much more evidence if we are to be much more serious about it. Indeed, such an attempt to be so literal in our interpretations faces obvious problems. I turn now to present and treat the most important of these.

*III*

TELLING THE TRUTH

We all say things like these: In telling Mary that he quit school, Ben may be telling her the truth. And, in telling her that he likes macaroni, Ben may also be telling Mary the truth. If we take this talk of the truth quite literally, then the most direct inference is that Ben may be telling her the very same thing each time. But, of course, this is absurd: That Ben quit school is one thing; that he likes macaroni, another. How are we to interpret these remarks so that we may, less directly, understand them as making quite literal references to the whole truth or parts of it?

In the first case, what Ben is really doing is telling Mary the truth *about whether he quit school.* In the second case, he is telling her the truth *about whether he likes macaroni.* These are two different things: The first *is* that he quit school, and the second *is* that he likes macaroni. So our typical use of 'the truth' here is elliptical. For example, in the first sentence, the phrase 'the truth' is elliptical for the longer phrase 'the truth about whether he quit school'.

Other sentences require but a bit more ingenuity to provide the completion for the ellipsis. In telling Mary each of these things, Ben was also telling her *the truth about himself.* But, again, he is not telling her the same thing each time. The point is, though, that in neither case does Ben tell Mary the *whole* truth about himself. That would involve his telling her the truth about whether he is tall, about whether he likes ravioli, and infinitely or indefinitely much more. So, the first time Ben tells her *part* of the (whole) truth about himself, *namely*, that he quit school. And, the second time, Ben also tells her *part* of the (whole) truth about himself, but *this* time, it is that he likes macaroni.

It often happens, of course, that in telling someone that something is so, one does not tell them the truth at all. That is, one does not then tell them the truth about *anything*. Thus, one will not then tell them part of the truth (about anything) either. In such cases, the propositional clauses which express what was told do not purport to refer to part of the truth. Their function is quite different. But, when we say *the truth was told*, we may always provide the completions to understand things quite literally: *These* propositional clauses *do* purport to refer to part of the whole truth about everything.

## *IV*

### PARTS OF THE TRUTH AND FACTS

When we dig down into the parts of the truth, we come upon parts which have no other such parts. These may be denoted by expressions of the form 'the truth about whether (or not) *p*'. They may *also* be denoted by an appropriate propositional clause, or that-clause. Indeed, it is only in this latter way that such "ultimate" parts of the truth may be most explicitly specified by us. We have already noted as much in the case of China and India: If China is larger than India, then the truth about whether China is larger than India is that China is larger than India. Otherwise, it is that China is not larger than India.

Unlike some other propositional clauses, or that-clauses, the ones just employed do *not* mean to denote anything which is true (or false). If we take a relevant sentence which *does* have such a that-clause:

That China is larger than India is true (false).

and try to connect it with one of our sentences:

The truth about whether China is larger than India is that China is larger than India.

the result is hash:

\* The truth about whether China is larger than India is true
(\* false).

We may contrast *our* key that-clauses with those employed
in, for example, simple sentences with the verb 'believe':

He believes that China is larger than India.

Here, the that-clause *does* denote something true (or false), as the
following connecting sentences serve to make plain:

In believing that China is larger than India, that China is larger
than India is what he believes.

In believing that China is larger than India, what he believes is
true (false).

We may expect, then, that what someone believes, while it may be
denoted by a that-clause, is never the same thing as any which is part
of the truth. Accordingly, if we should try to say of someone that he
believes something which is part of the truth, deviance should result.
To see this result, we compare:

?? Ben believes the truth about whether China is larger
than India, namely, that China is larger than India.

Ben remembers the truth about whether China is larger than
India, namely, that China is larger than India.

It appears, then, that while what is believed is at least often true or
false, anything which is part of the truth never is either.
    Now, facts also are things which seem never to be true or false.
Especially for facts of the sort purportedly denoted by that-clauses,
we may notice the following deviance:

?? The fact that China is larger than India is true (??false).

This is no mere redundancy, nor any mere inconsistency, as we may
notice from the perfectly grammatical sentences:

The true statement that China is larger than India is true.

The true statement that China is larger than India is false.

which, on at least one interpretation, are, respectively, tautologously redundant and inconsistent. The fact that relevant facts are also neither true nor false raises the idea that when that-clauses denote parts of the truth, it is a fact which, in each case, is being denoted. Accordingly, we have the idea that certain parts of the truth might just be certain facts. If this idea is right we would have some unity, and a large thrust toward the philosophically familiar. But, unfortunately, when we try to say of a promising part of the truth that it *is* an equally promising fact, only marked deviance is the result:

?? The truth about whether China is larger than India is the fact that China is larger than India.

Relevant connecting sentences only serve to confirm:

Part of the truth about China is the truth about whether China is larger than India.

?? Part of the truth about China is the fact that China is larger than India.

It appears, then, that parts of the truth are no more facts than things true or false. Rather, they appear to be some third sort of thing, which, despite their neglect by philosophers of truth, may well be the most deserving of our most careful attention.

*V*

THE OBJECTS OF KNOWING

My definition of truth is that it is agreement with the truth, the whole truth about everything. This *differs* from agreement with the facts, as our preceding discussion has indicated. But, why should we *prefer* our definition to one which gives facts the prominent role? Now, a large part of the motivation for our preference comes, as it ought, from the ability of our account to relate most systematically the main senses of 'truth'. Indeed, the word 'fact' even looks very different. No doubt, facts should figure prominently in the definition of some closely related notion, perhaps that of *factual correctness*. And, it *may* well be, also, that those things which are factually correct are, as a matter of necessity, precisely those which are true. But, if this is true, or right, or factually correct, it will take a comparatively indirect argument to convince us of that. More than an account of truth, or indeed any definition, will be needed in such an argument (if any such there be).

There is another large part to the motivation for our account. This motivation stems from the following intuition: When a man believes something which is *true*, then what he believes is *in agreement with* what might be *known* in the matter, insofar as anything might be known there. Putting the point more abstractly, and perhaps a bit more vaguely, the *things* which might be *objects of knowing* will, at the same time, be or constitute or serve as the *standard of truth* for things which might be believed, for what might be asserted, and so on. In particularly tricky or difficult cases, perhaps nothing may ever be known in a matter. Still, if there is a genuine question or matter, the relevant object or thing may be *there* even if nobody can ever know it. In a universe with no beings at all, the truth about whether there are any beings will be that there are no beings. And, this will be part of the whole truth about the world. Now, of course, nobody will ever actually know this thing; that is now the simplest matter of logic. But, we might acknowledge that *the statement that* there are no beings is nevertheless *true*. And this would be to acknowledge that that statement is in agreement with what is *there* to be known, even though, in the nature of the case, nobody is there to know it.

I submit that this intuition of ours is at least as deep as it is difficult adequately to express. Accordingly, I will now take great pains to argue that what is there to be known, if anything ever is, are parts of the truth or, in the (hypothetical) case of an omniscient being, even the whole truth itself. A particular consequence of my argument, then, will be this: Should someone *know* that China is larger than India, then the thing which he knows is, not a fact but, part of the whole truth about the world. How can we make good this long thrust toward our account of truth?

## VI

### The Direct Linguistic Evidence

There are, to be sure, certain locutions which suggest that people know particular facts. Thus we say, for example, 'Ben knows a great many facts'. But under scrutiny, these locutions look more like ellipses, or even idioms, than anything which is literal and complete. If we try to expand on our suggestive sentence, so as to say what (at least some of) those many facts are, we get a string which is at best badly substandard:

?? Ben knows a great many facts, namely, the fact that China is larger than India, the fact that whales are mammals, the fact that. . . .

Indeed, when we confront the shorter strings which the expansion forces upon us, the deviance becomes quite exceptionally acute:

* Ben knows the fact that China is larger than India.[3]

It appears, then, that our language has no straightforward way to say of a particular person that he knows a particular fact. The most direct linguistic evidence makes it look quite bleak for facts as objects of knowing.

If facts are out, we must treat anew such familiar sentences as:

Ben knows that China is larger than India.

Two alternatives suggest themselves. On the first, the that-clause makes no purported reference. On the second, it does, but not to a particular fact. While the first has some initial plausibility, that plausibility begins to evaporate when we consider sentences which connect:

One thing which Ben knows is that China is larger than India.

If Ben knows that China is larger than India, he knows at least one thing that Mary does not.

Sentences like these pressure us toward the second alternative: If we take them seriously, then there are things to be known though these are not facts. What are these things? They are, I suggest, each part of the truth. To further this suggestion, we may notice, first, that we may expand our connecting sentences easily enough, for example:

---

[3] This point, that 'know' doesn't take such direct factive objects is noted by the linguists Paul Kiparsky and Carol Kiparsky in their stimulating paper "Fact," originally published in *Progress in Linguistics*, ed. by M. Bierwish and K. Heidolf (The Hague: Mouton, 1970). They do not, however, seem to take it seriously enough. The point *seems overlooked* by Zeno Vendler in his book *Res Cogitans* (Ithaca, New York: Cornell University Press, 1972). This seems to occur even in Chapter V, "On What One Knows," where Vendler concludes that it is particular facts which are (often, usually?) known. He does, however, offer suggestive additional arguments for our *wanted* conclusion that the objects of knowing, unlike those of believing or saying, are never relevantly true (or false).

One thing which Ben knows, *and which is part of the whole truth about China*, is that China is larger than India.

And, this leads us to other new connecting sentences:

Ben knows part of the (whole) truth about China, namely, that China is larger than India.

Ben knows part of the (whole) truth about China, namely, the truth about whether China is larger than India.

Ben knows the truth about whether China is larger than India, namely, that China is larger than India.

These sentences, most particularly the last, strongly suggest that what people know, in case they ever do know anything to be so, are things which are each part of the truth.

This of course suggests some further ideas: First, in each case of a sentence of the form 'S knows that *p*', the propositional clause purports to denote part of the truth. And, second, the explanation of this is that sentences of this form always mean, at least roughly, what is meant by a paraphrastic sentence of the form 'S knows the truth about whether or not *p*, namely, that *p*'.

## VII

### AGREEMENT AND CONSISTENCY

The relation of agreement is much stronger than the philosophically more familiar one of consistency. If one thing is in agreement with another, then it follows that the first is (at least) consistent with the second. But something can be *consistent* with something else even while failing actually to be in agreement with it.

If I jump up and down, and our policy does not prohibit this, says nothing about such an action, then what I do is perfectly consistent with our policy. But it is not in agreement with it. If our policy *is* that we should jump up and down a lot, then what I do is, not only consistent with our policy, it is actually in agreement with it. When one thing *is* in agreement with another, then it is always in perfect, absolute, and complete agreement with that other. In this way, agreement is an absolute relation, just like the weaker relation of consistency. If what I say is not in *complete* agreement with what you say, at least *some of* what I say will *not* be in agreement with what you say. And, so, *what I say* will *not* be in agreement with what you say. Also, of course, if what I say is not *completely* consistent with what you say, then at least *some of* what I say will *not* be consistent with what you say. And, so, *what I say* will *not* be consistent with what you say.

If what I say is that China is larger than India, and what you say is that India is larger than Denmark, then what I say is completely consistent with what you say but it is not in agreement with it. If I say that China is larger than India, and you say that China is at least as large as India, then, while what you say is also completely consistent with what I say, I don't think that it is so much as in *agreement* with what I say. So, the relation of agreement is indeed a very strong relation. That is why it can play such a major role in an adequate account of truth.

## VIII

### Agreement with the The Whole Truth About Everything and Agreement with Appropriate Things Which Are Each Part of It

Everything we have said so far *may appear* to speak as much for the *following* theory of truth as it does for the account I offer: Truth is agreement with the *appropriate, or corresponding, thing which is part* of the whole truth about everything. In the case of the statement that China is larger than India, its *truth* is its agreement with the truth about whether China is larger than India, for in *this* case *that* is the appropriate thing which is part of the whole truth about the world. On this perhaps more modest alternative, when two things are both true, the property which they share is, not (being in) agreement with the same thing, but (being in) agreement with something which is correspondent with *the thing in question.* Almost anything which is true on our account will be true on this one, and almost anything which is not, not. On *our* account the truth of something *is its* agreement with *the whole truth about everything*, and it has that property just in case it is in agreement with the relevant part of the truth. On the alternative *its truth is* that latter. But, then, we *can think* of the former; what of *it*? Does agreement with the truth about everything have no name, no simple expression to mention it?

While still other alternatives suggest themselves, perhaps as compromises between or mixtures of these two, the dichotomy presented now allows us to ask the key questions which our own account must be especially well designed and suited to answer. The first key question is this: Which account allows for the simplest and most naturally sounding statement of what truth is, or definition of truth? Of the promising contenders, ours is the clear and obvious winner. But, then, why is that important? Well, first, one wants a simple account of something anyway; that's good methodology. But, in the present case, that's hardly the *main* point. For, we are not after a theory of galactic formation or insect behavior. We are after a theory of *one of our own common concepts*, and of *the meaning of one of our own common words*. Thus, we do well to ask, "When constructing a theory of things, and a language to express it, what *would men do*? Or, what might some brilliant men *have* done, especially in the case of truth?" Would they place in so (apparently a) central part of their thought and language a concept, and a term, whose definition we, and so presumably they, could easily, simply and naturally formulate? Or, would they put in such a place a term and concept whose definition would require a rather complex, awkward and difficult formulation? I think that the former course is by far the more likely one. Especially given my general views (presented in section 1) but really, in any case, this speaks rather heavily, I think, in favor of our simply expressed account of truth.

There is another large factor to favor our account though it is closely related to the first. Especially when we look at 'truth' in relatively splendid isolation, and do not confine our attention to 'the truth of this' or 'the truth of that', our own account gives a much better paraphrase than any more atomistic contender. When we say things like, "One must always seek truth", or "Truth is often not easily attained", our sentences have a meaning which gives them a certain inspirational, indeed, awesome flavor. Our own account provides paraphrases which capture this flavor rather well, "One must always seek agreement with the whole truth about everything" and "Agreement with the whole truth about everything is often not easily attained". More atomistic accounts do us *no* justice here. But, then, they, unlike an adequate account of truth, were never really designed to do any such thing in the first place.

Perhaps, our ancient geniuses felt many of our needs and, in each of our great, grand concepts, at once helped to fulfill many. Though it is not exactly the height of philosophical fashion, I think thoughts like these should be considered seriously when considering any great, grand thing: not only truth, but goodness, freedom, knowledge, and all the rest. Having bared my soul a bit, perhaps a bit too much, I return to think and write in a somewhat more fashionable and analytic style.

## IX

### How an Apparent Problem May Be an Asset in Disguise

When someone says something which we take to be true, we are wont to say:

What he said is the truth.

But, on our account, if what he said is true, then it is in agreement with the truth. Must we conclude, then, that the truth is in agreement with the truth, or is *in agreement with itself*? That is a puzzling, and an unwanted conclusion. Must we conclude, since what he said is true, and is also the truth, that the truth is true? That would also be puzzling, and unwanted on any account. Are we to conclude that for something to be true *is just* for it to *be* the truth? Unless we are prepared to say that being the truth may be the same thing as being in agreement with the truth, which seems absurd, this conclusion contradicts our account of truth. How, then, are we to explain such a sentence?

I take that sentence to mean:

What he said is *in agreement with* the truth.

This will solve our problem, as the short sentence will now present no problems for our account. But is this move perhaps only an *ad hoc* maneuver? I think not. Indeed, we can show that we need some such paraphrase in any case. We can show that taking the short sentence to be literal and complete leads to nonsense.

If what he said is anything, it is surely something which he *said*. If there is anything to say about this thing, then one such thing is this: He *said it*. In other words, we have:

He said what he said.

Now, if we take our short starting sentence so seriously as to think we have problems, we must also think that we must conclude:

He said the truth.

But, this last is nonsense. So, our starting sentence must be treated delicately, rather than swallowed. Our paraphrase provides just such a treatment.

Along the lines of our paraphrase, we have these connecting sentences:

He said something which is true.

He said something which is in agreement with the truth.

What he said is something which is in agreement with the truth.

What he said is in agreement with the truth.

What he said is the truth.

It should be clear that something like this is indeed what is needed here.

The problems we encountered in section 3, with telling, have nothing to do with the problems with saying. For example, we get just as much of a problem with:

What he said is the truth about whether China is larger than India.

* He said the truth about whether China is larger than India.

The problem here, then, has nothing to do with relevant parts. More particular sentences just require more particular paraphrases.

What he said is *in agreement with* the truth about whether China is larger than India.

And connecting sentences will be similarly more particular. Perhaps this is enough:

He said something about whether China is larger than India which is in agreement with the truth about whether China is larger than India.

For we must realize that what he said is now said to be in (complete) *agreement* with that particular thing, and surely not just (completely) consistent with it. In any case, certain related sentences will demand a more ingenious treatment. We must consider, for example:

> What he said was only part of the truth about that even though everything he said was true.

But, this might be paraphrased as:

> What he said was in agreement with the truth about that but, though everything he said was in agreement with the truth, it was only part of what might be both said and in agreement with the truth about that.

In any case, whatever the details for more detailed sentences, it appears that they may run smoothly along the lines of my account of truth.

This means more support for my account than one might first think. For, we don't even have as data to be treated any such sentences as:

> * What he said is the fact

> * What he said are the facts,

and so on. And, a perfectly fine sentence like:

> What he said is a fact.

means only something like

> It is a fact that he said what he said.

Thus, it is obviously quite irrelevant to our topic. So our original sentence:

> What he said is the truth,

which began by looking to be a problem, proves to be an asset in disguise. The very fact that the words 'the truth', 'the truth about that', and so on, turn up in such a direct connection with 'what he said' and 'is true', this fact indicates that it is *our* chosen entities that are to play the roles in any adequate account of truth.

## X

### The Predication of Truth and the Relevant Uses of 'True'

Truth is a certain property. It is a property of precisely those things such that, in each case, there is *the truth of* that thing. When we talk about a thing, for example, a particular statement, and say that truth is a property of that thing, we may say that we are predicating truth of the thing. Parallel remarks can be made about any other property; for example, redness. Redness is a property of precisely those things such that, in each case, there is something which is *the redness of* that thing. When we talk about a thing and say that redness is a property of it, we may say that we are predicating redness of the thing.

By far our most common and important devices for predicating properties of things are adjectives. The standard form of sentence for predicating begins with a referring expression, goes on with a tensed copula, and ends with an adjective. Thus, 'That is true' and 'This is red' are standard sentences for predicating truth and redness of that and this. In particular, it is the adjective 'true' which, in relevant uses, is our most common device for predicating truth of things. We ought, therefore, to look at 'true'.

While it has not always been for such a good reason as this, philosophers of truth have concentrated enormously on this adjective. (Our quote from Austin gives an example.) They have not, however, tried to separate systematically the relevant uses of the word from other uses which it has. That is, they have not tried to demarcate just those uses which pertain directly to the topic of truth, giving a rationale for this demarcation. Much less have they tried to define the word for those uses, to specify the meaning which it has in them and them alone. We will now try to support our account of truth by using it to remedy this situation.

The most natural extension of our account says this: Among those uses of 'true' which pertain directly to our topic, the most central is its use as a predicating adjective in standard sentences for that purpose, for example, as in the sentence 'That is true'. Other relevant uses, as in 'It is true that that is red', derive from this central one and are, accordingly, to be best understood as being so derivative.[4] The

---

[4] I suppose that this means that the prominent contemporary philosopher of truth from whom I differ the most is Peter F. Strawson, especially in his early paper "Truth," in *Analysis*, IX, 6 (1949). Of course, one should also see his later "Truth," in the *Pro-*

meaning of 'true' is the same for all relevant uses; it means, at least roughly, 'in agreement with the truth'. Accordingly, 'That is true' means 'That is in agreement with the truth', and, there being no qualification, we may understand what it expresses as logically equivalent to what is expressed by 'That is in agreement with the whole truth about everything'. The sentence 'What you said was true about him' then means the same as 'What you said was in agreement with the truth about him'. The meaning of 'What you said was true of him' cannot be expressed in a sentence obtained by direct substitution. But, it can be understood in our terms; we only need say that it means (at least roughly) the same. For in these sentences, 'of' and 'about' mean (at least roughly) the same.

Perhaps we may even say that 'true' *means* (just as roughly) *this much*: 'is in agreement with the *whole* truth *about everything*'. In that case, we would paraphrase 'What you said was true about him' in this way:

> What you said was, insofar as it was about him, in agreement with the whole truth about everything.

If anything, the sentence 'It is true that that is red', while philosophically familiar, presents even less of a problem. First, we may paraphrase it by the predicating sentence:

> That that is red is true (is in agreement with the whole truth about everything).

Additionally, we may also paraphrase by a direct substitution:

> It is in agreement with the whole truth about everything that that is red.

Now, *if* one always *demands* direct substitution, *of course* some problems occur with various relevant sentences:

> It is a true statement that that is red.

> \* It is in agreement with the truth statement that that is red.

---

*ceedings of the Aristotelian Society*, Supp. Vol. XXIV (1950), which is his part of the famous symposium with Austin. In that Professor Strawson was my own encouraging tutor for three terms, any value in the present work can only contribute to his already great reputation as an inspiring teacher.

But such failure of substitution does not count against our definition. For this typically happens when a predicate adjective is moved to a prenominal position.

A good definition of 'illegal' is 'against the law'. The sentence 'That was illegal in France last year' means, at least roughly, 'That was against the law in France last year'. But, however good this definition, we get no sentence at all by trying to substitute in:

That illegal act was worth doing.

We get only:

* That against the law act was worth doing.

So, if our definition of 'illegal' is a good one, all we should expect is this: First, we can directly substitute our defining expression in a set of central sentences with (virtually) no change in meaning and; second, we can understand other sentences where the word is used (and not just mentioned) in terms of their relations to the central ones.

With certain words, adhering to this criterion leaves many sentences unexplained. We might then expect either that our offered definition was not a good one or else that the word to be defined has more than one meaning, the offered definition then being, at best, good for only one of the meanings of the word. I think that the second alternative is what we find with the word 'true' and our offered definition of what it means.

Now, if this is right, our definition, and so our account of truth, may be tested in yet another way: by how well it separates uses of 'true' which have much to do with truth from those which have much less (directly) to do with our topic. This is no empty claim. When we compare the two sentences:

Her statement to him was true;

Her love for him was true,

we cannot help but feel that the first has much to do with truth, while the second has little to do with it. What explains this difference? Two routes join together. First, the first can be paraphrased in terms of our offered definition, but not the second.

Her statement to him was in agreement with the truth.

?? Her love for him was in agreement with the truth.

And, taking now the second route, we may say that only in the first of these sentences is 'true' being used to predicate truth. In that sentence, what we are bringing to the fore, and may go on to talk about is *the truth of* her statement to him. But, in the second sentence, we are predicating no such thing; it is badly substandard at best to try to talk of ??*the truth of* her love for him. What we *may* speak of here, and perhaps *are* predicating is faithfulness, or even *trueness*: Thus, we may speak of *the trueness of* her love for him. But of course this is a different matter; *our* topic is *truth*. Accordingly, our definition of 'true', along with our account of truth, lets syntax and semantics join in explaining the division between relevant uses of 'true' and those which do not belong to our topic.

*XI*

### Modification of 'True'

One cannot overemphasize, I think, our intuitive idea that truth is some sort of *absolute* and, so, that matters of truth are *not really* matters of *degree*. Matters of truth may be closely *associated* with certain matters of degree, for example, with matters of accuracy. But, then, we can be intuitively quite sure, for this reason alone, that truth and accuracy are different.

In classes in philosophy, elementary as well as advanced, students are often corrected for talking of truth by using 'true' with some modification which makes things look relative:

What you said is truer than what he said.

But, the students' sentence is perfectly grammatical and even may make good sense. The way to explain and preserve our intuition that truth is an absolute is *not* to *bar* that sentence, but to *understand it properly*. We do have the three forms with 'true' even in relevant uses, just as in ones far from our topic: 'true', 'truer', 'truest'. That is data which must be handled, never denied. If we can handle our students' sentence, all else will follow. But, how to handle it?

Looking at that sentence, the first thing to notice is that it is clearly entailed that what he said, at least, is *not* true. The next thing to notice is that it is *at least suggested* and *possibly* even entailed, that what you said is not true. If we suppose that it is even *entailed* that what *you* said is not true, we may *paraphrase* our sentence in any of these four equivalent ways:

> What you said is more nearly true than what he said.
> What you said is closer to the truth than what he said.
> What he said is not as nearly true as what you said.
> What he said is not as close to the truth as what you said.

If we suppose, on the other hand, that it is *only suggested* that what you said is not true, we may paraphrase by beginning with the quite unproblematic disjunct:

> What you said is true and what he said is not (true),

to get, for example:

> Either what you said is true and what he said is not or what you said is more nearly true than what he said.

This sort of paraphrase also *suggests* (though not quite so forcefully) that what you said is not true, and it *entails*, clearly, only that what he said is not true. I am inclined to think that this *is* all that is entailed. Accordingly, I am inclined to go with such a longer, disjunctive form of paraphrase.

Where *intuitively relative* properties are compared nothing like this does any justice. If we take, for example, the similar-looking sentence:

> What you said is wiser than what he said.

it is *not* entailed, or even suggested, that what *he* said is *not* wise; it might have been wise also, just *not as* wise as what you said. At the same time, no parallel to our vital disjunct even begins to do any justice to our sentence with 'wise':

> What you said is more nearly wise than what he said.

For this last *does* entail *at least* this much: that what he said is not wise. So, our forms of paraphrase at once let in modifications of 'true' and also bring out and preserve our intuition that truth, unlike wisdom and the like, is always some sort of absolute. But, also, how are we to explicate our sentence with 'truer' still further? And, how are we to bring it explicitly into agreement with our account of truth?

As the first disjunct is easy to handle, everything depends on our doing more with the second disjunct, with each of the four equally good ways we have expressed it. Now, according to our account the only way in which what is said might be, say, more nearly true is *by* its being more nearly *in agreement with* the truth. That this is the right idea becomes even clearer when we ask how might something which is said be *closer to* the truth: by its being closer to *being in agreement with* the truth. Accordingly, we paraphrase our second disjunct as, say:

> What you said is more nearly in agreement with the truth than what he said,

and, so, one of our equivalent ways of paraphrasing our original sentence becomes the long but faithful:

> Either what you said is in agreement with the truth and what he said is not or what you said is more nearly in agreement with the truth than what he said.

The ways of expanding the other, equivalent forms are equally clear, and equally in keeping with our account. Thus, what *are* matters of degree here are matters of *how close to* the truth things are, that is, really, of *how close to* being in agreement with the truth.

We may close this section with a few brief remarks about adverbial modification of 'true'. We do say things like: 'What he said was very true'. So, there are *some* adverbs of degree, like 'very', which grammatically modify 'true' even in relevant uses. But what are we to make of their function here? Concerning *truth*, no *logical* modifications are produced: When something which is said is very true, so far as truth goes, it is just plain true: It is also absolutely, perfectly, and completely true. There are no other possible things to be said which, while true, are *any less true* than it. The following is, in other words, *inconsistent*:

> What he said was *very* true and, though what you said was *also* true, it was *not as* true as what he said.

So, when adverbs and adjectives are properly understood there are no degrees of truth.

## XII

### THE FUNCTION OF AMOUNTS OF TRUTH

I now come to the most perplexing locutions involving 'truth'. An example is given by:

There is a lot of truth in what you said.

Here, it looks like we talk of amounts of truth, much as though truth were some sort of stuff. I will offer a perhaps overbold account of these locutions. This account will bring in my beliefs on the way we may *instructively view* language to have gotten started, and what theories and functions it was thus made to serve. So, for me, at least, rather a lot depends on what I am to say about these locutions.

Now, the very first thing to notice about our sample sentence is this: It *at least suggests* that what you said is *not* true; that there is *nothing* which is the truth *of* what you said; that you have here said *nothing* which is in *agreement* with *the truth*. Now, I am inclined to think that our sample sentence *only suggests* this, that it does *not* actually *entail* it. For the following seems, while a bit unusual, *consistent*:

What you said is true; there is, indeed, a lot of truth in what you said.

Still, even if our original sentence does not have the harsh entailment, its *suggestion* in that direction is extremely important. It must be attended to in further thought about the sentence.

Another thing to notice is that parallel remarks can be made right down the line for paraphrases of our sample sentence. We also have such talk of amounts with agreement:

There is a lot of agreement with the truth in what you said.

This too suggests that what you said is *not* true, but it doesn't seem to entail that either:

What you said is true and, indeed, there is a lot of agreement with the truth in what you said.

But, while this all gives support to our account, it barely scratches the surface in understanding the function of such sentences.

Now, perhaps the most important thing to notice about these sentences is that they *provide* nice, encouraging, *praising* ways of describing what someone said *in terms of truth even when what he said* is *not* true:

> There is a lot of truth in what you said, even if what you said isn't (completely) true.

In fact, these sentences are our *very best common device* for doing this. Compare the former with:

> What you said is very close to the truth, even if what you said isn't (completely) true.

Again, if we compare:

> There is a fair amount of truth in what you said, even if it isn't (completely) true,

and

> What you said is fairly close to the truth, even if it isn't (completely) true,

the former is *more* the sort of thing one *wants* to hear. And, the same difference emerges with:

> There is a fair amount of agreement with the truth in what you said, even if it isn't (completely) true.

> What you said is fairly close to being in agreement with the truth, even if it isn't (completely) true.

So, our account captures the brilliant power of amount talk in praising what is said, and so the sayer, in terms of truth. But, how does it do this? What is going on here?

Talk of amounts of agreement can be just as puzzling as talk of amounts of truth. One feels that just as truth is an absolute, so is agreement some sort of absolute thing. We have already noted this in section 4. But, it bears repeating here. Indeed, this has motivated our account all along and has served to make it most palatable. If, as we say, you and I agree about something, but *not completely* and, so, only in part, then we *don't* really agree about that thing. If your report and mine are, *in the main*, in agreement about that affair, then the two reports are *not* really in agreement about the event. So, what can be going on with all this praising talk of amounts, which seems puzzling in any case, and is especially so in the case of these absolute concepts?

I think that the fundamental idea is very simple: If your report and mine are, in the main, in agreement about the affair, then there are *things in* my report which actually are in agreement with *things in* your report, and, so far as these reports go, *these* things are the *main* things about the affair. Now, the things I'm talking about are exceedingly elusive. The reports may not be in agreement insofar as the content of their respective sentences is concerned. The things, which agree, go deeper than what is said by any particular sentence, or by any conjunction of the sentences. The sentences are just means by which we can say certain things. The sentences are important because there can be other things, vital third parties, *in* the things we manage to *say*. It is these third things which really do agree. And, so, it is they that allow, as we say, the two reports to "agree in the main".

While we like our reports to agree with each other, at least in the main, it is our concern for truth which is the point. We turn, then, from agreement between reports to agreement of something with the truth. We have already noted our lengthening paraphrase for: 'There is a lot of truth in what you said', namely,

There is a lot of agreement with the truth in what you said.

But, a shortening paraphrase is also worth noting:

There is a lot in what you said.

Now, if we are to take things seriously, we must ask what the words 'a lot' may mean to refer to here? In other words, a lot of what?

I think that these words are used here to refer to a lot of importance or value. But, it is not just importance in the abstract. It is the importance or value *of something* which *is in* what you said, or *of* some *things* which *are in* what you said. So, *the amount of truth in what you said* may be best understood by some such paraphrase as this:

The amount of importance of *whatever is true in* what you said.

This is born out, I think, by the *inconsistency* of such sentences as these:

> There is a lot of truth in what you said, but there is very little that is true in it.

> There is some truth in what you said, but there is nothing true in it.

> There is a lot of truth in what you said, but there is very little importance in what you said.

> There is not much truth in what you said, but there are many important things in it which are true.

So, we treat 'amounts of truth', or 'amounts of agreement with the truth', as ways of talking about the amounts of importance of certain things which are true.

It is something of a mystery to me how these true things might be *in* what someone said, or believed, and so on. Indeed, it is a mystery as to what exactly these true things might be. These things would *not* appear to be statements, or propositions, or even truths:

> ?? What you said isn't true, but there are many truths ( * true statements, * true propositions) *in* what you said.

A solution to this mystery would, for me, at least, consist in a further elaboration of the metaphysics embodied *in* our language. But, whatever the details of the solution, I think that what has already been brought to light may be seen to serve an important purpose. That purpose is the successful resolution of the following deep human conflict.

It often happens that a man says something which is not true, and what he says is of such a nature that nothing can be deduced from it which is both true and important. I take it that this is generally what happens when someone says something bold, fresh, new, and general, says the sort of thing which "contributes to our understanding in an original way". I take it that this occurs with what Newton said about the world, or with the most important, interesting, general things he said about it. I take it that the same is true of Einstein, of Marx, of Jefferson, and of Freud.

I think that there is in each of us a powerful motivating force which our language has us put like this: First, we want to *know* as much as possible. But, if we can't know various things, we would like to believe, with reason, as much as we can which is *true*, which is *in complete agreement with* what *would* be known if only it *could* be, what perhaps *is known* by an *omniscient* being. The truly creative thinker is driven by this force. He boldly strives to *know as much of the truth* as he can, *at least* to say and believe *as much as* he can which *is in complete agreement with the truth.*

But, the bolder and more creative his thinking and theorizing, the slimmer the chance that what he actually says and believes *will* be true. The truth, or at least truth, was his goal. Must his creativity almost certainly frustrate him in these terms? Do we have no place in our thought of these things to help resolve this conflict?

I think we may do well to view things this way: The ancient geniuses most responsible for our language were, intuitively, brilliant and sensitive psychologists. They *felt* this motivating force very strongly. They *also* appreciated that their limited minds, together with a relatively impoverished language, provided them with a conflict, encouraged frustration, and would lead to an inhibiting fear of that impending frustration. This fear could inhibit creative thinking. At the same time, they provided a relatively satisfying way of dealing with this problem, a relatively effective way of freeing future creative thinkers from this fear of frustration: the idea of there being a lot of truth *in* what a man says or believes. This is the idea that *in* what these men say or believe are many things, specifiable or not, which *are* in *complete agreement with* the whole truth about everything. In this way, the ancients let us *express* this powerful motivation. *And at the same time*, they *pressured us to talk* about the creative thinker coming out *well ahead of* the cautious bore *even as judged in these powerful terms.* Granted, they may have employed a certain amount of obscurity to accomplish this dual task. But, even, so, their expression of this fundamental motivation, and their resolution of its conflict with creative thinking, this still remains a considerable achievement, very considerable indeed.

Perhaps, I am totally wrong even *in* all of what I say here. But, with no boasts of creativity on my own part, perhaps I may hope and even believe that there is *at least some truth in* my account of truth.


## XIII

### SOME POSSIBLE CONSEQUENCES OF THIS ACCOUNT

There are two alternative responses to my account of truth. The first is to accept the idea that, since truth is agreement with the truth, there really is something which is the whole truth about the world. I suppose that this might be taken as a metaphysical discovery, or rediscovery, of some magnitude. Many of the consequences of this discovery may be appreciated by accepting many of the statements made in previous sections.

I am inclined to reject this first alternative. Nominalistically, if you like, I am inclined to think that there really cannot be any such thing as the whole truth about the world. Accordingly, I am inclined toward the second alternative: that there really is no such thing as truth. Once this alternative is chosen, many striking consequences appear to follow. Severe nominalists may be accustomed to these consequences, getting there by more familiar routes. In that case, I will only spell them out anew. But, in any case, I will now proceed to spell out explicitly what appears to follow from my account of truth once this second alternative is taken.

In terms of my account, a statement, what someone says, or believes, and so on, can be *true* only if there actually is something which is the whole truth about the world. Otherwise, there is no such thing with which the statement, and so on, could possibly be in (complete) agreement. Accordingly, we now must conclude that no statement, and so on, is ever true. And, should anyone ever believe or say that something is so, what he says or believes will never be true.

The radical consequences of our account hardly stop here. For, if there really is nothing which is the whole truth about the world, nothing can be nearly true, or at all close to being true, or even quite far from being true. On our account, we remember, that would require being quite far from being in (complete) agreement with *the truth*.

Coupled to our account, I will present the following plausible account of *falsity*: Falsity is, at least roughly, conflict with, or (in more philosophically familiar terms), inconsistency with, the whole truth about everything. I have worked rather hard and long on the details which support this account of falsity, enough to forbear trying to do them justice in the space I feel at liberty to take right now. Instead, I will ask the reader to accept the account provisionally, in order to see what consequences now follow from it. The first consequence of this account of falsity is that, in the relevant sense of the term, there is absolutely nothing which is false. This is because, as there is nothing which is the whole truth about everything, nothing can be in conflict with, or inconsistent with, any such thing. And, if we *combine* our accounts of truth and of falsity, as is only natural, then we get this combined consequence: In the relevant senses of the terms, nothing is either true or false: no statement, nothing which might be believed, nothing whatsoever.

In working out the details of my accounts of truth and of falsity, I did not seem forced to the position that, according to the concepts of our language, or to any theory embodied therein, each statement must be true or else false; similarly for what is believed, and so on. Quite the contrary seems to be the case, so far as the logico-linguistic matters go. While no statement can be both true *and* false, both in agreement with the truth and also inconsistent with it, at least certain statements *might be neither*. An example might be the statement that a certain person will soon jump voluntarily. But, then, what *is* the status of *this statement*? In terms of the general account of things into which my account of truth most naturally fits, the status of such a statement is that it is *consistent with* the whole truth about the world, while *not* being *so much as* in *agreement* with that alleged thing. When a statement has this status, then its *negation* is *also* consistent with the truth, in this case the statement that that person will *not* soon jump voluntarily. And, of course, that negation is also not so much as in agreement with the truth. (When a statement *is* in agreement with the truth, then its *negation* is *not consistent* with the truth, but is *inconsistent* with it. And, when a statement is inconsistent with the truth, then its negation is, not only consistent with the truth, but must be in agreement with that alleged thing.) What we may now say, then, is this: In the philosophically relevant sense of 'statement', any statement there may be must be either consistent with the truth or else inconsistent with the whole truth about the world. Now, if, as we have decided, there is *no such thing* as the whole truth about the world, then no statement can be consistent with such a thing, no more than any might be inconsistent with it. What follows from this is strikingly clear: In the philosophically relevant sense of 'statement', there are no statements at all. But, no one should suppose, it seems to me, that any of this turns on any technical developments.

For, it also appears that if ever anyone believes, or says, or thinks, or asserts that anything is so, then what he believes, says, thinks, or asserts, if it be anything at all, must be either consistent with the truth or else inconsistent with that alleged thing. But, if nothing at all can possibly be either of these, then it follows that there *never is anything* which anyone believes, says, thinks, or asserts to be so. And, it follows from *this* that *nobody ever* really believes that anything is so, nor says, nor thinks, nor asserts that anything is so! Now *this* is of course an *extremely* radical conclusion. Though this conclusion does not follow directly from my account of *truth* alone, it does follow from that account in conjunction with the most plausible and natural way of extending the account. So, I hesitantly accept this conclusion also, or would if it were possible for people to believe things to be so.

(In that our account leads to skepticism about belief, it is hardly surprising that it should lead to skepticism about knowledge as well. In any case, it does do this. If someone knows that something is so, then he knows the truth about whether it is so. But, there really is no such thing as the truth about whether the thing is so. For, if there were, it would be part of the whole truth about the world, and there is no such thing as that. And, so, nobody ever knows that anything is so.

In that our account leads to skepticism about knowledge, any consequences of that honored view will of course also follow from our account. One such consequence is this: If someone regrets that he did a certain thing, then he knows that he did it. Even if the objects of regret are different sorts of things from those of knowing, as facts are different from parts of the truth, a suitable *parallel* will hold between the objects so that the conditional here will hold. Thus, as nobody ever knows he did anything, nobody will ever regret his having done anything either. Likewise, nobody will every be happy or sad, upset or elated that anything was, is or will be so. And many similar consequences will also follow in like manner.) [5]

Though the many foregoing consequences of our account are puzzling, to say the least, we have not yet come to the most troublesome and, indeed, utterly paradoxical consequences of our account of truth. These consequences begin to present themselves when we begin to consider grammatically sound versions of strings made famous by Tarski.[6] Accordingly, we begin to consider the Tarski-inspired equivalence:

What is expressed by the sentence 'Snow is white' is true if and only if snow is white.[6]

[5] This paper, then, supports and is, to some extent at least, supported by classical arguments for skepticism about knowing, as well as such more contemporary attempts as in my "A Defense of Skepticism," *Philosophical Review*, LXXX, 2 (April, 1971). It is also in such a mutually supportive relationship with such of my later papers as "Propositional Verbs and Knowledge," *Journal of Philosophy*, LXIX, 11 (June, 1972), and "The Wages of Skepticism," *American Philosophical Quarterly*, X, 3 (July, 1973). In these later papers I discuss the relation between knowing and such things as regretting.

[6] I have in mind Alfred Tarski's paper "The Semantic Conception of Truth," originally published in *Philosophy and Phenomonological Research*, Vol. IV (1944). There Tarski has such at least mildly deviant strings as:

?The sentence "snow is white" is true if, and only if, snow is white.

Our slight change converts such Tarskian strings, I think, into perfectly nondeviant sentences. But, of course, that is a very small move. Of more importance perhaps is the apparently dire consequence of our account for theories of meaning, and so on, which would put truth at or near their center. I have in mind, of course, such Tarski-inspired attempts as those of Donald Davidson in such papers as his "Truth and Meaning," originally published in *Synthese*, XVII, 3 (1967).

Much as Tarski would have it, this equivalence looks quite pristine. It looks, at least, relatively unmetaphysical, possibly quite unproblematical. With or without any Tarski around, our own account of truth brings forth a rather longer equivalence with the same left-handed side:

> What is expressed by the sentence 'Snow is white' is true if and only if what is expressed by the sentence 'Snow is white' is in agreement with the whole truth about the world.

Now, I cannot see that any speaker and user of our language, English, can at this point fail to accept *either* of these equivalences, unless of course he opts out of seriously speaking the English language. If he is to stay in the community of English speakers, and is in no wise deficient in his appreciative abilities, he must accept them *both*. But, then, these two equivalences jointly lead to a third which, while it looks innocuous from one end:

> What is expressed by the sentence 'Snow is white' is in agreement with the whole truth about the world if and only if snow is white,

shows itself for what it is when the short side is put first:

> Snow is white if and only if what is expressed by the sentence 'Snow is white' is in agreement with the whole truth about the world.

Now, as there is no such thing for what that sentence expresses to be in agreement with, we must conclude that snow is *not* white.

That we should be able, indeed required, to reach such a substantive extralinguistic conclusion from what may *appear* to be *mere* considerations of language seems shocking; the fact that we would generally consider it a *false* substantive statement makes matters look even worse. But, of course, we could take a parallel course starting from equivalences concerning the sentence 'Snow is not white'. And, we would thus be led equally to the conclusion that snow *is* white. Putting two and two together, we must conclude, finally, that snow *is* white *and* snow is *not* white. In any case involving no future contingencies, nor the borders of vague predicates, we get a paradoxical contradiction.

At this point, those who have not already left me will, no doubt, be likely to do so. Blatant contradictions indicate a serious fault somewhere. But must that fault lie with my account of truth, or with my apparently natural extensions of it? Perhaps, instead, the fault lies with the very idea of truth, with truth itself. If that is right, then the fault will also lie with any language which gives truth a prominent role.

*XIV*

THE RANGE OF TRUTH

By writing in contemporary English, I have told a story about truth which my language naturally allowed me to develop. This story had as its central character an object that one would not naturally think to focus on explicitly: the whole truth about the world. By then doubting the existence of this thing, I made things look bad for my language itself, for contemporary English.

Now, if it is really the case that English embodies an *inherited* theory, and it is *not just* that we may instructively *view* it as such, then the same metaphysical story, at least in essence, could be told just as naturally in other, older languages. So, my account of truth *may* be an account of a concept with a very great human range. *If* a very similar essay could be written in classical Latin, or classical Greek, or classical Hebrew, and so on back, or in at least *some* of these, then I would be very happy indeed with my account of truth. If not I could, of course, conclude that truth was perhaps peculiar to my own language, and that the concept of *truth* had no place outside of my quite parochial way of thinking. Only other concepts, however closely related, might find any place out there. So, I would still stand by my account of truth in such an event, but the standing then would not be quite that important.

So much for thinking of the past, and even of contemporary linguistic strangers. What are *we* to do with *our* language if my account is right, and all those paradoxical consequences *are* in *our* hands? First we must get rid of a lot of metaphysical muddle. But, at the same time, we do not want to lose the baby along with any muddy bath water. The motivations captured by our ancient geniuses, the "drive to advance our knowledge, or at least our share of truth", these motivations should be allowed *some* expression in *any* language we devise, or in *anything much like a language*. And, we should also take care to find or create locutions, or things like locutions, which help dispel any fear this driving motivation might engender. If a decrease of creative thinking is the price of getting rid of contradictions, then contradiction may be the hobgoblin of small minds. But, my hope is that we can have our cake and eat it too. While my own talents for the needed task are meager, I hope for at least something like a language (and, so, for at least something like a way of thinking) which is *so* good as to do or be all this: It will be free of contradictions, be metaphysically quite pristine, and, at the same time, it will be no threat or hindrance to creativity. It *might* be that there is *already* something available to do all this: perhaps a Chinese or Indian language? But, more likely, perhaps, *invention* will be needed. Whoever may give help in this more creative task will, if I have not badly missed the mark, earn the thanks of future generations. For otherwise, we may only in vain seek after truth.[7]

---

[7] Many people deserve thanks for helpful conversations about the ideas in this paper. I single out for mention Rodgers Albritton, William Barrett, Gilbert Harman and Michael Slote, who were especially thoughtful in their very helpful comments.